Collective Wisdom

Collective Wisdom

Prominent Australians
Share Their Stories

Interviews by **Brett Kelly**

Photography by **Nathan Kelly**

50% OF PROCEEDS TO 'YOUTH OFF THE STREETS' INC.

Published by Clown Publishing
PO Box 1764, North Sydney NSW 2059, Australia
www.brettkelly.com.au

Distributed by River Grove Books

Design and composition by Bowra & Bowra, Sydney
Cover design by Natalie Bowra

Publisher's Cataloging-in-Publication data is available.

Print ISBN: 978-1-7640485-7-6

eBook ISBN: 978-1-7640485-6-9

First Edition

dedication

'People are meant to be loved, things are meant to be used.
Many of our problems stem from a disturbance of this reality
– people are used and things are loved'.
– Anonymous

the author

Young, thinking and very curious ... searching for wisdom, insights to success and inspiration, **Brett Kelly** is a first-time interviewer and author of *Collective Wisdom*. Brett is interested in business, loves sport, music and books and is passionate about the future character and direction of Australia.

the photos

Nathan Kelly has been working as a freelance photographer for the past six years. He has recently completed a Bachelor of Arts (Photography) at Sydney College of the Arts from the University of Sydney, and was nominated by *Commercial Photography Magazine* as one of thirty top graduates for 1996. Reading, music and partying are just a few of his interests.

foreword by

Senator Natasha Stott Despoja

This book is about inspiration born of determination. Brett Kelly, at a low point in life, dusted himself off and set out hopefully, on a journey of learning. What he learned (and shares with us here) is the wide-ranging views of 34 very interesting Australians.

They tell us what, or who, influenced their lives and also share their views on republicanism, taxation, drug abuse, abortion, racism, education and employment.

From Professor Gavin Brown's belief that education is about 'the excitement of, and respect for ideas' to Lindsay Fox's comment that 'Money is a by-product of job satisfaction', these are not just stories of success, but stories of successful thinking.

If you cannot find a role model out of this lot you are not trying. We all have people in public life who we admire (I'm a great admirer of Poppy King, to name just one). The short attention span of most media means we get only glimpses of what lies behind the public face. What, we wonder, is the drive and direction that propels them in their accomplishments?

This collection of interviews shows that if there is a single key to success, it is the one that opens the door to other people.

Natasha Stott Despoja
Deputy Leader of the Australian Democrats

contents

preface

This book has been made possible through the generosity of a great number of people, not least among them the prominent Australians featured. I would like to thank them all very much.

While my skill base is limited but growing, it is my sincere hope that in these oceans of wisdom and experience (to which I have had such generous access) I have managed to uncover just one pearl, one insight or distinction, that will contribute to the thrilling adventure of your life!

Collective Wisdom is a series of 34 face-to-face interviews conducted between August 1997 and March 1998. The interviews were recorded on audio tape, transcribed and edited.

All interviewees were asked a number of questions and were requested to respond to only those that they felt comfortable answering. None of the people interviewed is an expert across all the subject areas – as most Australians are not – and they are not presented as such by either the interviewee or the interviewer.

The editing process strove to maintain the colloquial and conversational style of the discussions, and the edited transcripts were approved by the interviewees prior to publication. Each interview is accompanied by a photographic portrait.

Each contributor was asked to comment on a variety of issues using a standard set of questions based on the following subject areas: Australia's future, unemployment, racism, drugs, education, the republic, tax reform, voluntary euthanasia, Aboriginal land rights.

The questions attempt to elicit personal rather than political responses. The idea is to examine each contributor's individual understandings and experiences of the issues.

acknowledgements

I would like to thank all those who have encouraged, supported and assisted me in the production of this book. To my very talented brother Nathan – endless sounding board and the creator of the wonderful photographic images inside – a special thank you.

To a very special group of people – without whose help this project would not have been possible – the personal assistants to the contributors: Margaret Jackson, Margaret McClenahan, Fr Lovegrove, Herny Clayton, Kaye McWilliam, Miriam Christie, Heather Barwick, Arlene Brooks, Margaret McCann, Sharon Middlehurst, Jill Saunders, Sandi, Jan Maree McPherson and Emma Mahon, Susan Santiago, Michael Ellis, Maybrit Prahl, Christine Kessler, Faye Anderson, Peta Domery, Lyriane Beuzeville, Kerri Clark, Claire Cooney, Kate Harding, Jacqueline Smith, Stephanie Wells, Margie Thomas, Tony Cudmore, Anna Cronin, Lyn Gall, Michelle James and Kerry Taylor.

I particularly want to thank Kathryn Lamberton, James Brennan and Natalie Bowra who are the original 'believers'; they encouraged and supported me when no one else would. Thanks also to Kiley and Emma – a super job. To Sue Wagner, my enthusiastic and professional editor; Bruce Pollack Publicity; and all my friends particularly Brad, Matt, Jane, the Maccas and, particularly, my family.

Thanks to James Falk and his team and to Nadia, Katarina, Anthony, Gary, Aart and Geoff at Valuad for your support.

When you haven't been working there isn't much money around, so I especially want to thank Garry and Maureen Welsh, Anthony van der Byl and Jacqueline Lion Cachet, Murray and Serena Crawford, Ted and Sharon Fawle, Dennis Karp, Trevor Gruzin, and FBK and JLK for their generous financial support, and even more importantly, the faith they have shown in me and the encouragement they have given me.

Ella Martin has made an enormous contribution – well beyond her proofing brief – as the 'eagle eye' of the project and has shown a terrific capacity to be flexible under time pressures.

There are numerous individuals who have contributed in many ways, not only specifically to this project, but also to me personally in the last 12 months. My warmest thanks to all of you.

about 'Youth Off the Streets' Inc

Founder and Director: Father Chris Riley.

Youth Off the Streets Mission Statement:

'Reclaiming and empowering chronically homeless youth by restoring social bonds. Providing accommodation, education, vocational, counselling and outreach services that respond to the physical and emotional needs of youth, in a way that respects the dignity of each individual without reference to race and creed. It is about maintaining youth in negative lifestyles; but about enabling them to step into their possibilities. This program challenges the culture of victimhood and celebrates instead the human capacity to triumph against the odds.'

Homelessness is one of the worst abuses and diseases known to young people anywhere in the world. Homelessness is about no love, no power, no future. It is about dislocation and not belonging.

To be a 'street kid' means that normally you are abused so badly at home or in your local neighbourhood that you have no choice but to leave home to live on the streets. 95% of the girls we deal with and 90% of the boys we deal with have been sexually abused. This has often happened at home, in their own neighbourhood or by someone they should have been able to trust. The abuse continues for them on the streets, because homelessness is the worst abuse of all. Homelessness means no friends, no family, always sick, hassled by police and security guards, ripped off by mates, involved in prostitution, usually drug dependent, hit on by pedophiles, often hungry and cold, no education, no future, no trust, absolute powerlessness.

To intervene or **reverse the cycle of poverty** and abuse, a major effort at many levels must be undertaken. The 'band-aid' solution is to feed, house and clothe young people; however, this method gives them a time out of the streets; but ultimately they end up back there because they lack the resources and skills to change their circumstances. Without the relevant structural changes needed, young homeless rarely live beyond 22 years of age and, if they do live longer, they are normally drug dependent and welfare bound. YOTS Inc. attacks the disease/abuse of the homeless problem at the structural level.

It achieves this by,

1. firstly, meeting the essential needs – clothing, food and accommodation;

2. it then challenges the young person to take control of their lives by making a commitment to leave their negative lifestyle behind them;

3. it provides them with the attachments and resources they have lacked for so long to bring out a change; and

4. stresses the importance of education and vocational training.

introduction

'We have decided to terminate your employment.'

It's not a great start to the day, and it's one that I've got in common with many Australians. And for me, like for anyone else, it was a shock, it was depressing, and it made me question just what the hell I was doing.

It was not until later, after months of to-ing and fro-ing when one contributor finally agreed to an interview, that I understood what it was I had been getting so wrong. The process of getting this interview – and others in *Collective Wisdom* – revealed some important things that I'd overlooked in my life so far, things that were so important they have changed my life direction. It was just a pity that I had to lose my job to be able to have the time to work them out.

When I was sacked – and there's no other way to put it – it was the first time that anything had ever gone wrong for me. And it went wrong in a big way. The boss called me in and let me know my work wasn't good enough, that I was different, and that I didn't fit in with the others. That was fairly in-your-face for a 22-year-old who'd always played by the rules, and who was working hard at being a success.

When you've never had things go really wrong, the first time they do it's a catastrophe. I'd had a good run. I was good at sport and at study. I'd talked my way into a prestigious merchant bank before I'd even finished my studies. I'd worked hard, but things seemed to work out for me too. It's not so difficult when all you do is follow a path seen as desirable by your workmates, parents and friends.

When things come that easy you don't think about them. You don't think about what's truly important to you, what success really is, or what you want your life to be. You just keep running along the same path, letting people assume that you want the life that they have. I'd swallowed the whole deal – that success is the fast car, the big house, lots of money, the 'important' job.

So when I lost my job I felt as though the worst thing that could happen had happened. Now I know it isn't such a big deal, but then, when I thought my career was a disaster, when screwing up my priorities had killed off a personal relationship, and a back injury had stopped my sporting career, it seemed things couldn't get much worse.

They could.

I thought about the managers I'd worked for, who thought nothing of working 16 hours a day, who didn't know their kids, who had beer guts and who were seen as successful and who appeared not to have much joy for life. That was where I was headed until I lost my job. With that model of success gone, I didn't know what to do.

Without a job my confidence was challenged. So I did nothing, my attitude stank and I had no idea where I was going. What I needed was to find some sense of satisfaction and passion in my life. And I can tell you, that wasn't going to happen the way I was.

I slipped into a routine of getting up late, reading the paper, watching *The Midday Show*, and wasting the afternoon. Without direction it's an easy thing to do. But after a while I started to notice something special about *The Midday Show*. The host, Kerri-Anne Kennerley, has a tremendous talent – her passion for her job. You can see her enjoying her work and it's this that makes her a great performer. I wanted that passion and energy for my life. The problem was I had no idea where to find it. I asked myself all the classic 'What am I here for?' questions. It's no surprise that I couldn't answer them, because no one else has been able to either. So, a little more humbly, I tried to work out my purpose for the next year. And it was then that some things started to happen. My mates had planned to go skiing, and I had decided not to go. At the last minute I changed my mind and went with them. I had committed to taking more risks, to be open to change, to live more for today and to just have a go.

I'd never been skiing before, so I was a bit clueless on the slopes. But because I wanted to improve, I took extra lessons and eventually got my skiing together. What made the real difference though, was observing the Austrian ski instructor up close. I learnt to ski by getting right behind him and doing exactly what he did – I just copied how he skied and suddenly I could ski.

Of course it was only skiing, but it started me thinking. I still didn't know what success was, I was still directionless. But I knew there were lots of successful people. It then became clear to me that you might be able to learn success just like you can learn skiing. You can watch the experts, copy the basics and then make the rest your own.

That's the real birthplace of this series of interviews – on the ski slopes. Just as I'd learnt from the expert skier, I wanted to get a glimpse of what made successful people successful. I wanted to learn what I could from them, and to find a few clues on how they tick.

I had suddenly found a passion. I started making lists of names of people to interview. I was almost obsessive, writing down names wherever they came to me. I imagined I could meet anyone I wanted to, anyone famous and/or interesting, anyone whose qualities, experience or achievements I could learn from. My mum despaired somewhat and would ask me when I'd go back to a normal life and get a proper job.

I made lists and lists of people. But I hadn't contacted anyone because I didn't know what to say. Why would they want to talk to me? I was young, 'between jobs' and that was about it. There are plenty of young people without jobs, so how was I going to get their interest?

It took a while, but eventually I came up with the idea of a book. I realised I could learn from the successful while helping others to learn from them as well by putting my interviews in a book.

I'm intense at the best of times, so once I identified what project I wanted, I scared myself with how focused I was. In five days I read eight books on publishing and wrote letters to every person I wanted to meet. I thought it would be that easy.

It wasn't. Everywhere I turned I was told how and why I would fail. That I should get a sensible job and 'just get on with life'. Every time I heard something like that (and it was often) it nibbled away at my confidence. It also made me more determined.

People in publishing tried to discourage me by saying: 'Books of interviews don't sell; you are not Ray Martin or Phillip Adams so who will buy your book? And anyway, you are not going to get the interviews you think you are!' A leading trade union official, who agreed to an interview, decided during the interview time I would benefit more from a 20-minute lecture on why the book would never be published.

So, people in the book business were saying I couldn't do it. Some of the people I was interviewing seemed a bit sceptical. And worse, some of my 'friends' made a point of letting me know I was unemployed, and that I should stop dreaming and start thinking about my future.

All I had was a see-sawing confidence in myself: confidence in someone with no contacts, no experience, no job, no publisher and no money. It's odd, but as the pressure grew, my resolve strengthened, and I decided *Collective Wisdom* would just have to happen.

But there were physical as well as emotional barriers to cross. To put together 34 interviews I had to make more than 3000 phone calls, send hundreds of letters and pass six months without earning an income. What's more, successful people are busy, with many demands on their time and energy, and you have to prove that you're not wasting their time, because they get a lot of time-wasters. I had to jump through hoops for media minders, managers and personal assistants. I changed my diary so many times I could hardly read it. I called back over and over to make it easier for people to speak to me. I did everything I could to help make the interview happen – and the most important thing was the fact to stay calm, pleasant, and always, always, always flexible.

Surprisingly, I managed to get 12 interviews done in the first seven weeks. After those first few interviews I thought things would gradually become easier. Was I wrong! The first interviewees had agreed almost immediately, then there was a period of more than a month without a single success. Every call I made or letter I sent led to a dead end. It was looking pretty grim.

But the breakthrough came with Bob Hawke. Not only did he contribute, he encouraged me at a time when I needed it. His interview then built a momentum that carried over into more interviews. By persisting through that five- or six-week period, I had got the project off the ground. And by persisting further the remaining interviews came through in waves of two or three at a time.

Then Peter Garrett set a major hurdle. When I contacted him, he asked for some sort of evidence that the book was going to happen. And fair enough too, because he was so busy. I could only give him my personal commitment. That was enough for him to agree 'in principle'. I knew that to get an interview with him I had to come back with something solid, to show that I was going to follow through. With that hurdle set, I moved on to prove to myself, and to Peter, that I could do it.

I was lucky too. Some people who had no time for an interview helped in other ways. Thomas Keneally was too busy, but offered to write review notes for the back cover. Kim Beazley made every effort to contribute, but fell sick at the last minute – while his media adviser spent a lot of time giving me tips and advice on how to get the book done. People were willing to accept constant follow-up calls, rescheduled appointments, reconfirmations and reorganisation. I was fortunate that such considerations were given.

However, I had a lot of trouble getting female contributors for the book. For this edition there are only seven out of 34, even though around half the people I approached were women. Sadly, they either didn't want to talk on the record about the issues in the book, or they didn't want to contribute to someone without a publisher and to a project as uncertain as mine.

And then there were the practicalities. How will I get it published? Do I know what I am doing? Above all else, how would I pay for it? These were basic problems, and I was surprised to discover that my confidence and commitment helped give me a solution.

I talked to everyone I could about the project. I rang an author of books on publishing, who took the time to advise me. I called the creator of a great tape series to ask for his tapes. And the more I talked to people, the more opportunities came my way. I met a publisher, who recommended an editor that was, and is, a total gem. Through her I found a book designer who was not only encouraging, but who offered to do the work for half price. Publicists and marketers offered support. This help from people who had been around for a while in the industry made it clear I was onto something. And all of them gave me help I had no right to expect, some without even charging for it. Suddenly, I had behind me a professional team with more than 100 years experience between them. I was learning fast.

The interviews themselves also came through people. Contributors introduced me to contributors I couldn't have reached otherwise. Gerry Harvey introduced me to John Singleton, who unfortunately didn't have time. Peter FitzSimons put in a word for me with Kim Beazley. The list goes on and on. And once things start to happen, luck runs your way as well. After I had interviewed Jeff Kennett, I was walking down Collins Street in Melbourne when I bumped into Malcolm Fraser. I interviewed him the next day.

Within six months I had done 34 face-to-face interviews, and had a great time doing it. Even now I can see myself talking to H.G. Nelson in a cafe in Bondi, doubled over with laughter for three hours. My cheeks are still sore. But even the less outrageous interviews gave me a lot. Putting the interviews together, and talking to the contributors themselves, showed me a lot of things I wouldn't have seen otherwise: from Edmund Capon's self-deprecating humour (and awesome secretary) to John Elliott's commitment to doing something rather than just going to meetings, to the need for persistence and honesty in achieving anything. In the process I ate Macca's with Peter Ritchie, chairman of McDonald's, discussed morality with Cardinal Edward Clancy, and politics with Cheryl Kernot. These are the sorts of learning opportunities most people would kill for.

All this was possible due to one very important group of people, the personal assistants of the contributors. A lesson I quickly learnt was that unless I could establish some kind of rapport with the assistants to the contributors then my request for an interview was never going to see the light of day. I tried hard to make helping me as easy as possible and I remained pleasant, completely flexible and respectful of their position.

But despite all this, the problem of how to publish the book remained. After talking to lots of people about the difficulty I was having, and how little support publishers seemed to offer, I decided to self-publish the book. In the end I didn't want to give control of my work to a company who hadn't helped make the project happen, or who had even discouraged me. I called myself Clown Publishing – because the serious players thought I was kidding about the book, and because I like the light touch clowns bring to their lives.

I needed a large amount of money to make my book a reality. But being out of work for six months meant I had absolutely none. I'd come to the end of my resources even though the book was ready to go. The money had to come from somewhere, and since no publisher would give it to me, I had to get a sponsor.

While I was trying to get a sponsorship together, I managed to find a great job. That was a winning move. With the help of my new boss, we put together a list of ten people who could act as patrons of the book. I approached six of them, and told them the story of the book, why I had done it and my need for funding. Oh, and I guaranteed I would pay it back no matter what, no matter how long it would take.

All six agreed to put up the money. I was stunned, relieved, overjoyed. I knew then the project could happen!

Through all the interviews I really had to learn some difficult truths about myself. When I was sacked, my boss said I needed to learn to listen – so for these interviews I really had to learn. I bought books on listening, particularly Hugh Mackay's book *Why Don't People Listen?* I worked on my listening skills in each of the interviews, trying to improve more each time, watching and copying others, until I had the pleasure of listening to Hugh himself a couple of months later. Funnily enough, our education system concentrates on teaching us to talk but rarely spends much time on listening skills. That personal development was one of the toughest aspects of the project.

This leads us back to Peter Garrett and that hurdle. And to the key thing that I have learnt from this whole exercise. Peter was eventually convinced that the book was a reality, not by me, but when my photographer brother Nathan sent him a letter with a photo taken at a Midnight Oil concert. The letter outlined the people I had already interviewed, and explained how the book was going to happen. That was enough to convince him. A letter and a photo, distributed by someone else, was what made the difference. It was what convinced Peter to do the interview.

That's the real gain I've made from the whole series of interviews. I wanted to learn what made successful people successful. Foolishly, I thought it would be something external, some skill or talent. But it doesn't seem to be like that. What seems to make successful people successful is exactly the same as what made my book a reality – the support, the help, the goodwill and the skills of people.

When I look at all the people I've interviewed, one of the things they have in common is a great skill at building relationships. They build rapport and relate to people with little effort. Not once did I feel ill-at ease in an interview, nor did I walk away without feeling I had got to know them in some way. They were friendly, generous and encouraging, much more so than I would have ever expected. In the main, they are people-people who can understand, relate to and work with others. Small touches come naturally to most of them. For example, Bob Hawke made a friend for life when he gave Nathan a Cuban cigar as a reminder of our visit.

They certainly have enormous reserves of energy and enthusiasm for what they do. And they are different and enjoy difference. If they weren't different they wouldn't be in this book. I am sure many of them weren't popular with their teachers at school. I'm sure many of them never fitted the mould school and work made for them. But merely being energetic and different doesn't *seem* to be enough without relationship skills.

The realisation that relationships make success has changed my view of success, and has changed my way of living. I had chased qualifications, skills, experience ... and let personal relationships flounder. I had some vision of being self-made, where I would be the total of my own efforts. Yet now I know all I can ever do is supply the energy and attitude to projects that coordinate people's abilities, ideas and enthusiasm. Everything is done with people.

That's the shift in my life – one that's happened through writing this book. You can't be successful unless relationships are the primary part of that success. With those relationships, you achieve more, your life is richer and more interesting, and you have a lot more fun. The differences between people, and their unique experiences, add an extra dimension to your life. Putting this book together is a classic example. Not only have I succeeded because of others, my life and vision is richer for all the people I have met and all the help given to me.

Everything worth achieving is achieved with people. This may be obvious to a lot of you ... it certainly wasn't to me. No one is truly self-made – after all, we start as the product of a few minutes joint effort. By seeing through the eyes of those who have contributed to *Collective Wisdom,* I hope you will be able to see how important others are to your success. No individual can solve the difficult issues we face as a society, but people working together in harmony have shown that anything is possible!

Brett Kelly
April 1998

the interviews

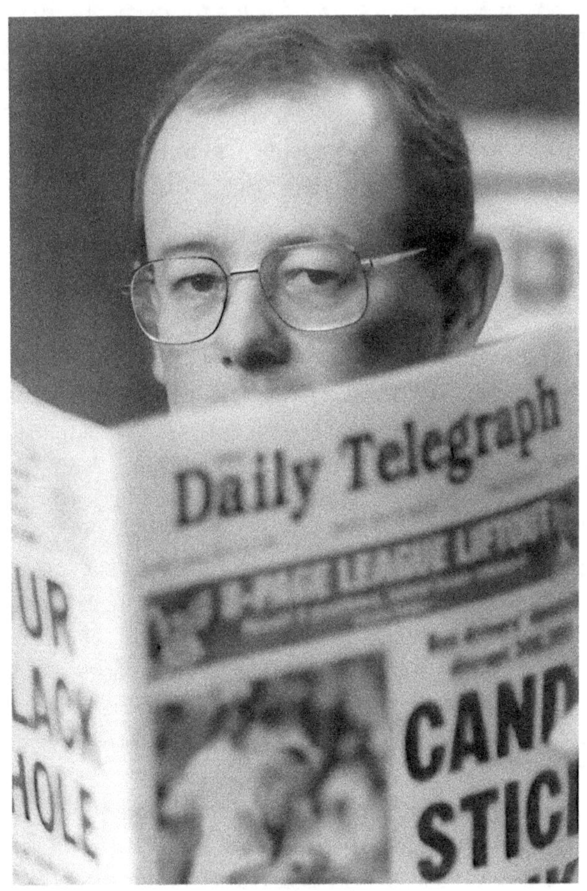

Col Allan

Editor, the *Daily Telegraph* (Sydney) News Limited

'Get into it'

BRETT KELLY: *Mr Allan, was there an idea, person or event that really had a significant impact in your life?*

COL ALLAN: Only that I was born before TV, and I grew up prior to TV. So for entertainment, I read. It's a dying art, you know – I think not enough young people read. And I grew up in a country town, so I suppose reading opened my mind and created my imagination in many ways. Of all the things that have occurred to me, perhaps the most important was having precious little else to do as a child other than read.

Is there a motto, quote or thought that really summarises your approach to life?
Flat out.

Just get into it?
Get into it!

What are the most critical issues facing Australia in the next decade?
Well, I think economic management is always the most important issue in any modern society. And very competent – visionary – economic management is the most important issue in this country, without a doubt.

Why is that?
It's not just about the creation of wealth. For a society to function, and for people essentially to enjoy their lives, and for them to believe there is a future for their children, we need an economy that is both stable and will continue to grow. So that our children can at the very least enjoy the standards that we enjoy. Those of us in the generation that is bringing up children, like our parents, would like to believe that we're leaving the country in a better shape than we got it.

What do you see are the best things about Australia today? And on the flipside, what are the things we need to do better?
I think that the nation's great strength is its egalitarianism, without any doubt. You go to any other society – West or East – there is no society on earth as egalitarian as the one that we have. And the dangers are anything that attacks that, including racism and economic discrimination.

Is there a personal experience of unemployment, perhaps a friend or family member, or a story you have done, that has given you a real insight into this issue?
Well, I haven't been touched by it, nor has my family, but I don't think you can do the sort of job that I do and not be very familiar with its consequences, and the human impact of unemployment. We see that constantly, in crime, drugs, and so on. So we have a strong feeling about unemployment.

What are the rewards from the job you do, apart from the money?
Ahha! Well, I work very long hours here, and I guess anyone who does any job purely for the money isn't going to succeed in the first instance. Financial reward is certainly part of working, and part of building a career, but if that is all there is, then my view is you are going to have a fairly limited career and limited success.

I think daily newspapers are fascinating, difficult – like wrestling a crocodile every day. So publishing a newspaper, to see the end result of a day's work very quickly, is one of the joys of the industry. It's a flawed business though. I'd like to think that we have tried to set pretty high standards here – certainly higher than existed previously. What that means, of course, is that you don't always meet those standards, so that can be frustrating. But a lot of the fun is in trying. I mean, anything that is easy is not really worth doing. So if you set standards that you are meeting two or three times per week instead of six times per week, it is kind of frustrating. But on the other hand, if you are meeting these standards every day of the week you are either a genius or you are setting your standards too low – and I tend to think it is the latter.

Is there a real sense of satisfaction in setting goals?
Absolutely.

Is there any merit in the idea of a work-for-the-dole or national service type scheme?
I take the view that there are two classes of welfare in this country, necessary and unnecessary. Clearly there are some people in our community who are unable to care for themselves, some people who through no fault of their own need assistance from the rest of the community, and I think it is proper that we do our best to take care of those fellow citizens who haven't been as fortunate as us.

On the other hand, I do think the system has been policed very poorly over a long period, and it has encouraged people not to work. We have made it too easy. So therefore I think that we need to be more vigilant in determining who are genuine in their need for any sort of welfare, not just unemployment benefits.

The USA is currently enjoying what we like to call full employment – a remarkable thing for a nation of 260 million people – and that is simply because people have to work. You sleep on the street otherwise. They don't have the universal and generous welfare provisions we have in this country.

Somewhere in between is the right position. I don't say we have to get rid of welfare just because I've got a job, but I think there is a lot of abuse and a lot of waste in the amount of money we spend on welfare. And I think the other danger for Australia is that you get generational welfare.

There was a very interesting study done in Philadelphia a couple of years ago – they were horrified to discover how many people in three generations were on welfare. And we are in real danger of creating a culture where you have parents in their 40s and 50s on welfare, and they are setting that standard, that pattern for their children.

In your experience, is Australia a racist nation?

No, it's not. I don't believe it is. It comes back to that wonderful equality we have here, the egalitarian nature of our society. Australians are essentially very tolerant people, they are willing to give everyone a go.

I think that it's possible that Australia is developing a racist undercurrent only because of the shrillness of a very small minority. But we are not a racist society, nor are we in danger of becoming a racist society. We need more immigrants in this country, not fewer. The USA is a complex, extraordinary society, but its success and its wealth have been largely built on immigration, both from Asia and from post-war Europe.

What is education, and what should it be in the '90s?

Education in this country is in deep trouble and I think it is one of the great problems we are facing. Education has been taken over by modernist views, taken over by people who count, by computers, and it is a terrible thing. I could talk for hours about this!

You know, kids don't study Shakespeare any more. What is the importance of Shakespeare? Well, one, it is difficult to read so you know it is challenging. Two, as children we were asked to read, but more importantly to comprehend it. You were asked to mount a case, for example – and this was something I enjoyed as a child – defending the role Brutus played in the assassination of Caesar. I think that anyone, if you read it, think about it, can mount a strong written comprehension case that Brutus was right to do what he did. Equally you could argue that he was a treacherous son of a bitch. But the point in all of this is that it encourages people to think and argue, in a very conscious way.

And do you know what comes from this? Ideas. People who teach themselves to think creatively about situations and problems develop creative minds. I don't believe children are born with creative minds. I think everyone potentially has a creative mind, but a classical education, in terms of the language and reading, forces your mind to become gymnastically active in understanding that you don't have to be right or wrong, as long as you can provide evidence that you are thinking.

What is happening today is the education system has been taken over by teachers who grew up in the age of numeracy, so they are not challenging kids any more. We see in the HSC, for example, the weighting, the importance of mathematics, science and those disciplines. And at the same time we see the importance of English and history being pushed down. It is an appalling mistake and we will pay for it ultimately. It will affect the economy of this nation in my view, because we are not encouraging people to be bright, to be thinkers.

In the USA, every degree has a liberal arts component. Is that an improvement?

My problem is that this damage is done way, way before university. This is happening in homes. Kids are watching too much TV and not being forced to read. I was talking to a lawyer who has turned off his TV in the house Monday to Friday. So the kids have got to read. I think it is fantastic. They only get to turn the TV on at weekends.

It was very difficult, he explained, at first, but the kids are now enjoying themselves and having conversation in the house.

I see this as a real problem. TV is a pure entertainment medium. We need to be entertained, but we have nothing else in our society at the moment – people watch TV and think they are getting information, but they are not. It is not helping us.

What role has formal education played in your life?

Not much. I went to the ANU in Canberra and I learnt two things there. I learnt how to play very, very good billiards and I got to understand a little bit about women. And indeed they threw me out after 12 months.

Are education opportunities plentiful and well distributed in Australia? And is there a danger where you have an increasing focus on 'up-front' university fees?

No, I think it is pretty reasonable and pretty fair. The problem remains high school. Kids are discriminated against in less affluent areas of Sydney, Melbourne and Brisbane. I think they should be getting the best teachers, and better resources.

My view is that governments assume that kids in some of those areas are not going to do very well so there is not much point in throwing resources at them. I don't believe that your intellect is determined by your postcode. But leaving aside the discrimination that occurs in some urban and country areas, I do think we are pretty fortunate in terms of higher education. I think the kids get a pretty fair go.

Your story on Mount Druitt High and the rest of it. Was that not a clear example of under-resourced areas not getting a fair deal?

Ah, the argument about Mount Druitt. Kids in that school were being taught in their final year at high school by people who weren't much older than them. Teachers in their very early 20s. You wouldn't find that at North Sydney Boys' High. You need to teach kids in their last year of high school, and at the same time, we need to understand that some do come from difficult backgrounds, there are broken families, there are economic pressures in some parts of western Sydney. They need more mature, better experienced teachers.

The reality is, teachers are like everybody else, they don't want to live too far from where they work. So the solution is to create some serious financial incentives for quality teachers to get into some of these less affluent areas.

If your kid had a drug habit, would you want society to treat them as a criminal, or as an ill person requiring treatment?

I've got a pretty clear view of that. Until the politicians change the law, people who sell and consume illicit drugs are breaking the law. The laws are in place because they represent the greater will of society and I don't listen to the shrill rantings of a handful of social engineers and left wingers who think that we should be taking care of drug addicts. If that's the case, let the politicians change the law and then let's see what the public says at the ballot box.

So if what we have been doing for the last 20 years hasn't worked, should we be looking for alternative solutions, rather than throwing another $100 million at the drugs problem?

I don't think we should decriminalise drugs. I do agree though that we need to spend more money helping people to break their habit. The government's done a fine job. It's got a two-pronged attack. But part of the problem is that the lawyers and the courts have gone soft on this stuff. People who sell and deal drugs are not punished in the way society wants them punished because there are all these liberal judges and liberal politicians who have this peculiar view. And we reject it. It's wrong.

If we accept that what we're doing doesn't work, is it time to look for another solution, to have a more open-minded approach?

Really, we should be building bigger jails and throwing more people in them.

If they are dealers?

Absolutely. And you make it stick, you throw them in jail and you tell them they will get out in 20 years. Now I'm not saying for a moment that this is going to kill the drug problem. It's not just a question of deterrents. That's important, but we are effectively encouraging an illicit drug culture in this country by slapping people over the wrists and then making a big racket over how much it is costing us. You do one thing or the other.

Is tax reform desirable? Does our system work? And how might a consumption tax fit in?

I think people make a mistake when we talk in this country about tax reform. The discussion is all about a consumption tax, but that's only part of the subject.

The country's crying out for tax reform. We pay too much tax, all of us pay too much tax. I don't get carried away with this idea of the black economy – there is no doubt there are some people making heaps of money avoiding tax. But it's a small part of the issue that we have an incredibly difficult Tax Act. There is an immense amount of red tape for business. We pay too much company tax in Australia. Payroll tax is outrageous – the idea that you would tax somebody because they are employing people, it's bizarre, it should be removed. And indeed the whole regime of sales tax.

Some of the examples John Howard used – a family goes out to purchase household items and pays a wholesale sales tax on them, but if you buy a Lamborghini you don't; or if Kerry Packer buys a jet, there's no tax. The whole thing is an appalling mess.

I think this government will reap a significant reward from the Australian people if they get it right and undertake a very significant overhaul of tax, and introduce a goods and services tax at around 12 percent.

Should Australia be a republic, and why?

I'm a republican. It's an emotional thing. But it's very difficult when you get into this discussion and people ask, are we going to be better off? Because you can't point at a bag of money or any very tangible benefit. And yet I become quite annoyed every time I hear the Queen of England described as the Queen of Australia. So I think it is important for us, for our children, to really look at the issue. The whole republic debate in this country seems to have become a debate between young and old – and that is probably good.

I am less inclined to change the flag than I used to be. The flag is a different issue – it is both a more emotional issue and a more difficult issue. And I think republicans who link the flag back to the republic are making a mistake. They hurt their cause in a sense.

Can you imagine a situation where voluntary euthanasia might be useful, and do you see a role for it in the next decade?

Yes, I do.

Do you think people are already pretty much accepting the concept?

Look, I don't think it's an issue most Australians think about all that often. It's not on the radar screen of most people. But if you ask the question, why not ... most people work hard and enjoy their lives and they should enjoy their deaths as well. What the hell!

One final question. I am looking at native title and at our system of government. The idea of a federal government using legislation to effectively change the outcome of a High Court decision – is that desirable?

Well, you know the High Court is not infallible. The High Court and the Parliament both draw their power from the people, and I think that sometimes the judges forget this. They are appointed by politicians who are appointed by the people. So the power and the will of the people must always win in any struggle on any issue.

My view about native title is that the Aborigines have done themselves great harm in not only politicising the issue but in making extravagant, outrageous claims. In terms of public relations they have done themselves a great disservice. And we require certainty – it is very important.

I don't believe that this is going to be a major issue at any election because there are more important things. The economy, tax, education, are the issues that people will contemplate as they fill out a ballot box. Not native title.

Thank you very much for your time.

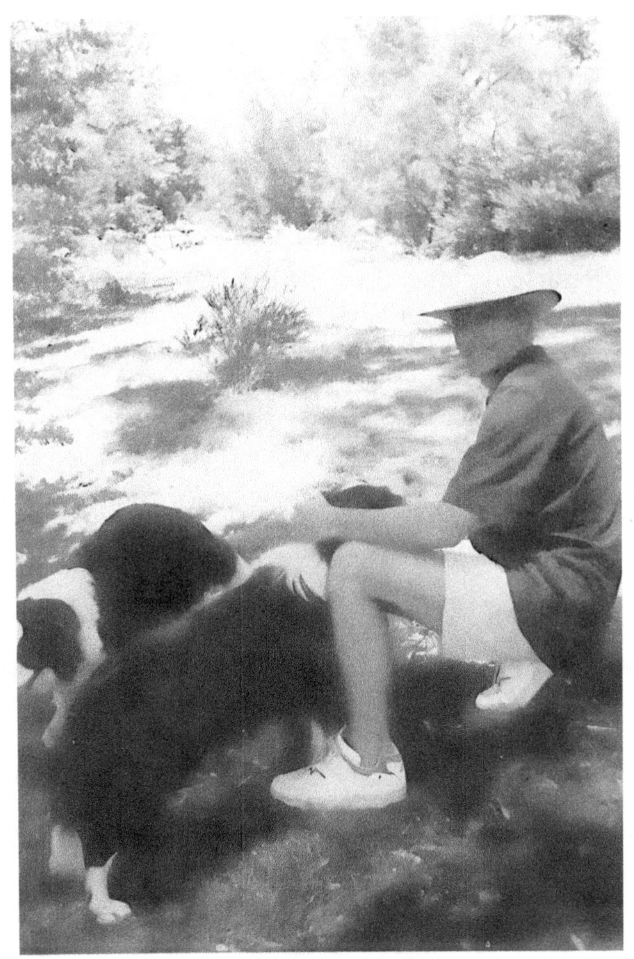

Peter Brock

Motor Racing Legend

'Bite off more than you can chew,
then chew like hell'

NATHAN KELLY: *What was the idea, person or event that had the single most profound impact on your life?*

PETER BROCK: There's something in those moments when you are faced with the absolute depths of despair, you have a feeling of extraordinary futility, that something has gone just so far out of whack in life that you are forced to sit back and reconsider the directions that you have been taking. That's when you learn lessons in life, through adversity.

I've had a few of those in my life because I've always worked on the basis of embracing life. I've never thought, I'll just do this little project, it'll be enough. I've got to have about 10 things on at once. So I've probably packed enough life experiences into one life to have accelerated my learning curve somewhat, but I suppose as long as you learn from these levels of adversity, well, it's all okay.

I can think of no one person who's had a profound influence, but I've had, as I've said, motor sport issues, business relationships, personal relationships. A handful of those probably have made a difference in my life.

Is there a motto, quote or thought that best summarises your approach to life?
Well, this is partially tongue in cheek but I've always had a great enthusiasm for life, a great vitality, and I'd say 'Bite off more than you can chew, then chew like hell.' It's just, *do* it! The greatest sin you can commit is to do nothing.

What do you consider the most critical issues facing Australia in the next decade?
Accepting that change is inevitable, change and reform in all areas. Change of the planet, change of the face of Australia, change of relationships. Understanding our position as part of a whole, that Australia is really a part of this world we live in. So we have to get rid of any isolationist ideas and a feeling of, stuff them, we're all right. We've got to be just as concerned about the state of the game in Lithuania as we are in Tasmania. That's a fact. Think globally and act globally. So I think there's going to be enormous change, and people have got to be able to cope with that change.

What do you see as the best things about Australia?
Well, the people. There is a level of friendliness and an outgoing nature here that is at least as good as anywhere else in the world. We are in danger of losing that because of the changes in society, but still that thread does exist. Australians are very open – they usually just say it as it is, and that's a good thing. We're not pompous, we don't put on an act, we're pretty open and honest.

You only need to travel to know that we are indeed very fortunate because we have this vastness, and because we are a new country we have a great potential not to make the same mistakes as other countries have made. I wouldn't say we're on that path at this point, we have been slavishly following Europe and the United States.

We live on an extraordinarily old and stable continent, with a great history and tradition, particularly through the Aboriginals – that consciousness of the planet

still exists here. That understanding of nature, of the land, of everything belonging to the land that makes the land what it is, whether it's an emu or a snake or a tree or a billabong. Aboriginals understand this far better than Europeans do, but I think Europeans are starting to learn a lot about that nowadays. Particularly with the debate about our national identity in both the Wik and the Constitutional issues.

The downside about Australia and Australians – do you think there are things that as a country we could maybe do a bit better?

Racial tolerance. We kid ourselves that we're tolerant, but you get with many people in positions of power and when you talk a little, tête-à-tête, and you find that they're as racist as the next person. And that stuns me, to think that people can be that way. You've got to be honest and say that a particular race may exhibit a certain character trait different from another one – that's just realistic. But to think that one is superior to another is bizarre. I think we need to learn that, and we are in a fantastic position to do so because we are probably the most cosmopolitan society that exists.

We've all had a different life experience, so it's understandable that we all have a different perception of things. As long as we understand that, and learn to tolerate and accept it, I think Australia will do well.

Is there a personal experience of unemployment, either your own or that of a family member or somebody you know, that has given you a particular insight into the issue of unemployment?

Well, our family hasn't had that, so I'd be stretching somewhat if I said I had a very close experience. But I do feel that a lot of people who are unemployed are often lacking in self-esteem and self-confidence to believe that they can actually do it. So they have a mind-set about a scarcity syndrome – you know, I'm not going to get any jobs because there's nothing out there for me. And the more you believe that the more it becomes self-fulfilling. To turn that around for young people is very, very difficult.

People often have unreal expectations, and maybe the job they're looking for simply doesn't exist. But when you say, here's a bit of manual labour, let's go plant some trees, it doesn't take long for them to say, oh, hang on, this is not me, I've got blisters on my hands, this is not my caper, I'm more into computers. Well, you can only have a certain percentage of the population involved in the computer industry, that's a fact – someone's got to make the planet kick along, provide food and shelter and all those things that people demand.

So it's a difficult one. I think it's a lot to do with people's understanding that the community has many facets – we need people who are prepared to work picking up refuse and others who are involved with making food available, others making shoes and others taking care of our spiritual wellbeing. As long as we have that type of thinking – we're much like a primitive tribe, we all have certain things we contribute to the group – we'll get along fine. But if everyone thinks they've got to have a university degree and they've got to be involved in the arts or filmmaking or whatever, well, I don't think everyone can do those things.

Do you agree with the basic concept of a work-for-the-dole scheme?
Well, yeah. I think people have to gain self-esteem. I couldn't think of anything more debilitating than to think, I'm not contributing anything, I'm just taking. Once people begin to accept that, they think, the country owes me a living. Look, there's no doubt that in this country we are all going to survive – some better than others. But from a personal development point of view we really need to be looking at making a fair contribution to society, to community.

Whether that is, say, going to an old people's home every afternoon and spending a couple of hours just sitting down chatting to people – that's a fantastic contribution. Not only do you gain wisdom from the elders, which that opportunity is sadly lacking, but at the same time you are providing company and brightening the lives of people who are otherwise cut off from the rest of community. So it doesn't mean you've got to be physically doing a job that results in the sale of product, for instance, but you've got to be out there getting involved in society and the way it works at all those levels.

So work-for-the-dole has its advantages, and I would say that its greatest advantage is in giving people a sense of self-esteem from doing something to get that money.

Do you think that there's an acceptable level of unemployment?
There's always going to be _some_ unemployment because there's a certain number of people out there who aren't prepared for that particular experience in their life. It's not appropriate for them to be working, that's reality. If you look within that person you would say, well, that girl there should be staying home with her kid or be looking after her sick mother. Yet she might be out looking for a job and the mother is suffering from cancer or something. Perhaps if she spent time looking after her mother, that would be a great contribution to community.

So you've always got to be looking at life, I guess, instead of looking at statistics. I think that your contribution to society is the major issue. People shouldn't feel that because they're not working they can't do any damn thing – there are a million things to do, like come out here and water some trees.

I'm astounded by the number of people who talk about their high ideals about the environment, yet they'll walk past litter on the footpath and walk past trees dying of thirst. I feel like, look, you've got this wonderful theory but you're not putting it into practice. We tend to be so high tech that we don't think in a basic practical manner. I'd love to see that turned around. That's going to take some strong leadership.

Society is edging towards more and more labour-saving devices. I've got a machine down there which can dig dams and big holes and one guy can get on it and do a fair amount of work in one day, like building a water storage unit, where 50 years ago it would have taken 10 blokes all summer to do the job with horses and carts. It would have been very labour intensive. Well, that world has changed – every facet of life, from turning on an electric stove to cooking dinner.

So there are less and less jobs out there. So you've got to change your mind about what is an acceptable job. The trouble is, we've had our heads filled with these ideas ... I'm very happy to go out and get involved in manual labour around the farm. People say, 'you're crazy, you could pay someone to do it'. I could, but I enjoy doing it. It gives me a great sense of satisfaction – you get your fingers in the dirt and while you're working it's like a form of meditation, it's relaxing.

Are there rewards in work besides money?

Well, I've never been motivated by money at all. That may surprise you. Money has never been the issue in my life. I've never cared about money. I've always just assumed that money is going to exist to go on to the next project in this dream of life – and basically it's happened. I've somehow scraped up enough to go on and do the next thing. If I wanted to go overseas, well, somehow I'd find a couple of grand to get an air ticket. I've never worried about how I was going to exist down the track, it's just the immediate concerns that seem to inspire me. I've never been involved in long-term planning – except that I would always want to be compassionate, caring, understanding and make a contribution to society.

I suppose you could say in the overall scheme of things that's basically what humans want to be. They like to look at others and say, gee, that person's pretty decent, I'd like to be like that. As long as they're ticking along they learn like that from other people.

So what motivates you to get into a car and drive around Bathurst for 1000 kilometres?

The simple answer is that you're doing something which is extraordinarily fulfilling from a personal point of view, that you have to overcome a number of personal obstacles to do it. Those obstacles are shutting off outside influences, learning to focus on the moment without allowing the noise of the other cars, television people, to distract you. So that gives you a great strength and resolve, to focus on your ability, just to be in that moment. That's a difficult thing to achieve.

Do you think that also applies to life?

Absolutely. You realise after a while that indeed life is the journey, not the destination. It's all about enjoying what it is you're doing and giving it your best shot and not worrying what the outcome might be but knowing what you're doing is going to control the outcome. The more you focus on the outcome, the less you can put into what you are doing. So I say to people, work on what you're doing right now, enjoy it every minute of the day. If this means getting up in the morning and cooking some breakfast, enjoy it, make it a nice breakfast; if you're having a cup of tea, enjoy your cup of tea. If you get caught in a traffic jam – you complain that you haven't got a spare moment, well now you've got a spare moment in a traffic jam it's all in the way you see things. So enjoy the moment and you will find that life unfolds very nicely.

In your experience is Australia a racist nation?

I believe it is, yeah. I'm not saying that it's overtly racist and there's going to be some racial war, but there is an underlying element there that must be addressed. Australians are not going to be able to move on to the next step and become a truly powerful group of people who can create change everywhere unless they understand that we're all in this together and there's no good making snide comments about Aboriginals or Vietnamese or Greeks or Italians or anyone else. It's the life force, the soul that's inhabiting the body, which is the thing you've got to address all the time.

So there is a need for Australia to be realistic. If you said to the Aboriginals, we apologise for the way we treated you, yeah we do. Of course we know terrible things were done, and we're terribly sorry today, and we would never ever do those things again. And then you can all move on. It's a simple thing to say, isn't it? I mean, we all know that it is a contentious issue at this point in time. But the wounds do exist, and they must be healed. Somehow we need to say, look, hang on, we're all in this together, we're all brothers and sisters, all the planet.

What is your concept of education?

Life is. The trouble is, though, that kids get caught up in the concepts. The academics have been to a large extent responsible for this belief that unless you do certain things on a certain campus you're not fit to live, you're not smart, not intelligent. Well, isn't it curious when you look around that some of the most brilliant ideas, inventions, new directions, that mankind has ever had come from people who are not formally qualified? As I say to people, 'don't give yourself a hard time.'

If you develop a thought form that says something is impossible within certain limitations, you're actually limiting yourself from some brilliant new idea that could be out there just waiting for you to pounce on it. A person who is open-minded, loves life, has a great ambition to see things get better, they'll get the ideas. So I see *life* as being the educator and I see the education system having to rapidly take stock of itself. It's going to have to take a far more spiritual point of view and say to people, 'here's who you really are' – like a Monty Python film, this is the so-called meaning of life, this is what it means, this is why you're on this planet.

If a child of yours had a drug habit, would you prefer society to treat them as a criminal or as an ill person requiring treatment?

Criminalisation has got no part in society – it hasn't worked. I think we're starting to realise nowadays that that person who commits the most horrendous crime, either against themselves or against others, is the person who needs the greatest level of love and compassion. Yet that person receives least, gets hatred, revenge. When in fact he or she is crying out for help.

The person who has a drug habit for instance is saying to you very simply, there is something wrong with life, I don't like it, I'm not fitting in too good. I signed up for life on this planet, but I'm trying to remove myself from it a bit. So they take some substance which just alters their consciousness a little, to pull away from the disillusionment they find with life.

As soon as you understand that that's the basic cause, you'll be able to say to that person, okay, well, let's get you back on track. It may take some time, but that's the approach.

You've said that what we've been doing over the last 20 years hasn't really been effective. Do we need to look 'outside the box' for solutions to the drugs problem?
I see no difference between drugs and the extreme of that problem, youth suicide. It's the final step. Youth suicide is just saying, 'well I'm getting out of this sense of reality, like permanently, I'm out of it – not just to escape it for a bit or to distort it for a bit, I'm getting right out of it!' So I'd group them together.

I group a lot of so-called driving accidents here, too. They're not accidents. They're people who just don't want to be there, they're doing something to upset the applecart – not too sure what it's going to be but they're prepared to put themselves enormously at risk. And a lot of the single-vehicle accidents I believe are suicides. They just drive off the road, bored. And with their friends, and they're just going crazy. Slow down or you'll be killed – do they slow down? Bang! Because they just don't like it, they are totally unhappy with life.

Now, to me, you can put band-aids on these things, give them a few Aspros but you've ultimately got to get to the fundamental reason – what's causing this person to do this in the first place? You've always got to honour the fact that every person is allowed to experience life, you can't force people not to do things. But you give them the guidance, the understanding, the wisdom, and perhaps you can get them through it with the least amount of heartache. Ultimately it's their responsibility and their choice. You've got to allow them to do that.

Talk about fencing off swimming pools to stop kids drowning – you can't do that with people. Think of every creek, every beach, every pond, every dam on a farm. It's like playgrounds, or stopping kids climbing trees. These are life's experiences – you fall down, you get hurt. That's life. Ultimately, you've got to accept that stuff is going to happen in life.

So I don't get too carried away with the law and order side. I'm more in line with the point of view that you take away the cause for a person to go down into those depths. Just say, 'look, here's an alternative, here's a choice, it's up to you', and *keep* offering those choices and support them all the way through. Don't withdraw the support if they fail, that's the point. That's what people do, they withdraw the support, say, well bugger you, you're on your own. But they need support *because* they've done something which you wouldn't do, because they didn't know any better. Help them, get close, increase those bonds, don't decrease them.

Do you think Australia will be a republic? If so, when? And why would anybody care?

I don't care. I mean, it will probably go that way, but I think we've far more major problems than a republic. I would see the evolution of the earth as being the major problem that exists at this moment.

And whether or not we become a republic is insignificant?

It really *is* insignificant. How you can hype up some sort of emotion out of that, I don't know. Because our Anglo-Saxon roots are becoming more and more tenuous as each day goes by, because of the influences from other countries. And I think there's no doubt that we are developing a stronger sense of nationality.

Could you imagine a situation where the option of voluntary euthanasia would be desirable?

Well, it's already in practice. The fact is that I think everyone knows around the traps that when an elderly person is suffering some severe debilitating disease, in extreme pain and discomfort, that these things slowly but surely and quietly get done. I don't know why it had to be raised, to be honest with you. I thought the system was just ticking along. I mean, everyone knows that there is a certain time to be arriving on the planet and a certain time to be leaving and these people, they're just going to go. That's all there is to it. It's a difficult one. If a person makes a decision from an intellectual point of view rather than a spiritual point of view, it's very difficult for everyone to get it right. I think people are finding ways anyway, that's my opinion.

Do you see the introduction of voluntary euthanasia laws in the next 10 years?

My view of what's going to happen over the next 10 years is probably totally different from anyone else's. I'd say that people are going to have to change so radically in their understanding of life and what it means that voluntary euthanasia laws will become irrelevant in the next two or three years. That's my opinion.

What's your understanding of the native title debate?

I don't know. I'll be absolutely honest with you. I can't figure it out, I can't see where it all sits. There is actually no doubt in my mind that Aboriginals are quite rightly demanding that they need some sort of understanding about where they're coming from, particularly with their heritage and their culture and those things that they hold most dear. Their attitude to the environment is understood by very few white people. I'd like to think I'm one of those.

Traditional Aboriginals live totally in harmony with the planet around them. I think that if the white community can become more in tune with their point of view we'll have gained an enormous amount. We should be using their skills, I suppose, trying to understand what are they on about. Because you can't put it down in dollars and cents, you can't put it down to mining rights, you can't put it down to land ownership. It's something different from all that. And surely

we've learnt by this time that our European way has not got all the answers, that there's a lot we can learn from those ancient people who have a totally different relationship with the earth. I think it's time we stopped and looked and said, okay, what are they on about? Let's learn from that.

Thank you very much for your time.

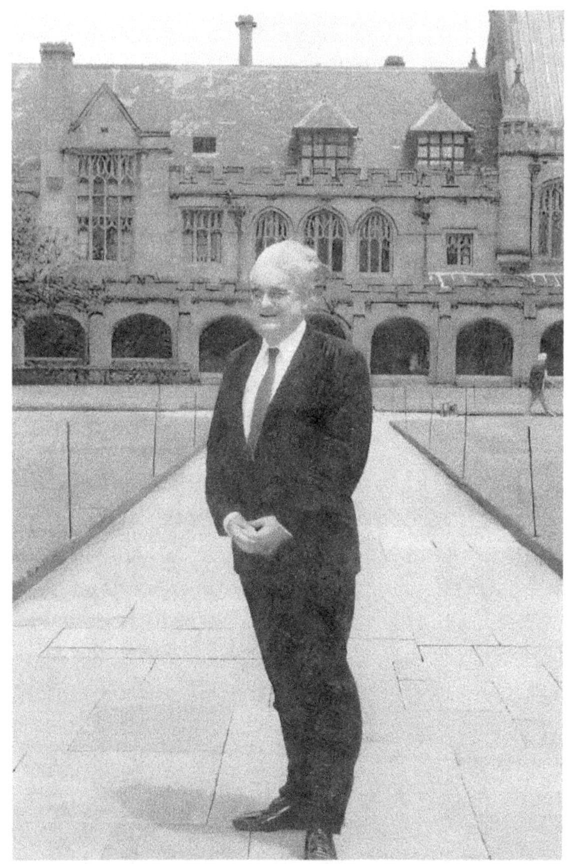

Professor Gavin Brown

Principal & Vice Chancellor, University of Sydney

'To be fearless'

BRETT KELLY: *Is there an idea or event that has had the single most profound influence on your life?*

GAVIN BROWN: One person who had a very big influence on me was my maths teacher at high school, a guy who by that time was over 70 and was still teaching. He came from a poor mining family in Fife. He had a double degree in classics and chemistry with a PhD in chemistry, and he still didn't speak English properly – it was very Scottish. In other words he was a very, very intelligent and cultured person, but at the same time he was still part of his original mining community. He was just a marvellous person.

And he inspired you to follow an academic career?
Yes.

Professor, is there a motto or a quote or thought that really summarises your approach to life?
I think it's to be fearless. If things are worth doing, they are worth doing to the full degree. You don't mess around and worry about other people's ideas, you decide what are the important things to concentrate on, and go ahead and do them.

What do you see as the critical issues facing Australia in the next decade?
There's the ongoing quest for a new national identity that comes out in a whole lot of ways. It comes out in terms of finding the right kind of reconciliation with the indigenous peoples. It comes out in questions about what sort of links one should have with Britain, the republic debate, and so on. It comes out for a relatively small population based at the edge of South-East Asia – how do you integrate with that region, how do you make sure that the country continues to generate its own wealth?

What do you see as the best things about Australia today?
It's got an extremely stable government structure. It's got all kinds of marvellous influences of every possible variety. I mean, it does things in a way which is incredibly harmonious. It's also got a terrific climate – and people do actually know how to enjoy themselves.

What do you see as the things maybe we could do better?
I think that we should be more competitive in all the areas that we're not so competitive in these days. We're still pretty competitive in sport – I'd like to see that kind of spirit translated into a whole lot of other activities.

Is there a personal experience of unemployment, perhaps of a relative or friend, that has given you a particular insight into the issue?
My father was a bricklayer, and in the winters in Scotland he was often laid off because it was too frosty to work. He would get a job clearing snow off the roads

or something like that to make money, but pretty regularly Christmas was a period when I expected my father would be laid off.

Have you found rewards in work apart from the monetary compensation, and if so, what are they?

Very much so – I would not be doing my present job if I was in it for the money. The principal reward is the way in which, by providing support to other people, you can give them an opportunity to achieve more than they might otherwise have achieved. I think that becomes very addictive. It's one of the reasons why you move from purely personal achievement to management, because it allows you to multiply.

Do you think there is an acceptable level of unemployment?

I think there is some sort of inevitable level of unemployment, but that's not quite the same thing as acceptable. *Any* unemployment is obviously undesirable. What I find particularly terrifying is where you start seeing second generation unemployment.

So presumably you think it should be less than what we've got?

I think we should be working extremely hard to find ways in which everybody has an opportunity. You get a kind of personal satisfaction out of making a useful contribution to society.

The concept of a work-for-the-dole or national service type of scheme, do you see any merit in that? I'm not looking for comment on particular government policy.

The obvious disadvantage is that it's not preparing people for long-term effective employment. On the other hand I'm quite attracted to the schemes which give people a degree of self-respect. Similarly those schemes which provide interest-free loans for people who are very poor – this enables them not to be ripped off by getting behind with huge debts. I personally would like to see these schemes having a small rate of interest, again because of the self-respect factor – I think it's very important.

In your experience is Australia a racist nation?

No, I think there is a very, very remarkable respect for multicultural development. There could be lots of national conflicts, carried over from Europe for example with our European migrants, and that's been remarkably absent. I believe it is not at all racist in terms of Asian migrants either. I think it's one of the most tolerant societies I've experienced. I think it's very important that it stays that way.

There's a lot of talk about education, training, preparation for work and all the rest of it, but at its core, what is education?

Education is giving the excitement of and respect for ideas – that's what it is at its core. So teaching should incorporate this, and there should be a process for encouraging people to be learners, who are going to continue with critical appraisal of ideas throughout their lives. Similarly, it is all about facing challenges and new ideas, and in some respects creating them.

What role has formal cultural education played in your life?
Not as much as you might expect. I was actually called in and questioned severely when I was a university student about non-attendance at lectures, as I didn't find lectures terribly useful. It was suggested to me that if I didn't attend a few then they might dispense with my presence. So in that sense the formal classroom experience may be severely over-rated. It may suit some people's personality but it didn't happen to suit mine. I was still holding very well in what I was asked to do, and of course there is a great amount of benefit you get from being at university in terms of the other activities, sport and other things.

Do you think educational opportunities are plentiful and well distributed in Australia?
There is a problem about people having the support that enables them to live while getting an education, yet there's been too much focus on fees. This misses a large part of the point, which is that if you are going to have an education but deny yourself gainful employment, you starve while you are doing it, and you have to support yourself through that period. I believe that we haven't achieved an effective way of making education available – it is a very very difficult problem.

Do you think that significant 'up-front' fees are going to affect the quality and equity of opportunity in our universities?
I assume you mean adversely. I actually believe that we ought to have a system which is much more flexible than the present options. I favour a system in which universities receive anchor public funding and are able to charge top-up fees at their discretion. Of course this requires a system of scholarships and deferred federal loans. That would, I believe, increase both quality and equity of opportunity.

I didn't mean adversely, because I've just read your article and its observation that it's fine if you charge fees, but you then enter a global market – so if I was going to pay $25,000 to come to university here, I could pay that to go to a US university or any other university. But we want to see quality as well.
That's the other thing. Universities are certainly not in the business of making a profit but there's certainly a need to increase cost recovery, and to have that money available to enhance the quality of what they do, such as hiring and paying good staff.

If your child had a drug habit would you want them treated as a criminal or as an ill person requiring treatment?
It is a pity we didn't go in for the heroin trials. I think that in every example where one has attempted to deal with sociological problems by prohibition, new problems and tragedies have arisen.

Given that for 20 or more years we have tried the prohibition approach and it hasn't worked, is it time we looked 'outside the square' for a new solution?
Yes, but there is a lot of controversy attaching itself to countries like Switzerland and Holland that try and determine a solution. I mean, you can send two different observers there to see what they have found, and you get two different stories back.

Not specifically the ACT proposed trial, but the idea that the government might supply currently prohibited drugs on a program to AIDS sufferers, how does that seem?
It seems to me that would be a reasonable thing to do.

Tax reform, possibly including consumption tax, is it desirable?
I believe so. I think that the arguments that say it is socially regressive are not valid. It is possible if you are on a high level of income that you also have the sophistication and the means to arrange to not be heavily subject to income tax, so a consumption tax can help ensure fairness.

Do you have any primary concerns you would like to see addressed in that agenda?
Obviously if one were going to make a major reform in the tax system then one needs to be very sure of one's planning. It is important to set in place measures which preserve social justice. On the other hand, you don't want to screw up the rational system you're trying to put in place. It's actually a very difficult subject we don't know the ideal answer.

Should Australia be a republic, and if so, when? And why should Australians care?
I touched earlier on the idea that I think Australia needs to re-evaluate its relationship with the United Kingdom and certainly Australia needs to assert its own national identity. Whether that translates into becoming a republic is a different issue, and it's one of those technical constitutional issues on which I'm not going to speak.

Can you see it happening before 2000 or 2001?
I'd be amazed if it did.

Do you see any real benefits for Australians in becoming a republic?
Well, I can see very real benefits for Australia in asserting its own identity.

Can you imagine a situation where it would be desirable to have the option of voluntary euthanasia?
I certainly don't rule that out as an option that people might want to take. Obviously it's something that needs tremendous safeguards, so it doesn't permit a situation where unreasonable pressure could be put on people to use it.

Given the idea that the legislature and judiciary should be separate in a constitutional monarchy, do you think the Howard Government's Ten Point Plan is desirable in respect of that separation?

Actually I think it's the government that should be making the law rather than the judiciary, so in that sense the government has every right to legislate. That's got nothing to do with the rights or wrongs of the particular plan. In practice, however, most law gets made by a kind of interactive process and there is a sense in which what goes on in the courts does actually change the law. But that should always get picked up by the government of the day as soon as possible and actually be enshrined in the law, so that the law at the end of the day gets made by the legislature.

Terrific. That's all. Thank you very much.

Edmund Capon

The Director, Art Gallery of NSW

'A pox on whoever invented the word accountability'

BRETT KELLY: *What was the idea, person or event that had the single most profound impact on your life, to date?*

EDMUND CAPON: I can tell you *who* had the most influence. It was very professional in that respect – it was my English teacher at school, who suddenly managed to open the door to an appreciation of the intangible. Through the magic of literature and poetry and, above all, not through the material, if you like, or the language, but the notion that behind that language there was the expression of the human experience.

Is there a motto, quote or thought that you feel really summarises your approach to life?
How rude can one be here?

As rude as you like.
'A pox on whoever invented the word accountability.'

What do you mean by that?
Because we seem here, in a place like this, to have to rationalise and be accountable in detail to people who, firstly, are in no position to make judgements about this process of accountability, and secondly, the yardsticks of accountability are irrelevant to an institution like this, which is dealing basically with the qualities and intangibles of the human imagination.

What are the most critical issues facing Australia in the next decade?
Obviously the republic – get on with it.

You think that that is critical?
Absolutely, fundamentally the only real issue. And maybe we should have a Civil War to do it, because that's probably the only way to do it.

It is critical or merely symbolic?
Critical in every conceivable way. I mean, this country is like a middle-aged man still living at home. It's unbelievable – I simply can't understand it. I'm bewildered by it. People in Britain are totally bemused by the fact that this country still has their queen as its head of state.

What do you think are the best things about Australia?
The best thing without doubt is its spirit. There's an incredible spirit in this place – there's a wonderful mixture of a spirit that is underwritten by convention, yet is determined to break convention. That is a magical mix for a wonderful spirit.

So what do you think are things we could do better?

One of the worst things about Australia is indecisiveness. The country is totally, totally bound by indecision, and that is a leadership question.

Is there a personal experience of unemployment, with a friend, family or whoever, that you feel has given you a particular insight into the issue?

I have been fortunate in not experiencing unemployment myself, but I'm very conscious of people who are unemployed. In one case, for example, one who does not *wish* to be unemployed, but is being too particular about what they want to do. My feeling is that if you're absolutely *determined* not to be unemployed, you can probably find something. And the other example is one who is clearly comfortable about being unemployed, with a lack of energy and drive. These are very hospitable people, in the sense of communicating with people, society, but the lack of purpose I find quite debilitating.

Have you found rewards in the work that you do apart from the monetary compensation?

Absolutely. I believe firmly – I've always believed this – I would rather have 100 percent part employment than 60 percent full employment. With all the technologies and machinery that can do the things which the human hand once had to do, the need for a reasonable level of employment inevitably is going to lessen the amount of work that we each do. I'm a profound believer that if it comes to one job available and there are two people there to do it, then rather than give one person the job and put the other out of work, every single time I would say share, share the work. I believe that the economics of employment are rather unjust, socially unjust, because they actually push for full exploitation of the 'one person, one job' and push people out of potential employment. The other agenda, of course, is to say that the high rate of unemployment means you can keep wages down. That, for me, is complete anathema. If there's a finite amount of work to be done, and people to be employed, it should be spread around.

So there really isn't any acceptable level of unemployment?

I don't think there's any acceptable level of unemployment. No. It may be an idealistic and impractical point of view, but if anybody wants half this job – just let me know!

Do you agree, in general, with the idea of national service or a work-for-the-dole scheme, or some sort of scheme where people if they were unemployed could find work? Would it be a good idea?

Well, in my scheme of things, that wouldn't arise. As a short-term solution, I'm not totally opposed to it, although it sounds rather insidious and nasty. You can see all the potential implications of cheap labour and exploitation, etcetera, which are very uncomfortable. But if there was a total change in the employment ethic then we wouldn't have this situation.

One of the things that totally bewildered me about employment here was actually a payroll tax. Here we are worrying about creating jobs and creating employment, so what do you do? You tax people who are employing them! For me that is one of the most bewilderingly stupid things. My answer to this question is a bit ambiguous, I suppose. I don't feel comfortable about a work-for-the-dole scheme, but it might work well – it could. You can see how it could be perceived as an indignity though. Maybe we could find some ways around that – not by saying 'this is dole work' but by saying 'here is a group of 100,000 people who need some employment'. And basically do what happens a little bit here and in other places, whereby you are given people on a training scheme or something like that. Obviously there are better ways than just saying because you're unemployed you've got to go out and sweep the road. Though at the same time, you go out and look around a place like Sydney, look at the mess. I travel on the trains quite a lot, and I think some of that unemployment benefit money should actually be directed not towards paying the unemployed but giving the railways that money to employ people to clean the trains. Isn't there another way around it? Instead of paying unemployment, give a company that money to employ a person. I know it's complicated, but we could do better.

So, do you think in your experience Australia is a racist nation?
I don't feel comfortable with generalisations. I really don't. The reality is that there are people in this country who believe, very, very profoundly, that the colour of a person's skin affects their intellectual, emotional and social capacity. There's no doubt about that. But whether that makes Australia a racist country is very much another question. I think, when you ask questions like that, you tend to say well, what is the attitude that's actually represented in government? And it seems to me, if you ask that question, the answer is yes.

At the federal level?
Yes, absolutely. I mean, what does one mean by 'racist'? Because you're born with a certain attitude that you are actually superior to another. There's no doubt as to whether you could call Australia a racist nation. I don't feel comfortable with that, because I actually don't know. I know people here who feel that way very strongly. But that's a very big generalised question.

What do you see as education? Do you see it as all classroom or a mix of work and life experience? And do you feel the opportunities for university and TAFE are well distributed?
Well, education is two things to start with. Mainly it's about experience and learning from experience. The fact is that in the first stages of that pattern we have to be taught. It might be unfashionable to say that – here everyone thinks they should express themselves – but frankly, what are you going to express if you have no knowledge? You've got to have teaching, and people have to learn from instruction. This is the training program for everything else.

Now knowledge in itself is not learning – it's information. So I see education in three very distinct phases. The first stage is being taught and that's the most important thing and it's underestimated now you know, we don't want to impose on children, we must let them express themselves. Fine – they should learn to express themselves, but they still need to be taught and they have to learn by dedication, devotion. Great minds do not work without discipline. Or great painters. Great writers do not write without discipline. Nothing in fact can be achieved without discipline. Discipline is part of the 'being taught' process.

The second part is where you have a mixture of being taught, like being fed the ingredients but you're actually making the stew at the end of the day. And the third part, this is where we have the 'real drama' ethic at the present time in universities – which are amongst the most dull institutions in this country, because they have become vocational training centres. Now this is a dictate of necessity to some extent. Universities are meant to be about liberating the mind, but in fact universities now constrain the mind. So that's my big beef, and whenever I go to a university they always come up with the same strategy for employment – specialisation, specialisation. People come out of universities for the most part with no more inner vision than when they went in, and that to me is a total reversal of what it should be about. Again it's two things. One is the pressure of specialisation, getting a job, which is perfectly understandable. It's also in the teaching – we lack horizontal minds in teaching, it's all vertical, so we produce little pegs in holes.

My feeling is that the universities are rather disappointing. The wonderful atmosphere of spirited debate has been reduced to very specific goals and achievements.

Edmund, touching on access to universities ... ?
Disaster, disaster. Just going to university to follow up on a profession and get a job is the worst possible reason, to me. The university's role should be absolutely the opposite. I feel passionate about education. My solution is very simple – that we halve the defence budget – or the attack budget – and put that into education. Does the future lie in defence or in education? It's education, isn't it? OK, so you put your money here, you don't put it there.

Australia has a huge illicit drug problem, particularly heroin among young Australians. If your child had a drug habit would you want society to see them as an ill person requiring treatment or as a criminal?
I can try and transport myself into that situation – obviously it's an ill person requiring treatment. The terrible thing is the people behind it.

What we're doing isn't working – is it time to look 'outside the square'?
I suppose instinctively I worry about legitimising things which are dangerous. The best thing in the world is simply not to have them. So in a sense making them illegal is obviously not likely to be effective. Obviously if there was no heroin we wouldn't have a heroin problem. Surely that would be better. So how do you remove it?

You don't remove it by making it legal, that's for sure. I don't know. Obviously it needs more review and a new approach. My concern is, what are the alternatives? Assuming you can't absolutely demolish production. That should be the ultimate objective, shouldn't it? The only one that's going to be effective.

There's been a lot of talk about tax reform. Is tax reform of some description desirable?

I think tax reform is a seriously exciting concept. It really gets me going. I think I'd love to sit down, and think and breathe tax reform ... [snoring sound]. I don't know. What pisses me off, and it really does, is the fact that the bulk of the tax revenue comes from the average worker at whatever level, and they're paying their tax regularly. A source of great disgust to me is those people, few in number I agree, that have vast amounts of money and make tens of millions in one deal and hardly pay any tax. Hate it! ...

I basically believe in a fairly high tax, in a highly provided-for society. We all have an inherent dislike of tax but my own view is that, in a developed country such as Australia, a fairly high tax and a high level of service is always appropriate. So far as the consumption tax is concerned, to me the only benefit of that is that it might embrace all that money that is in the society that currently avoids tax. So if you're going to do that it's got to be compensated for in other ways, I suppose. There is a certain logic in that, I think. Because there's a lot of money going around that is not taxed, where it of course should be ... its owners are happily using the services paid for by taxes.

Do you think Australia will be a republic by 2000? What are the chances?

Receding rapidly. I mean, you see, the problem is that 2000 or perhaps 2001 have a degree of opportunism and urgency about them. If it's not done by 2001, people will say it doesn't really matter any more. Of course it matters, but the lethargy here about the republic absolutely staggers me. I'm bewildered.

Could you imagine the situation where the option of voluntary euthanasia would be desirable?

Absolutely, no doubt about it. You really need to go to old people's homes, retirement homes, to know the alternatives.

So you definitely see a role for this?

Absolutely.

Would it be a worrying shift in this society, if on the one hand we have laws to protect and value life, and on the other we're killing off people?

You're not killing off people. People are being allowed to make that decision for themselves. That's not being killed off.

The Wik Decision and Mabo. Rather than having a separation of legislature and judiciary you've got the government taking over with the Ten Point Plan. Do you approve?

That happens everywhere. They make the laws, they are empowered to make the laws ... Certain decisions that are made there might have an impact on new law, of course. I think it's a hard thing to say that they *don't* have that power. Because of course once the law is made, it's passed over to the courts. It's not a bad system, is it? After all, the government has a fundamental responsibility to make laws, and the making of new laws is going to be influenced to some extent by how laws relating to that new law have been enacted in the past. And that ostensibly embraces some notion of public attitude.

I think that what you're saying is that the High Court made a specific decision which the government didn't like, so it changed the law. But at the same time, how do you get around that? I'm not saying that it's right or wrong. We've empowered the government as the *law-making* body but not the *exercising-of-law* body. To a large extent in a society such as we enjoy, it is the public perception of that exercise of law which is the greatest influence. I think that, generally, existing laws are changed largely through the pressure of public opinion – and maybe, just, that is what the government *believes* it is doing – but I would suggest it is misreading public opinion.

If it's good enough to have a Ten Point Plan regarding Aboriginal land rights is it good enough for government to have perhaps a five or ten point plan clearly communicating where they're trying to take Australia – a national vision?

We have to have a corporate plan – I went to Woolworths to find mine.

Why do it? I mean governments lie, politicians lie, why bother? It would be pure fiction, it's a nice idea but would it be worth the paper it's written on? However, leaders have visions. This country has experienced a few leaders, not too many. History has experienced a few leaders ... leaders have vision. I think ultimately it's not up to governments. I think it's up to leaders. But Whitlam had a vision, and Keating; Mao Zedong and General de Gaulle did. They were great leaders, they were visionaries. So don't rely on governments for vision, rely on leaders.

Thank you very much for your time.

His Eminence
Cardinal Edward Clancy

Roman Catholic Church

'Faith conquers the world'

BRETT KELLY: *Cardinal, is there an idea, person or event that has had a profound influence on you?*

EDWARD CLANCY: Yes, I would have to say that that would be my dad. He would probably have been the biggest influence in my life in all sorts of ways, not always easy to identify. He was a man, I think, of great wisdom, balanced judgement. He was a very committed and dedicated Catholic but not demonstrative about it. It shows up for example in my decision to become a priest. He never in any way pressured me to become a priest but was always supportive. In that and in many other ways I'd say he probably was the single greatest influence in my life.

Is there a motto, quote or thought that best summarises your approach to life?

As a bishop I have a motto, which of course I chose. It is 'Faith conquers the world'. It is taken actually from the first letter of St John in the New Testament. Faith conquers the world. I think today we have a big confrontation between faith and what St John called 'the world'. To him the world means all that is evil in the world. He used the word 'world' in that sense of a secularist world that denies God and the values of the gospel. It is not new, that confrontation between faith and the world, and I think there is a great significance in that saying of St John's, that faith must overcome the world. So that was my chosen motto, and it is one by which I can easily live.

What do you see as the most critical issues for Australia in the next decade?

They tend to show up if you ask what are the worst things about Australia today. I think among the critical issues is the Christian faith, number one. We live in a Christian civilisation; we have inherited a Christian civilisation; it was Christianity that overcame barbarianism in the beginning and established our civilisation, its values, its norms, and they are very much under threat now. Whether or not they survive depends on whether or not our Christian faith prevails. I think we stand or fall on the ability of our Christian faith to maintain the basis of our civilisation. That is a big issue, not just for the churches but for the whole civilisation.

Issue number two, I think, is the family. It is a truism almost that the family is the basic unit of society. When the family begins to fall apart, society begins to fall apart. The family is under great stress today, and one might say even that it is falling apart. Not the least worry today is the size of the family, now barely sufficient to maintain the present national population. When we speak about an increasing population we speak in terms of immigration; but we can't depend on immigration to maintain our numbers. If the family does not become larger we get into the situation that Japan is in, top heavy with elderly people. Things are right out of kilter, out of balance, and in the end you don't have enough young people to maintain the older members. That is the sociological outcome of it all. So I think the limiting of families to one or two children has all sorts of implications for the future of our society and our world.

Another major issue is abortion. I think that it is the most damning indictment of our society today, that in excess of about 80,000 babies are killed every year in this country. You know, when I was growing up, abortion was considered shameful in the extreme and people were horrified at the very thought of it. Today it is accepted by society. When you stop to think what abortion really is, it is frightening that our nation would be involved in it. So I think that is another major issue.

I think that social justice is a major issue. While you have such a big gap between the rich and the poor, social justice will always be a major issue. I am not a communist, I don't think that everybody should be on the same income – certain people have skills and talents that others don't, and I suppose these should be transferred into financial terms – but there shouldn't be this great gaping gap that we have today. There is grave injustice here.

Employment, or unemployment, of course is a major issue. We shall get to that. Drug abuse is another obvious one. There is much talk about that at the moment. Education and health care, they are major issues also and they make headlines every day. If they weren't major issues they probably wouldn't attract so much attention.

Cardinal, there is a theme that runs through there for me. I am not sure whether you agree, but there seems to be an issue of the value of human life that runs through, as I understand it, central to Christianity, that human life has intrinsic value and I suppose that is concerned with all these issues?
It is a point that the Pope has made constantly throughout his pontificate, that every human being has an innate dignity, that is, a worth, a value, almost infinite value, present even in the poor old derelict lying in the gutter. He is made in the image, in the likeness of God. He is someone, some mother's son. Until we realise the dignity of every human individual from the moment of conception we are going to be in serious trouble. The innate value of life, or dignity of the individual, is indeed a common theme.

What do you see as the best things about Australia today?
Freedom, there is great freedom in this country, even though we do go over the top sometimes, where it becomes licence rather than freedom. Freedom and tolerance: I do think we are a tolerant people. And friendliness. I think that we are universally experienced as a friendly people. In my own moving around the world and visiting other countries I understand this perception.

What are the things that we can do better?
Abortion and unemployment are concrete kinds of things but I think, on a more theoretical level, the 'value vacuum' in society today is a concern. So many people just don't have values, not real values, those basic Christian values, the gospel values which have determined our Christian civilisation over the last couple of thousand years. People nowadays make their values up as they go along. The values today

might be different from the values tomorrow. The 'value vacuum' – yes, we can do better on that, as also unemployment, abortion, family.

When we talk about value vacuums and breakdown of family and abortion and social justice, all of those things, I suppose in the past it was a very church-centred society. The churches have been increasingly marginalised by other interest groups. What can the church do to arrest that decline?

I get that question from time to time – I got it from Alan Jones on the radio not so long ago. The fact of the matter is that today, all the churches can do is present and promote the gospel. They can't force it on anyone. Right from the beginning the Lord sent out the disciples two by two; he said, if you go somewhere and they welcome your message, stay there and accept their hospitality; do whatever has to be done and then move on. If they don't want you, shake the very dust from your shoes and go elsewhere where they do. So obviously the church can't impose itself upon people. I don't think, ultimately, that the church can be blamed if society walks away from the gospel.

That having been said, we live in the era of the mass media, the secular media monopolise mass communication. What they broadcast at saturation level has little to do with the gospel. They promote disvalues. Now that makes it very difficult for the church even to find a voice, and to make itself heard. So the church is right up against it in that sense, but the church has continued to do what it can, and we make what use of the media we can. A lot of people have the idea that the media are a kind of a neutral agency that one uses at will. But 'the media' really means the people who control the media and while there are many good people in the media, by and large, they are apostles of this secularist philosophy.

What is unemployment? Have you ever been unemployed?
What was your first job?

So, what is unemployment? I would say that unemployment is the absence or the lack of gainful and rewarding work. What is an acceptable level of unemployment? There is no acceptable level of unemployment. Not even 1 percent or 0.1 percent. Again it is a question of human dignity. Every person must not only be worthwhile but *feel* worthwhile and that means work, that means doing work. To say that in practice it is difficult, or, as some would say, impossible, to employ everybody in this technological age of ours, is not an excuse. Our society must devise a system in which everybody does have satisfying work to do.

Is the idea of people who can't get work being offered some sort of work by government and being paid for it, whether it is still called the dole or it is an actual wage or whatever; do you think that sort of scheme might have some value?

Ah yes, if people don't have work then somehow or other they still have to live and it is up to the government to provide them with at least the minimum whereby to do so. But I think that most people, the overwhelming majority of people, would prefer to work for what they get rather than just get it for no effort at all. Not everybody perhaps, but most would. And therefore I can see merit in a scheme whereby people did some work with the proviso, however, that it not be perceived or perceivable as some sort of a judgement, or a punishment of people who can't find work. It is not their fault if they can't, try as they might, get work. The scheme should be voluntary, but I do think that people's dignity demands that where possible they work for what they receive.

Are there any suggestions that you think would make a difference in the fight against unemployment?

Well, I think that there has to be some redistribution of wealth, and I just don't mean the Robin Hood thing, taking away from the rich and giving to the poor, it is more subtle and more difficult than that. But things are radically wrong when you get so many people who are very rich, and so many who are so very poor. We have a great big gap there. So means have to be found whereby the wealth of the country is more equally distributed. And there *are* ways of doing it, I am sure there are. I think it means a greater willingness on the part of those that are very well off to share their wellbeing and their fortune with others – not just by means of handouts but by some other mechanisms as well.

Secondly I think that in giving jobs, giving work to people, there should be a preferential option for the poor, and a preferential option for the young. It is easy to take on an adult employee. They have got some experience, they are more available, and that doesn't give a young person a chance. I think there will always be occasions when it is reasonable to choose somebody who is older and more experienced but there are many, many situations where there is not much difference and one should give preference to the young. For example, of two-income families, many could become one-income families, and while it is true in many cases that they need the second income to survive, I think in too many cases it just serves to maintain the standard of living to which they have become accustomed. So it means people being prepared to accept a lower standard of living in order that others may have a higher standard of living. There are many things we can do to make it a better city, a better country to live in, and this means work being made available; it means some of our taxes being distributed for that purpose. It is one of the acknowledged ways of providing work.

Do you feel that Australia is a racist nation?

No, I think one can't say that Australians are racist because we run second only to Israel in terms of per capita immigration. Israel is about 100 percent. We run second to that and yet we have had virtually no real trouble in Australia – little tensions turn up here and there, and we have the Pauline Hansons surfacing from time to time. But any country which for this length of time has had such a great diversity in its population, and no real violence in the streets, can't be called a racist nation.

At the same time, both the question and the answer are somewhat simplistic. I think that under pressure there can always be a certain antipathy to somebody of another race, but it doesn't necessarily add up to racism. Somebody like Pauline

Hanson can stimulate a fear of people one does not always understand. That sort of thing is always there, in every nation, I think. But are we racist? No, I would strongly maintain we are not.

What is education?

I think it is the development of one's talents and capacities. We all have certain talents and capacities that are developed, that need developing, through education.

The church through the Catholic school system is very involved in that area. How do you think you are serving people in that area?

I think we are doing pretty well actually. I think that our Catholic school system is doing a very good job, and parents certainly think so. There is a flow from State schools to private schools generally. I find our Catholic school communities are caring communities; there is this personal relationship, more personal than in many other schools. Whether or not they are preparing children sufficiently for the difficulties of later life and work, I don't know that I can answer that question. One could argue that because in later life so many run into all sorts of difficulties and so many don't get work, that we are not preparing them adequately, but I think that it is unfair to put all the onus on the school for that sort of preparation. Society itself, government, parents, all have to accept a share of that responsibility.

What role has formal classroom education and training played in your life?

It played a major role. I am of another generation, but things are not so different from today. I think that formal classroom education and training are still of great importance.

Is it the best place to learn about life?

There are all sorts of ways to learn about life, all sorts of facets to life, but I think classroom education and training is an essential component.

You touched on the flow of children from State education into all sorts of private education, suggesting that the quality of private schooling is generally superior to public school education. Do you see that opportunities for education are plentiful and well distributed in Australia?

With regard to your preliminary remarks, it is worth noting that I did all my primary education in the State school system and my father was a teacher in the State system, so I understand the State system and owe a lot to it. Are the opportunities plentiful and well distributed? They are plentiful but not well distributed. In the city there are plentiful universities, TAFE and all sorts of possibilities for people who want to learn, but the opportunities are mostly in the cities. Some of them are in the large country towns too, but a lot of people in the country don't have those facilities and they don't all have enough money to pay for them. So yes – plentiful but not well distributed.

In terms of well distributed, I was also looking at it from a socioeconomic perspective; to go to a private school generally has a cost associated with it where public education doesn't. It appears that university education is increasingly shifting to more 'up-front' fees. Do you see that as desirable?

No. I think it stands to reason that with the gap between the rich and the poor, and the increasing number of poor people, they are going to be disadvantaged every step of the way including education, and the fact that education *is* going to cost more means that they are going to be even more disadvantaged. It is probably worth saying that the Catholic school system educates a young person a lot less expensively than the State school system does. In Catholic schools there are levies, but they are in the State schools also. I don't think that the Catholic school system makes education more difficult for people, or less available, but certainly when you get to tertiary or beyond, then costs go up; and if universities favour fee-paying students as against subsidised students, there will be those who are greatly disadvantaged.

Here I am not looking for comment on the ACT's attempt at a heroin trial, but it appears that our efforts to attack the drug problem are not succeeding. Are you against the idea of illicit drugs being supplied to addicts under specific programs? And further, if what we are doing now isn't working, should we be looking 'outside the box' for an answer?

Somebody once said that it is a bad principle to legalise your problems – there is a lot of wisdom in that. I think for a start that any system of providing drugs, if it is not aimed at curing the person with the addiction, certainly I would be totally against it. If it is something that is going to gradually get them off the addiction, you would have to look at it. But I think the main trouble is in looking only at the superficial outcomes of drugs. All these other things we have been talking about – family dysfunction, unemployment, poverty, the atomisation of the younger generation today. Some young people don't belong to stable families, they don't belong to the church in any meaningful sense, they don't belong to any kind of association – they are very much loners even though they knock around together. When it comes to the crunch they have got nobody to look to with confidence, to lean on, to counsel them.

You were saying that there are deeper causes that need to be addressed?

Our government and society likes to brush over those, and just look at the immediate causes – oh this child ran away from home and got on to drugs so the reason he got on drugs is because he ran away from home. There may well be all sorts of good reasons for running away from home. We have to dig deeper to find the real causes. Unless they are addressed, unless they are solved, the problem of drug use is not going to go away.

When I put these questions together they weren't actually as topical as they've now become. I am not really looking for, as I have said in other questions, a political comment on what was proposed by Dr Hewson in his GST or anything like that, but really further to say – do you think that the tax system serves our nation well?
Anybody who has had to fill in a tax return would agree that we are not being served well and that the tax system needs to be reformed. Our knowledge that there are so many loopholes and so many people managing to find them confirms this. I think there is all sorts of evidence that the system needs reform – and simplification.

So we open the door to reform: one option is the GST. What do you feel are the critical issues that we should keep in mind when we are looking at tax reform?
The central thing is that whatever system we adopt, the main burden doesn't fall on the poorer people in society. Those with most should pay most, those with less should pay less. That should be the central principle.

What role can the church play in the tax reform debate?
We need to be concerned with principles – that is, moral principles. The church has a role in proclaiming moral principles. It hasn't any special expertise in economics.

You have touched on concern with the value of human life, and you also spoke of abortion. Another issue I am looking at is voluntary euthanasia. Do you see it playing a role in Australia's future?
Euthanasia is of course the deliberate intervention to terminate a person's life, in order to spare that person from suffering. It doesn't mean withdrawing futile and disproportionately stressful medical support that is unavailing – that's not euthanasia. To take a person's life is murder. To take one's own life is suicide. Neither is permissible according to the traditions of our civilisation. Will euthanasia play a part in the future? You are asking me to speculate – I don't think it will. I certainly hope it won't. I think the good sense of the community will prevail into the future, as it did recently when euthanasia became a political issue.

Do you see fundamental dangers in the widespread introduction of euthanasia legislation?
Absolutely. Anything as morally flawed as that will create all sorts of problems. For a start it's the thin edge of the wedge without any doubt, although that seems not a good argument in the public debate. Experience has shown elsewhere that when you introduce euthanasia, after a while you start not to consult the person, who may be only half conscious anyhow, or you increase the categories of people subject to euthanasia, people who could live to 100 but are mentally or physically impaired, for example. All those abuses are wide open once one has introduced active euthanasia.

The Prime Minister has a Ten Point Plan which appears to be an effort to circumvent the umpire's decision in terms of the High Court's findings in the Mabo and Wik cases. Do you see a situation where the government is putting a plan in place to negate the power of the judiciary, so as to bridge that separation that is fundamental to the operations of a constitutional monarchy such as ours? If so, is that a desirable precedent?

I wouldn't wish to speak on the intentions of the government, but I would say that the end result of the Ten Point Plan would be to leave the Aborigines worse off than they presently are, with less rights than they already have.

Moving away from that, but just in general, keeping the judiciary and the legislature separate – is that a good thing?

Oh, I think so, yes I do. I think that it's only while they remain separate, in tension somewhat, that we get the best deal and justice is preserved. If it were left to the politicians to both make the laws and interpret them, we would have good reason to be anxious. But on the other hand if it were all left to a handful of judges, again the balance would not be there, so I think the two should be kept separate and kept in tension.

Do you think that Australia will ever be a republic and what are the chances of that happening by 2000?

I think it will inevitably be a republic. I mean, 67 percent of our people are immigrants from countries other than Britain. That figure might not be quite right, but we certainly have a very big percentage, and an increasing percentage, that come from countries other than Britain and who have never had an allegiance to the Queen. Apart from that, we are a mature nation now, more or less, and it just doesn't make sense hanging on to the apron strings of England. So I think, yes, inevitably it will happen.

Is there a superior form of government to the one we have got? Do you see that as being critical to the republic issue?

That is a good question and a question that has to be asked. We don't want to have a republic just for the sake of having a republic or to shake off the embrace of Mother England just because it is Mother England. We need things like peace and justice and the government to deliver them. We need to take care that in adopting a new form of government we don't end up with worse. We're better to stay as we are than to adopt a worse, less effective form of government. Being a republic is not an end in itself.

Thank you very much for your time.

Ken Done

Artist

*'Look to this day. Yesterday is already a
dream and tomorrow is only a vision'*

BRETT KELLY: *Is there an idea, person or event that has had the single most profound influence on your life to date?*

KEN DONE: My parents had the most profound influence in my life because they allowed me to leave school when I was 14 to go to art school; they allowed me to choose the path that I wanted to follow at a time when most kids' parents would say no, stay at school.

Is there a motto, quote or thought that summarises your approach to life?
'Look to this day. Yesterday is already a dream and tomorrow is only a vision. But today, well lived, makes every day a dream of happiness and every tomorrow a vision of hope.' This is a quote my father had in his study.

What are the most critical issues facing Australia in the next decade?
Understanding that we are mature enough to make our own decisions and also mature enough to understand our real place in the world. So I feel, it just comes down to education and communication. Some kind of belief in holding onto those values that made Australia, and yet with a clear understanding that Australia at the end of this century, end of this millennium, is very different to what it was at the start of the century or even in the '40s when I was born.

What are the best things about Australia today?
Number one is our geographical position which enables us to have, in a sense, a world view from a slightly different position. The second, I think, is the inherent fairness which you find in Australia, and the fact that Australia is a genuinely multicultural society working well, changing laws, changing things, without violence in most cases.

Are there things which you think we could do better?
We could do better at being more tolerant, we could be more appreciative of some of the skills that we have in this country, we could be better at our understanding of the responsibilities that we have to indigenous people. It's just like any human being's life, we could *all* be better. And so it's just a matter of whether you're optimistic about the future or pessimistic about it.

Is there a personal experience, either yours or that of a friend or relative, that you feel has really given you an insight into unemployment?
I had my first business when I was 11 and I've told this story before. How long do you want it? I'll give it to you briefly. I had a great mate, he had a set of ball-bearing wheels. In those days, I'm talking 1951, if you had a billy cart mostly you had old pram wheels on it or something. This kid had a great set of ball-bearing wheels, so I decided that I would go into partnership with him, he'd put his wheels on my billy cart and we would start a manure business. I did this terrific poster that had

a series of drawings of animals down one side and various prices that we would charge for manure. So every Saturday – I lived in Springwood in the Blue Mountains at the time – this kid and I would go out and hide behind the trees and basically watch animals and see them make some product, and if they did we'd go out and bag it. Then we'd go and sell it, essentially to my mother and my aunt, and it was a terrific business. It ran for about three weeks. Until this guy decided he wanted his ball-bearing wheels back. So I saw my business collapse at that time. That taught me that for me it is about control. Not in a megalomaniac sense, not in a dictatorial sense. But as a painter or designer or even as a businessman, I like to give people great degrees of responsibility and certainly reward creativity – but essentially I like to take things in the direction that I believe they should be going. So there's some self-confidence in it, I suppose.

Have you found rewards in the work that you do apart from the monetary compensation?

Oh sure, if it was just money I wouldn't be doing it. I'm sure that you'll find this with anybody that you talk to. Most artists are expected to be starving or dead, well I'm not. I *see* no reason why artists shouldn't make a reasonable living. So you have to remember that even though I went to art school when I was 14, I was 40 before I had my first exhibition. I'd worked for a long time before I was ready to show things, and the first things I showed, I wanted them to be simple things that would reach a wide audience and that people would be happy in buying and having. And I saw no problem in reaching a wide audience. So every problem I'm trying to solve, I'm trying to think, who am I talking to? Now obviously if it's something in the design business, if it's a pair of socks – now there's a pair of socks, I'm showing you a wonderful pair of striped socks, this is not the Sistine Chapel or the Mona Lisa, but it should be thought of not only as a pair of socks but as a good pair of socks. If I'm making a painting – this big picture here about the feeling of being underneath the reef – you could see that as purely decorative, which I'm quite happy with, or you could see it as something that gives you joy about the amount of colour, or you could also see it as a strong political statement saying the reef is a beautiful place and therefore we should preserve those kinds of things. I like to work at a multiplicity of things and a multiplicity of attitudes and a multiplicity of problems that I'm trying to solve.

What tangible things, apart from money, have you got from work?

Well, art essentially is interesting because it is one of the few things – I suppose writing could be another – where you have to get better as you get older. I mean I'm 57, I hope to be quite good when I'm about 65 to 70, and yet I've worked for 50 years. I can't think of a time when I wasn't painting and drawing. So it's a journey, and the harder you work, I think you might understand, the further up that particular track you go. But artists are really part of the whole road of people you're influenced by, all kinds of different people. In the end you have to find your own path, your own track. The rewards, apart from the monetary ones, are the intellectual ones. Knowing more about yourself, understanding more about your successes and your failures.

Is there an acceptable level of unemployment? We hear people say unemployment is too high.

I don't think there is an acceptable level of unemployment. I suppose it is naive to imagine that there'll ever be nil unemployment. Clearly there's a point where you do have to have people seeking jobs and moving around. I think there is nothing more important than that all people feel a sense of their worth, and the concept of working is absolutely paramount, absolutely prime. And given that fact, you know there will be some people who for various reasons need to be supported by the government. I would look for situations where any government's main thrust is finding work and building up a climate in which business operates successfully, because it's business by and large that creates employment.

Can you see any merit in these discussions – not looking for comments on particular political suggestions – about a work-for-the-dole or some similar scheme?

Sure, I've got no problems with that. I know there are varying degrees – some people would go as far as saying it's slave labour, other people think it's a fantastic idea – I think I'm more towards the end of 'it's a very good idea'. Anything that gives people even the skills of being at a certain place at a certain time – you said you'd be here at 10 o'clock, you were here at 10 o'clock – this is absolutely prime. I think there are probably a lot of people that need to know those particular lessons, the lessons of punctuality, the lessons of learning from other people. The lessons of accepting there is certain knowledge that can only come with time, and feeling satisfaction after a day of work – whether it be mowing a lawn, weeding a nature strip, or developing a computer game – these are all good feelings to have. Better feelings, I think, than lying around becoming despondent.

Are there any concerns that you would have about that sort of scheme?

I don't have any concerns about this scheme, I mean I'm not an expert on it ...

Not that particular scheme, but I'm sort of having feedback whether it should be compulsory or it shouldn't be compulsory ...

Yes, I certainly believe that you shouldn't continue to pay the dole to young people after a given period of time. It is necessary to have the drive and desire to find work. You're not necessarily going to find work lying on the beach at Byron Bay, as great as Byron Bay is. I'm not against the beach culture at all, but I think that when you find a situation where you have two or three generations of a family that have all lived on government handouts – or artists, a case I understand better I suppose – where artists believe that somehow the government owes them the money ... I've never had a grant, I've never had any assistance, and I believe that if you're passionate about what you want to do, you'll find ways of doing it.

Ken, in your experience is Australia a racist nation?

No, I don't think Australia is a racist nation, although there are the seeds of racism within all of us. I mean, I'm Australia's goodwill ambassador to UNICEF, so I often find myself in refugee camps in Africa and Vietnam and places. I was always brought up to think that all people are equal. Yet I've been in lots of situations in lots of countries where clearly one group feels slightly different from another group. Whether that is India or Nepal or Africa or North Sydney, people have these feelings. They're basic human things, they're only broken down by education and understanding. It would be sad, I think, to see Australia less tolerant, because it is a pretty tolerant society.

Ken, I was interested you said you left school at 14. I ask people broadly, so what was your education?

Well, education is – I'm going to give you the classic answer ... it's for your entire life. I mean I left school at 14 to go to art school, it's just that I was more interested in studying art in those years than algebra or geometry. I continued my education till 18 or 19, but it just happened. I think if you're a painter or musician or something like that you need to be studying those things early. I was grateful my parents had the understanding to let me do those things. But no, education is what you listen to on the news in the car, and what you learn from the problems that you tackle during the day – it's forever if you want it to be forever.

What role has formal classroom education played in your life?

I think quite considerable, but again if you think I started school at four so there was sort of 10 years of 'school' but then there was another four years of art school so that was classroom in a sense. I don't think you can ever add up the balance between what you learnt from the classroom and what you learnt from the streets. I happen to have a business that's quite successful, that I guess has a pretty good reputation and turns over quite a bit of money, but there's lots of it that I don't understand or I'm not intelligent enough to really participate in, so therefore I use people to fill in those gaps as I like to concentrate on the big picture.

At the moment we have 'up-front' fees for universities. Do you see that as likely to affect the quality and equality of opportunity in tertiary institutions?

Yeah, I think it's a bit of a worry. It would be a great sadness for bright students from disadvantaged families to slip through the net and not have those opportunities. I'm not quite sure how you balance that, but bright is bright wherever it comes from and you shouldn't be allowed to simply buy a degree.

Are educational opportunities plentiful and well distributed in Australia?

I don't know that much about it. I've been a bit disappointed with the quality of the students that I've seen coming out of the art schools. I think that maybe over the last 10 years or so there's been a lot of conceptual thought come out of art schools whereas there needs to be always a great emphasis on basic hand skills. It's like being a musician. If you go to the conservatorium, for the first five years you learn how to play the instrument, not to make some comment on music at large. So I think almost inevitably we need a slight return in the art schools to more hand-based skills, so that when you go into a gallery and see something that purports to be a work of art you look at it and understand that someone has worked very hard and acquired skills to do that, rather than seeing in an art gallery a half-eaten sandwich and pair of fireman's boots in the corner and someone telling you it's a piece of conceptual art.

I'm looking at the issues of illicit drugs. Last year there were 900 deaths from heroin in Australia. If your child had a drug habit, should he or she be treated as a criminal or as an ill person requiring treatment?

It's an addiction, there's no question about it. I was disappointed that the heroin trial in Canberra wasn't allowed to continue. I think we've got to be a lot more inventive and a lot more open in the ways that we deal with drug addiction and the education that goes with it. I'm not a smoker and haven't been for 20 years, but I'm a drinker. I enjoy wine and I handle it, and I guess I have some knowledge of its effects. It's important that society as a whole has the same amount of information about the number of illicit drugs that are available. It's naive to suggest that young people won't try drugs, they simply need to be informed about what it is doing to their bodies.

If we've been doing something for 20 years and it hasn't worked, is it time to look 'outside the box' for a solution?

I think it's very important to look outside of the box. They've got to look more carefully at the Swiss exercise, and the one in Israel where they are trying a different kind of detoxification. If you can take the criminal element away from it clearly that would make a difference to law and order – I think you try anything. I think there's nothing sadder than seeing people hooked on *any* drug, whether it be alcohol or heroin. And it's also very important that it be understood that drugs are not a kind of key to creativity. That it is the wrong message, for society to somehow feel that drugs open the mind to great works of art, music and so on.

Do you feel that our tax system serves us well? And is tax reform desirable?

Yes, I think tax reform is very important. We have no schemes, we're probably fairly naive in the way that we organise our tax. I'd be all for a GST – I think it makes a great deal more sense. I think that there are too many schemes used by the rich to avoid tax and there are too many tradesmen still working for cash. I would be happy with the GST tomorrow.

Ken, Australia as a republic – when do you think it's likely to happen and why would anyone care?

It will be like being 25 and wishing you'd had a 21st. It will be too late. We should be a republic by the year 2001. We should have a new flag by then. We should be seen as something unified and not divided. I believe I understand precisely what the new flag will be and should be, and if I had my way we'd have the new flag and the republic on 1 January 2001, or 26 January, Australia Day. Because I think if we don't, about five years after that people will say, we really should have done it then. The eyes of the entire world will be on Australia at that point in time. I'd prefer  it actually to be earlier – before our athletes walk into the stadium at the Olympic Games carrying the flag that represents Australia of the past. I'm not against the old flag but it doesn't genuinely represent who we are and what we've become in our maturity. It's like seeing a product and the product is called Australia. It's the greatest opportunity we've got, I think, to show our sense of maturity at that time. So if I had control I would want to show what those assets could look like and the symbol that they were carrying. However this won't happen, so the next possible thing would be that there'd be serious debate and I would hope reconciliation, not just between us and Aboriginals but between all Australians, to understand that 100 years after Federation is precisely the time when we should stand up and say 'this is the Australia that we've become and this is the Australia that we want to be for the next 100 years'.

You've sort of alluded to it, and so have a lot of people I've spoken with – at the end of the day, what's the value of the symbol?

Well it's just that – it's a symbol. It's not a picture of something. In fact a number of people who have made attempts to design the new Australia flag fall into the trap of wanting it to be a picture of Australia. That to me is as bizarre as if people in Switzerland sat down and said, can't we have a mountain in the corner. Well I mean you can't, and you don't need it. It's simply a symbol, and so our symbol will be, I believe, the Southern Cross. Every piece of research says that most people feel passionate about it, it has history, folklore, it has heritage. So to me it is just a matter of saying, what is the strongest and most powerful way that you can place the Southern Cross within the rectangle of the flag? That's question one. Once you've answered that, then question two is, what colour should this be? So that's two very simple questions, and once you know the answer to them, there is the new Australian flag. It shouldn't be thought of as the Ken Done flag, it should be thought of as everybody's flag, in the sense that it was always there. The Southern Cross was always there. All I've shown is that if you move it to the north, south, east and west of the rectangle you put it in the most powerful position, and that the colour of Australia should be blue and gold. Gold for the wealth of the nation, gold for the quality of the people and the aspiration and feelings of Australians, blue for the sky, the sea and as a continuation from the past. If you had that as a flag it wouldn't favour any groups. It was here before the Aboriginals were here, it doesn't single out any one group of people – Irish, Scots, Greeks, Italians, Australians, Aboriginals, it doesn't matter.

Can you see a situation where voluntary euthanasia – to have that as an option – would be desirable?

Not sure on that one. Desirable if there are enough checks and balances. I certainly think that I have a great deal of respect for people who have the courage to in fact go through with it, and I have seen people in such dire circumstances that you can understand their need to have the dignity of deciding when they go. But it's a matter of the checks and balances that go with it, so that it's not just open slather, with people feeling they can somehow tidy up society by lopping off all the ill ones.

Finally, Ken, I'm not looking specifically at native title here but I'm saying, well, Mr Howard came up with a Ten Point Plan and really the intent of that is to somehow change the High Court's decision – what do you think about that as a precedent? If rather than having a separation of legislature and judiciary you've got the politicians taking over the whole show?

I've done a symbol for reconciliation. You can make a black hand and white hand and make them go together and make them become Australia. I've given this symbol to be used by various groups in this particular debate. I've tried to follow it and I think I'm getting too confused now. Like a lot of other people I'm confused about where we're at. Although I don't feel a personal sense of involvement with, let's say, the lost children, I think it was a very sad thing. Just like famine in Vietnam, and the war, was a very sad thing. When I was in Vietnam in my role with UNICEF of course I was sorry for that situation, without having been there or been part of it. So I personally can't quite understand why it's impossible for a government to feel sorry in the broadest sense. Again, I have Aboriginal friends and I've been in the outback enough to know that the sense of understanding and relationship with the land that Aboriginals have is really quite special and unique.

But I feel it's not necessarily more special than how hard I had to work to buy my piece of land or how much I love it. If Aboriginals made claims on my little plot of land of course I would be furious. As I understand it, the Howard Government is trying to find this balance, trying to find an answer to this very very complex situation.

I was a bit concerned that people were saying recently this legislation should go through quickly. I don't actually think there needs to be a rush, I think it's a very important decision, even if it took another year – and if that year was done without some of the rhetoric that seems to me to become extreme on both sides. I've heard Noel Pearson speak rationally and quietly and calmly about it, I've heard him also be irrational about it. I've heard the prime minister speak rationally, calmly and clearly about it and I've also heard him say some things that I didn't quite agree with. I don't know ... like all Australians, I hope that we can find some balance, that miners, pastoralists, suburban dwellers, city dwellers and Aboriginals all in the end feel that they've been treated well, given the fact that in all cases there probably needs to be some compromise.

Thank you very much for your time.

Mark Ella

Former International Rugby Representative

'Attack is the best form of defence'

BRETT KELLY: *Is there an idea, person or event that has had the single most profound influence on your life?*

MARK ELLA: I guess growing up in La Perouse, we used to watch a lot of the rugby league finals when they were played at the Sydney Cricket Ground, through those heydays with up to 50,000 people sometimes watching the matches. In a way, I wanted to play at the SCG and overseas and have thousands of people screaming out for me. That sort of inspired me. It was something I always wanted to do, and when I finally did achieve it, it was very satisfying.

Do you have a motto, quote or thought that really summarises your approach to life?

Yeah. There are a number of cliches I guess that are used in sport and in life in general. There is one particular cliche, 'attack is the best form of defence'. In a lot of ways that sort of summed up the way I played the game of rugby – I'd rather attack with the ball in hand than play a defensive game. A lot of players are now more defence oriented, whereas I was always ready to attack. Whether we were behind by 50 points or in front by 50 points, you still attack. I mean there weren't many times in my playing career when I thought, let's just settle the game down, and play it nice and safe. It was always, let's have a go, particularly with my brothers – it was good fun.

What do you see as the most critical issues facing Australia in the next decade?

I think social welfare, the difference in social classes that we are creating in this country. It is true that the rich are getting richer and the poor are getting poorer. We are not giving, in terms of the social environment, a fair opportunity for every young child. Obviously, those whose parents have got money get the best education, the best opportunities. Those that live in poorer suburbs are being basically neglected by this government. I guess we need equality in our society, that gives every young girl or boy the opportunity of receiving a decent education, having the opportunity to play sport or whatever. It just seems there is an imbalanced society at the moment.

What do you see as the best things about Australia today, and what are the things we could do better?

I guess it's our nature, our lifestyle and our personality that are great. You know, we've got a fabulous country and natural highlights all around us: you go to Queensland with the beaches, Sydney Harbour, Ayers Rock. It doesn't matter where you go, there's some spectacular landscape. We should be selling ourselves more to the world. Again, when I travel overseas the Aussies are always natural. You can pick them out in a crowd, not because they're boisterous and loud, you know, but they're having a bit of fun. That's our character that makes us unique around the world.

Mark, is there a personal experience, either your own or that of a friend or relative, that you feel has really given you an insight into unemployment?

Well, I've been lucky to a certain extent – I've never had problems with being unemployed. I guess in a lot of ways that's because of my nature. Some of my brothers are still unemployed and it's taken them an awful long time to secure a job. A lot of them, either relatives or friends that I know, haven't the confidence to actually go through an interview process, to hold a steady job. In a lot of ways they're underselling themselves and getting the menial tasks, the government jobs, the council jobs. Really crazy, because they've got a lot more intelligence than what they give themselves credit for, but they just lack the social skills. It comes back to the education system – to be actually confident and go out and do it. I feel sorry for these guys because I mean, obviously they've left school, they're in their early 20s, if you lack confidence in your early 20s you're not aggressive enough to go out and sell yourself. If you're going to go through life like that, then that's a tragedy.

Mark, in the work that you've done have there been rewards apart from the monetary rewards?

I played rugby as an amateur anyway, so I didn't receive any financial rewards. I've received different acknowledgments in terms of Australian awards, various Sporting Halls of Fame – I mean they're not monetary, that's an honour. But I get a buzz, you know, when I've been to Buckingham Palace a few times, and met prime ministers and different people from all over the world, and that to me is what it's all about. I haven't done anything for monetary gain, not in terms of a professional career. My life is good fun, and that's really what I want to do, just to be able to live a comfortable life and be happy.

Do you believe there is an acceptable level of unemployment?

Ideally, you don't want unemployment, but there is always some. Unemployment is just a part of society, you've got to have unemployment. But again, are we doing enough to stem unemployment? That is the political issue, more than anything else. We just don't seem to be highlighting or targeting the right issues to get people, the people I spoke about before, back into jobs.

Do you find the whole idea of national service or work-for-the-dole repugnant, or do you think there might be a scheme, either compulsory or voluntary, that may have some merit?

I think this could benefit us where long-term unemployed people cannot get a job. Then they should be looking at some scheme, whether it be a work-for-the-dole scheme – I'm not too crazy about national service – that gives people training and skills instead of just keeping on looking for work. Yeah, I think that there's benefits in working for the dole.

There's been a lot of talk, with Hanson and other various factions, about Australia being a racist nation. You've travelled widely and you've had great life experience, do you feel Australia's a racist nation?

A good question. Many times I would have said no, we are not a racist nation by any stretch of the imagination. I think, to a certain extent, what Hanson is showing, we could have been hiding as a nation. I'm talking about Aboriginals also – I'm not talking against Aboriginals or Asians, I'm talking about the whole of our community – I think we are all racist. There's a lot of underlying tension out there between Australians, between neighbours, and I believe we're underestimating the power of it, or underestimating Australia's racism.

A lot of people I've interviewed have said, look, people are scared of difference. Do you see it as that, or is it something more sinister?

No, I think it's again our nature. We've been brought up, you know, to work hard, respect our families, get a house. Property seems to be fundamental in our lives, secure that and then you go on and have kids and whatever. But I mean, protecting what you've got is important and we are scared of others taking what we've got, or coming into the country ... 'they've been in Australia five years and they've got bigger houses, more cars, they're going on better holidays'. So we're jealous that other people, other races, come in and do the hard work that we haven't done and then get more benefits. So, difference is part of it, but I think jealousy is also another curse.

Talking about education for young Australians. What do you see as education itself – does it need to be in a classroom, or is it more about life?

I must admit I went to school in the '70s, and it was a waste of time. I guess I started being educated as soon as I left school – when I got into the real world. So you've got to have a mixture of good formal and good life education. You need the basics – English, mathematics, grammar, and those who want to go on to university have obviously got to specialise in certain subjects. But there's got to be a mix. Because it doesn't matter what you do at school, how intelligent you are, the results you get, your life starts – and your education starts – once you walk out of school.

OK, so in terms of educational opportunities, do you think they are plentiful and well distributed in Australia?

For the jobs available – the field I am in is marketing and other white collar jobs – it's hard because they are specialist areas and there are limited opportunities, whilst there are many people studying in these fields. I mean we've got about 18 million people, and there's not all that many opportunities. What we've got to do with the business professions, accounting, banking, whatever, is try and create more positions. But a lot of companies and industries are not so keen on expanding the opportunities.

Looking at it in terms of university education, do you think the idea of increasing up-front fees to do your course is going to be a positive step for equality in education?

No, it's not. You are almost buying positions in the university – there's no equality in that. How is somebody who lives where I lived at La Perouse going to get into university? Their mother and father are lucky to put them through school, let alone through university. So there is, I think, a great inequality in this system.

It's been said to me that we're very competitive in sport but we're not as competitive in business. Do you think there could be some correlation in terms of sport – you encourage the best no matter what background – whereas in terms of education we're going towards a system where if you can pay, you're in?

That's it. Whilst in sport you're right in saying the elite players or elite people will get pushed and they don't care who you are, in education we need to create an environment where you've got to keep a competitive edge, but also cater for the masses. And it can be done.

I'm looking at illicit drugs, in particular the heroin problem with young Australians. At a personal level, if you had a child with a drug habit, would you want society to view them as a criminal or as an ill person requiring treatment?

I'd like to think they'd be seen as having a sickness and get community support. But again, the criminal element comes in when they can't get the drug or they've got to pay for the drug. So we've got to ... again, it's a hard question. A lot of other countries have run different schemes with various levels of success. I guess we've got to regard it as an addiction and it's got to be treated by specialists, rather than just throwing people in jail. Because that achieves nothing.

Do you think it's now time for people to sit down and canvass other approaches to the drug problem? Look 'outside that square'?

Well, exactly. It hasn't worked. We've still got the same problems we had about 20 or 30 years ago. In this day and age, the government is under more pressure to come up with results. But the government – and the lobby groups – are reluctant to make those changes, radical changes, that are needed, because they think drug users are criminals and we're supporting criminals, and that's not true. It hasn't worked. So therefore we've got to look at different options, and until we take that step we'll always struggle.

Mark, tax reform. Some sort of consumption tax they're talking about at the moment, but in general do you feel tax reform is necessary?

Yes, the tax system sucks. I think a consumption tax, a GST, as long as it's not going to go overboard, is quite acceptable. I mean again, because I've travelled to most other countries, everybody pays VAT, GST, and it's quite normal. As long as, then, your personal tax and company tax drop accordingly. We need a complete overhaul of the tax system – I think Howard's doing it now – and some sort of consumption tax is the way to go. We have to do it, it's part of life, we must accept it as Australians. It seems to work in the majority of countries I've been to, and as long as it's fair and equitable to all it's not a problem.

Will Australia ever be a republic?
Hope so.

Before 2000?
It's hard to see it happening before 2000, but we've got the centenary of Federation coming up in 2001. We need to do this in the new millennium, that's for sure. I'd like to hope it would happen before the year 2000, before the Sydney Olympics, but I doubt it. We need to be an individual country, we don't need the monarchy any more. We need to review our Constitution, so I agree. I've been to Buckingham Palace, I met the queen, terrific people, but we need our own identity. We're old enough, we're 200 years old, why are we stuck with some ancient system run out of bloody London?

So, do you think there are benefits from this?
Mainly for our image within the Asia-Pacific region, I mean we are island people, not tied to the Commonwealth. Whilst there will be tangible benefits I think it's more for our international image. To me it is important, if I'm talking to a company, that the person I'm dealing with can make his own decisions. Not that I'm saying we *don't* do that now as a nation, but we've still always got this tie-back – we need to break the umbilical cord. So with that company I can talk openly, I can negotiate, knowing that there's no tie-back, nobody looking over their shoulder. You're dealing with a republic, an individual country that's grown up, basically.

Could you imagine a situation where the option of voluntary euthanasia would be compassionate or desirable?
I'd probably support voluntary euthanasia. It is a decision that should be up to the individual. To pass it at a government level you need a whole new way of thinking and it will be an issue that will get bigger and bigger. Basically I support it, I think there is a role for it. People should be able to determine what they do with their life, how they spend their money, who they marry and when they want to die.

Finally, Mark, here I'm looking at Aboriginal land rights, particularly with Mabo and that whole area, but I'm looking at two levels. First I'm saying, well if you have a High Court (the judiciary), and a government (the legislature), and the idea is that they're separate, the High Court is meant to be the umpire. When it makes a decision ...
Well, you'd think if the highest court in the land, the High Court, has made a decision it can't be overturned by the legislature ...

So the idea that you have a government that puts a Ten Point Plan in place which effectively seeks to circumvent what the High Court intended, is that desirable?
It's a bloody joke, and that's why there's so much ruckus at the moment. Not only is there pressure coming on the Howard Government by Australian Aboriginal people but there is an awful lot of just normal Australians getting behind it. And  there's also a lot of international support for the Mabo decision, and you can't have a government overturning the High Court.

Thank you very much for your time.

# John Elliott

President, Carlton Football Club

*'With courage mightier than the sun, he
rose and fought and, fighting, won'*

BRETT KELLY: *Is there an idea, person or event that has had the single most profound influence on your life?*

JOHN ELLIOTT: The most important thing was the very happy family life I had. I was one of three boys and I can't recall ever having heard my parents have an argument. My father was very influential in terms of setting what he regarded as the moral standards that we ought to live by, and we were fortunate enough, although he didn't have a lot of money, that we all went to a private school. He had a very high expectation of education. So he, I think, framed my attitude to life.

Is there a motto, quote or thought that really summarises your approach to life?
I have two. 'When the going gets tough the tough get going.' And the other, which I found in the *Reader's Digest,* is: 'With courage mightier than the sun, he rose and fought and, fighting, won.'

You have had some highs and lows, rough and tough times. I guess these mottoes have been handy during such times?
Highs and lows, well, really, what are they? In the end, you stand for what you believe in. And I won't compromise. When I was charged [recent matters involving charges relating to prior commercial dealings] I knew I was innocent, and as a result I was the one least perturbed by it.

What are the most critical issues facing Australia in the next decade?
I think the most important thing for Australia is an attitude change. Australia has had a very easy progress through its 200-odd years, it really hasn't had any major downs. The quality of life in this country has been achieved with little or no work for the small population we have, and as a result there isn't the fierce desire to compete in the workplace to create wealth, to create jobs or a better life. It's all happened too easily.

I heard somebody say, 'It might have been better if Australia *had* been invaded by the Japanese, so that we had to fight them off our shores, and then we might have felt much more parochial about making sure that never happens again.' Which is what's happened in Europe. So I suppose that attitude change I think is the most important issue.

Yet I'm not sure this change in attitude will happen because, as I say, the quality of life is better in this country than anywhere else, for not much effort. We're highly competitive in sport, we expect a high quality of life without working, but today we live in an economy where the world is becoming one.

In the '60s or '70s Australia could have got a huge amount of investment that would have set this country going before Asia and Eastern Europe and these other countries became 'opportunities'. We didn't take it because our laws were outdated. We made it difficult for foreign capital to come here and we were very parochial. The most important thing we've got to do now is to change the tax laws, to start attracting investment in this country, otherwise there are not going to be jobs for any of the kids.

Is there anything you see that could achieve that attitude shift in quick measure?

Well, the quickest way is, in fact, to put in a value added tax, to lower income tax dramatically and to provide tax incentives to people who invest. We've got a highly qualified, educated workforce and at the moment there's not enough investment in this vast country. Things like the Wik decision, all they've done is made us a laughing stock in other developed parts of the world. And we've now got to get back to basics and say we're going to employ our people, and to do that we've got to get investment in the country.

Is tax reform inevitable?

Your question's not good enough, because tax reform is *not* inevitable; the question should be whether it is desirable. It's not inevitable because of the attitude of Australians. It's the most important fundamental change we could make in the country. We're one of only two countries in the developed world that do not have a major indirect tax system. But it should only be implemented so that we reduce personal income tax marginal rates dramatically, to under 20 percent, so that the people who go out and work and produce, keep the money they earn.

What are the primary concerns to be addressed by any tax reform agenda? You seem to be hinting that there should be more incentive to get out there and do something.

Yeah, that's right. But I'm not hinting. I'm making it very clear that I would rather see an income tax rate maximum of about 15 percent, and then also tax consumption. The revolution and change in New Zealand is dramatic. Today Australia looks a backward country compared to New Zealand, which makes us a laughing stock. Australians don't seem to care.

What has a consumption-based tax system got to offer Australia?

The thing it does is provide incentive to those earning, because it's not taking it all to pay for roads and defence and everything else in the country. You are funding them via consumption, so it creates a great incentive for people to work, and it creates a great incentive for people to invest, which will help create work.

What are the areas of most danger, that need to be most carefully watched in any tax reform agenda?

That the government doesn't just treat the implementation of the GST as if it is gaining an additional tax. I know in the Liberal Party they are very clear and decisive about that. Socialist governments are sometimes different. They find an easy way to raise the tax bill by just increasing indirect tax, 1 percent or something, once it's in there. But in essence, when it's initially brought in, the income tax is reduced dramatically. Because people see the income tax all the time, but they don't see the indirect tax in the price of a bottle of milk.

So is there room for some sort of bipartisan, mature approach where people sit down and say, well, these are the objectives we need to achieve, how do we do it? Is it possible to put politics to one side on this issue?
No.

No?
I don't think it is, because Keating tried to bring it in in the mid-'80s and got dumped by his own ACTU and Hawke. When John Hewson tried to bring it in, Keating saw an opportunity to stay in power longer. Then Howard, to win the election, said I won't do it in my first term of office. Now the High Court has upset the illegal tax system of the States, and the result is you're seeing the Labor Party trying to make political capital out of it.

The biggest problem in Australia is that the governing party, whether it be Labor or Liberal, can't get a majority in the Senate, so any major political reform is going to be exceptionally difficult to get through. My view is that the House of Representatives needs to be reduced back to what it was, 123 or 125 seats, so we only have 60 senators instead of 72, that is, 10 in each State instead of 12. So that when one of the major parties wins a decisive election, they get majority control. Then they can implement their policies. I think that's a huge problem in Australia. We must have consensus and leadership in reforming, whether it be drugs or the education system or the tax system.

So what do you see as the best things about Australia today? You've alluded to our quality of life and our natural competitiveness in sport.
The best thing about Australia is that it's a wonderful place to have a holiday, that's the way the world sees it, and it has great quality of life. But the other thing is, we have a huge land area which can be developed to feed Asia. We have probably an immense amount of mineral wealth that hasn't been discovered yet which can create wealth for the nation. We have a highly educated workforce which can be used to help the Asian countries as they grow. What I mean by that is, educational institutions bring them in, and people in Asia want to come here to have their important medical treatment, operations and so on. In other words, we should be providing the service industries for Asia.

You've strongly suggested that one of the worst things about Australia is that life's a bit too easy here. Is that the major thing that you think we could be doing better at? An attitude shift in that area?
Attitude is critical. A lackadaisical approach in adopting competitive attitudes, in everything but sport, is our biggest problem. I suppose the other thing is, there are no national goals and we've had no strong political leadership since Sir Robert Gordon Menzies. In those days, the business community, the population and the

politicians all had a goal, to make Australia a better place. Today we seem divided much more and that comes because we haven't had an outstanding leader, like a Margaret Thatcher or a Ronald Reagan.

What's your experience and understanding of unemployment as an issue?

It's a major problem. When I left school in 1959 I went to university, and when I came out of university I had a choice of probably the 15 biggest companies in Australia, who all wanted to employ graduates. So I decided which company  I'd go to. The whole thing was if you were educated you'd always have a job in Australia. It was only the unskilled who were at risk. Today everybody is at risk. There just aren't enough jobs to go around, and that's because there hasn't been enough investment, and that's because the tax laws are not good, so it's a major problem. And you know, it's not going to be addressed by government, it's going to be addressed by private enterprise being given the opportunity to invest here.

Do you think you had some sort of ethic that predisposed you to success in your working life?

Very much so. My father didn't give me any money. I had to do my paper round which got me the equivalent today of $1.40 a week, which allowed me to live as a young man of 14. I could see that if you went to university and got educated, you would get a job. So I went to university for that sole purpose. Not to be an educated person, but because I thought it would help me get a better job.

Today there's kids out there without work, who have a uni degree and they still can't get a job. What's your feeling on that?

That's the sad outcome of the matters I've raised previously, that I think my generation has stuffed it up. People ask why have you been successful in business, and I say, well there's no competition in the country, everybody else is going to the football or the beach. So the attitude change, and the change in rules related to tax, I think are most important in solving the problem over the long term.

Is there an acceptable level of unemployment, and if so, what is it?

I think in today's environment it comes down to, there are certain people in this society who can never get a job and you've got to look after them. They could be mentally handicapped, they might be physically handicapped, you know, through their environment they've been most unfortunate. I don't know what that level is in this country. My guess is it's about 3 percent. But I don't have any great statistics to support that. In America they now regard a 'base' level for unemployment as about 4 percent.

So is unemployment an inevitable reality in a global economy?

No, no – it's a reality only in those countries that don't bring about the proper reforms to stimulate their investment environment. You know, if you look at Asia, particularly the emerging nations, they're not worried about unemployment. They're turning people from peasants into educated, employed people.

Do you think there could be value in some sort of national service or work-for-the-dole for young persons struggling to get a job?

I have argued for 20 years in the Liberal Party that there ought to be work-for-the-dole. You've got to create the work ethic in people. The other problem I see with young people is they're not taking any interest in the political system, and the result is that nobody is arguing their case very strongly. When I was 26 years of age I got involved in the Liberal Party because I wanted to see Australia change. Today you find very few young people getting involved in the political system, and until they do, I don't think they'll put the pressure on for the fundamental reforms that will get them jobs. And young people now have to take part of the responsibility because that's the other problem in this country – everybody leaves the politics to somebody else, so as a result we get the politicians we deserve.

In your experience, do you feel that Australia is a racist nation?

I think Australia is probably the least racist nation in the world. Both in its laws and in the attitude of its people. Perhaps not *the* least. I think America probably accepts people better than anybody else. Australia is not racist, but I think you've got pockets in the country. There are people in rural Australia who have been very badly treated in my view – I call them the forgotten people, nobody cares about them, they've lost their political influence – who feel upset that the Aboriginals, for example, get priority treatment versus ordinary Australians living in that area.

So I don't think we're very racist at all, and when you look at the Asian countries, of course, their immigration rules are far more stringent than Australia's. I mean Japan won't let anyone into the country except Japanese. And Malaysia is very racist. Singapore. China. And on it goes. The sad thing is that because of the quality of our media in debating this, the parochial nature of our press, they have created that problem, in my view.

We spoke earlier about the strong influence your father had on you. You emphasised that education was a foundation for that. Today, classroom education and training, the whole area, is changing. What do you see as the relevance of extensive formal university classroom training?

It is absolutely critical. I will still say to any young person today, the more education you get the better equipped you are to do something. I suppose the important thing is, I don't hold with the classical theory that says you ought to go and be educated because it makes you a better person. I think it does, it makes you a more knowledgeable and probably better person, but if you know what you want to do in life that's the thing you've got to focus on. A lot of kids today, from what I've seen, don't know what they want to do. Partly because they are not sure what opportunities are out there. For a start you've got to do something you like doing, become good at it – today the job opportunities may or may not be there.

What is a person's role in creating opportunity? There are young people out there starting businesses, and Australians in the past have been entrepreneurs, have invented lots of things. Is there an argument to encourage more people to seek their own business as an opportunity?

Too many people want to go out and run a business before they've had training – they read about entrepreneurs and think, I can become one of those. My own view is you've got to become very good at something. You've got to in fact be respected by your peers before you are likely to be able to attract investment from other people – people thinking, this guy's smart – to get the capital base to do something. If you haven't had the training or the experience, you will very likely stuff it up. So I think it's a mistake here that everybody thinks they can become an entrepreneur. My guess is that there's not a lot of people aspiring, let's say, to be a top accountant or a top economist or a top something-or-other, or to become the best salesman or the best marketing manager, before they branch out into something. There's the odd case, people like Lindsay Fox who drove a truck and built a big trucking business, and there were a lot in Australia who did it in the '50s. It's harder now. But I think you've got to be good at something before you can expect to run your own business. You've got to know what you're doing.

If you had a child who had a drug habit, would you want a society that viewed them as a criminal or as an ill person requiring treatment?

Well, it's a loaded question. Nobody would answer the question in any other way than that you'd want them treated as an ill person.

Do you think that our approach to the drug problem is effective at the moment?

No, I don't. Society is changing. My generation looks on people that take drugs as, you know, what's wrong with them? Whereas today, I'm told, everybody gets exposed at a young age. When I was young we took up smoking and drinking beers. Now they're doing that as well, and other things that weren't available then. So my own view is that it's very sad that the federal government ... the very conservative response of the *Telegraph* in New South Wales, they should take most of the blame for stopping the trial in the ACT. I'm not sure that would have solved everything, but we have to find *some* new ways to solve the problem. We need to have an innovative mind, to try things in a controlled way. Nobody seems to have a solution around the world. I do believe that countries like Singapore and others are cracking down hard on the pushers and the people behind the drug trafficking that are making a lot of money illicitly. I'd be very hard on them, but not on the recipients.

Should we accept that what we've done in the past 20 years hasn't worked in relation to drugs and that it is time to look 'outside the box' for an answer?

Obviously the answer is yes. The world's got to look at new ways of doing things if they're not solving the problem. You look outside the square.

Will Australia ever be a republic?

Yeah, it's inevitable. When, I don't know. The thing that we need to concern ourselves about is that we keep the stability that the monarchical system has created, and I'm still not sure how you select or elect the equivalent of the governor-general. I think the issue is a bit of a red herring, other than that Australia is getting mature enough, and it ought to be its own country.

I find the republic somewhat of an irrelevant issue, so I don't get heavily involved in it. I don't treat it as something that I spend much time on. But I would not be for change in this matter unless the republicans can come up with something that keeps our same level of stability. Whichever way you look at it, it seems to me that in a republic you're going to politicise the office, which is a bit of a worry.

What difference is the republic going to make to the man in the street? Do you see that it would make any difference?

In one sense it does. In that Australia now has moved a long way away from Britain and I think it would be better if we were just Australia now. But unless you're going to keep the stability I don't think there's a lot of benefit in it.

Has there been, or could you imagine, a situation where having the option of voluntary euthanasia might be desirable?

I think it should be available. I think about it for myself as I get older. I don't want to be here as a vegetable. Australia today has an aging population and in the next 15 years the workforce is going to be a much lower percentage of the total population. People are living longer because of the improvements in medical care. But the animal kingdom, you look at it as the survival of the fittest. I'm not suggesting we shouldn't be trying to perpetuate the lions among people; it's terrific to think you can live on this earth another 10 or 15 years because of medical science. But there's no point being here if you've got Alzheimer's disease, in my view. There's no point being here if you've got a terminal illness that's going to create great pain. I think the whole thing needs a radical look at. And I don't think the community will be able to afford it. My guess is in 15 years' time those people who are paying higher taxes to support the aged will increasingly be interested in euthanasia. So it might have a role.

Mr Elliott, thank you for your time.

Peter FitzSimons

Journalist & Former International Rugby Representative

*'The heights by great men reached and
kept were not attained by sudden flight,
for while their companions slept were
toiling upwards in the night'*

BRETT KELLY: *Would you tell us about yourself?*

PETER FITZSIMONS: I was born and raised in Sydney, educated at Knox Grammar School, Sydney University, schooled in America, an Arts degree from Sydney University, lived in France for four years, Italy for one year, returned to Australia in 1989. Got picked for the Wallabies, played seven tests, work now for the *Sydney Morning Herald* and the Doug Mulray Show on 2SM, bit of this and that, here and there. I've written six books.

Is there an idea, person or event that had the single most profound impact on your life to date?

OK, for me, I'm at the age of 36 and I'm happy. I'm going all right, not without problems here and there, but basically I'm fairly happy and fairly fulfilled in my life. The most profound influences on me were having two very loving parents, growing up in an extremely loving, close family. Once or twice in my life I have sort of semi fallen over but I had seven strong sets of hands to pick me up, dust me off and get me back on track, and that was my family. Having a strong family and a good education I think was extremely important to me. I went to an all-boys private school and it is fashionable now to sort of pooh-pooh and portray us as a mob of wankers and the rest of it – and maybe there's something in that, but it did give me a very good grounding in a lot of areas. Sydney University similarly, doing an Arts degree allowed me to know a little about a lot, where I think if I'd done Engineering or Medicine or whatever perhaps I'd know a lot about a little. Being able to travel, my rugby helped me a lot because rugby allowed me to live in other parts of the world. A man I was quite close to in Italy said to me, *'Viaggi, viaggi, viaggi, leggi, leggi, leggi,'* which means, 'Travel, travel, travel, read, read, read' – I've done those two things and benefited from them. I've got three children now and what I would encourage them to do would be exactly that. To read a lot, to travel a lot, to concentrate on their education. I think the most crucial foundation stone that I want for my children is to have a very good education. I say to my wife, if we can give our children only two things, they are a lot of love – I want them to grow up in a stable, loving family and a good education.

Is there a motto, quote or thought that best summarises your approach to life?

I teach my boy Jake, who is now four, and he says it: 'If at first you don't exceed, try, try again'. What he means is 'if at first you don't *succeed,* try, try again'. It sounds trite but I think that it's good, that persistence, not being put off easily. Two things my father taught me. The Latin quote: *'Per ardua ad astra'* – 'through hard work reach for the stars'. The other quote he told me that I remember, 'The heights by great men reached and kept were not attained by sudden flight, for they while their companions slept were toiling upwards in the night', and I remember studying for my HSC, repeating to myself, 'toiling upwards in the night' – it was because of that quote that I liked working at night because it made me feel I was working hard. But that basic principle, basic point, that I want ingrained in my children, and that was ingrained in me, is you've got to work hard. It sounds like a Speech Day speech but it is the truth, there's no other way around it, you have to work hard to succeed, to be fulfilled. I note in the paper the other day that one in five teenage boys gambles once a week, in Lotto or Scratchies or whatever. And I find that figure ridiculously high because I think that the whole thing of pinning your hopes on winning the lottery is not the way, it's fine every now and then but if you include it in your lifestyle it's like there's an easy way ahead. And there isn't an easy way ahead, I think it comes through hard work. But not such hard work that all life is crushed out of you. Many people do that I think – in fact, at the moment I'm being interviewed I'm fully aware that I'm working way too hard, and my wife is working way too hard and we've got  children, and you know we've both decided we are going to relax a bit, so it's not just success, success, success. In fact, success shouldn't be defined wholly or at all in terms of material success. For me, what I want is to be able to have a family that is loving and stable, and also financially secure – which is why we are working so hard.

What are the most critical issues facing Australia in the next decade?

Certainly black and white reconciliation, Wik and Mabo, getting that sorted out and not going on with this wretched Ten Point Plan brought forward by John Howard. I also think greenhouse gases and sorting out our environment. Our position in the world. Are we a European outpost? Are we a part of Asia? Where should we head, what should we do? Deciding whether we're a republic or a monarchy – it appals me to think that anybody should think we should stick with the monarchy. I'm particularly appalled by ambitious politicians who pin their flag on us remaining a monarchy. I couldn't think of anything more stupid to do. Of course Australia should be a republic and will become a republic.

What are the best things about Australia today?

I think our multiculturalism is a great thing. All sorts of cultures and nations around the world are trying to work out how to get along with each other, but we at our best can get along with each other and multiculturalism has shown that – or at least it could show that up until two to three years ago.

Which are the things that we could do better in Australia today?

The worst thing is that I think in the last few years we've semi lost our way. There's a sense of the nation flip-flopping around, seeking direction. We're looking to our prime minister to provide that direction, but anyway ... I fear that in the last few years we have lost our way.

Is there a personal experience of unemployment, or that of a friend or family member, that has given you a particular insight into the issue?

I haven't been unemployed *per se*, but I've gone through periods – I remember when I was about 23 or 24 and I was out of university and sort of independent for the first time, there were times I would feel an enormous magnetism between my back and the couch or the bed and I sort of couldn't get up. I was just ... I don't know, tired or unmotivated or whatever. As I say, I went through that for a week, even two weeks at a time. It was my older brother David at that time who said, and another friend called Angus basically made the same point, 'You've got to *do* something, you've got to get up and get moving'. Eventually I came to the conclusion that you may as well find a career path and work at it. In a sense I find I feel most fulfilled at the end of the day if I've done a lot of good work.

Have you found rewards in work apart from monetary reward?
Certainly. I work as a journalist, I like nothing better than writing a good article, making an impact on certain things.

Is there an acceptable level of unemployment? We hear people say that unemployment is too high.
The acceptable level of unemployment ... I wouldn't know. I do think that unemployment is an enormous problem. I believe it is the role of government to find ways to minimise it, and it is the role of the employed to be conscious of how lucky they are to be employed and to give the government support in taxpayer dollars or whatever to minimise that unemployment. I think one of the things that the government should provide resources for is training, to get people started. One of the great problems of unemployment, of course, is to give people the skills to get off the unemployment queues – which is not to say that everybody who is unemployed is without skills, because that is nonsense. But I think that if they are unemployed, it is for the government to provide them with the opportunity to get the skills they need to be employed.

What are your ideas on national service or a work-for-the-dole scheme?
Well, the disadvantage is that if you want to build a dam or something, and you pay people $60 a day or whatever, you get this whole army of unemployed people that are being exploited. But the advantage is, if they could get the scheme to work properly, people would feel fulfilled. Instead of getting a handout, they would have some sort of fulfilment, that they've done an honest day's work for an honest day's pay. It's a very difficult question.

In your experience, is Australia a racist nation?
I wouldn't have said so three years ago, I would have said definitely not. Now I wonder, in the era of Pauline Hanson. Thankfully I think that her era is passing. Certainly three years ago Australia could take a very, very deep bow on the international stage for our race relations and for knowing just who we were, where we were going. As I say, I think in the last three years we have semi lost our way.

What do you see as education?
Education is an understanding on many different levels of the world around us and how to proceed in that world.

So what would you say describes a formal education and the role it has played in your life?
As I say, a fairly huge role. But I think I have learnt as much kicking around as I have in the classroom.

What do you think of the quality of education in Australia?
I think generally our education is very, very good. Certainly my experience was very good, but again for my last six years that was from a private school perspective. But many of my close friends were from a public school perspective and they are highly educated people. I think generally the education is there if you want  to take it. The experience of my private school was, 'you'd bloody well *better* take it or there will be big trouble'. There was at Knox a sense that 'close is not good enough, you will be the very best you can be or you'll be on detention after school'. Whereas I think that for motivated people in public school, as I understand it from friends, there was less of that high expectation, but nevertheless the educational resources were there for them, once they decided to take them.

Do you think a university education is a handy thing to have, and do you think increased emphasis on 'up-front' fees is the way to get the best people in there?
I think Gough Whitlam did a wonderful thing in 1972 – it was in fact Kim Beazley senior, Education Minister – basically making universities free for everyone, and I think that is the right way to go in terms of the inequalities in Australian society. Those inequalities will never be wiped out, but we can at least maximise equality of opportunity.

If your child had a drug problem would you like them to be treated as a criminal or as an ill person requiring treatment?
I think it was outrageous that they got rid of those ACT heroin trials. Of course heroin is a terrible, terrible problem, but to think that the solution is to give more money to Customs and more money to the police force is ludicrous. They can't keep drugs out of maximum security jails, to think that they could keep them out of the Australian continent is just ridiculous. If my child had a drug habit, one thing I would want would be for that child to be absolutely sure what they were paying for, what they were getting, that it was of a controlled quality. I would be appalled if my children had a drug habit, but a friend of mine, who was a journalist I worked with at the *Herald,* died of a drug overdose a year or so ago, and I understand it was because the stuff that she had got off the street – it wasn't pure, or it was too pure, or something. I can understand why people take heroin the *second* time, after the big kick they get out of it the first time, but if ever you saw a drug with bad press it's got to be heroin. It is an enormous problem and the methods that are being used so far to diminish that problem have certainly not worked. The ACT heroin trial, whatever else, it was going to be controlled, and it was a start at looking for a different way of handling the problem. I understand it has worked very well in

Switzerland and I think also in Holland. Some sort of system where people who absolutely physically need it, who are so far gone that they're going to get it – pure heroin, or at least a controlled substance, a clean substance – I think that could be the way to go. Yes, it's time to sort out the drug problem outside of the conventional tactics. I mean it's got to be semi legalised and very controlled.

Is tax reform desirable?

I'm not really into it. I don't fully agree with a consumption tax, I believe it will do the Howard Government damage bringing it in. I know that people say it's worked very well in New Zealand. My primary concerns – I would like big business to pay their fair share, it nearly kills me what I have to pay in tax every year, but I would like to see the people with the clever lawyers called to account. I'm not really into this subject, but I wonder if a flat tax wouldn't be the right way ... I don't want to hear any arguments, I don't want to hear any loopholes, I don't want to hear any reasons, if you earn $100,000 a year you will pay $25,000. I mean, in fact, not quite a flat tax, but if you're poor and you're earning $30,000 a year you'll pay 15 percent and there'll be no exceptions. It doesn't matter if you are earning a million a year – maybe you'd take that rate up to 30 percent or whatever – but I would love to see all the bullshit done away with. If you were going to put anybody on the unemployment line, it would be the clever lawyers and accountants, if you know what I mean.

Should Australia be a republic?

Absolutely! It is ridiculous that 100 years after Federation we're still tied to the apron strings of England. I find it deeply embarrassing that we remain a monarchy now, and just absolutely ridiculous. I also find it deeply embarrassing that on the Australian national flag we've got the Union Jack in the top left-hand corner. If it were my decision I'd say to England, we will leave your Union Jack in the top left-hand corner of our flag if you'll put a little map of Australia in the top left-hand corner of your Union Jack. And can you imagine the outcry if that was put to the British people? OK, from here on in we're going to put a map of Australia in the top left-hand corner of the Union Jack! And everybody would say, that is the most insane, ridiculous, embarrassing thing we've ever heard of. Well, I say exactly the same for the Australian flag. Things are changing in Australia, in how we view ourselves. Fifty years ago, the majority of us viewed ourselves as an outpost of Mother England, out in the colonies or whatever, certainly 100 years ago that was the case. The Aborigines were not necessarily thought of. Now we see ourselves as a multicultural nation for a start, we see ourselves as independent of Britain, we acknowledge Aboriginal ownership of the land, at least *prior* ownership of the land and to a large extent continuing, and what the flag says, if you look at it – the Southern Cross and the Union Jack – it says here we are, we are an outpost of Britain beneath the Southern Cross. Well, we are no longer that, we don't see ourselves as that, I believe we're not like that, we're drawn from all nations, we have a great Aboriginal history – that should be acknowledged in the flag that we fly.

What are the benefits to Australia from being a republic?
That when we walk on the international stage we're not red with embarrassment about still being a monarchy.

Could you imagine a situation where it would be good to have the option of voluntary euthanasia?
Yes. I think anybody who has nursed a dying parent, as I have, could never be against euthanasia. When my mother passed away from bowel cancer, and I was with her, with all my brothers and sisters in the last week, she had reached a certain point where I believe her only conscious thought was pain. Enormous pain. And anybody who's been through that must believe in euthanasia. 

What are your feelings about the Wik decision and the Ten Point Plan?
It's absolutely outrageous! I think it will be a blight on the government and on this generation of Australians if the Howard Ten Point Plan goes through. In 50 years' time when they look back they will say, what *could* they have been thinking? I believe that the Wik and Mabo decisions ... for 200 years in this country there has been a great dividing range between black and white Australia and that's been terrible. Then the Wik and Mabo decisions forced, at long last, forced a passage through that great dividing range to achieve black and white reconciliation. And for the Howard Government to use the legislature to close that passage and reinstall the great dividing range is a national shame and a national disgrace. I believe that the Wik and Mabo decisions should stand.

Thank you very much for your time.

Lindsay Fox

Entrepreneur

'The basic value of caring and sharing'

BRETT KELLY: *Is there an idea, person or event that has had the single most profound influence on your life?*

LINDSAY FOX: No, I don't believe so – I'm the product of a happy home. That in itself is a combination of a mother, a father and a brother, and I guess it's a good foundation.

Were your parents very strong influences in your life?
Very strong.

Is there a motto, quote or thought that really summarises your approach to life?
Probably the basic value of caring and sharing. Many people weren't as well off as we were. I can even recall as a kid getting out of bed before I went to school and there were strangers in the lounge room sitting before the fireplace. My father pulled them off the street. He gave them shelter, and this was something that sort of happened through a lot of my younger life.

Did that develop a sort of attitude in you?
I think it gives you an understanding that even in those circumstances – my father was a truck-driver, probably making ten pounds a week and we lived in a 15-foot-frontage house – it doesn't matter the level, as long as you understand the values of caring and sharing. For somebody who is not as well off as you, you can always do something. Even all the way down to the bottom of the line, in a one pound a week rented house. That's where we lived.

What are the most critical issues for Australia in the next decade?
One of the most critical issues in Australia today is long-term unemployment. How to overcome it? The only way, I believe, is to bring industry back to Australia, so that there can be long-term sustainable jobs. We just don't have that today. There needs to be a political approach that is bipartisan, that covers issues of national importance. Jobs is one of those – at the moment we've still got politicians who play games for re-election rather than take decisions that have the national interest at heart.

What are the best things about Australia today?
The best thing about Australia is probably the spirit of Australian people. The commitments within communities and regions of Australia. There is still a tremendous amount of pioneering spirit, a tremendous attitude of 'can do', a commitment. In two world wars, Australians in tough competition were probably the greatest warriors that there were. This is all part of our folklore, we've had great sporting heroes, we've had people committed to the wellbeing of Australia. We've got to maintain that, because it's what differentiates us from the rest of the world.

What do you think are the things we could really work hard to improve at?
We've got to break some of the traditional attitudes of 'that'll do', or 'it's good enough', 'she'll be right mate'. We have to overcome that and create a standard that is as good as anything in the world, in all we do. Many years ago my principal, George Langley, at Melbourne High School, emphasised all the negative points of the Australian attitude like 'she'll be right mate' or 'it's good enough'. Those are still the problems today, 45 years later. We have to overcome that.

Is there a personal experience, either your own, or that of a friend or relative, that has really given you an insight into unemployment?
I've spent the last five years looking at unemployment around Australia, two days a  week. I've seen the impact on communities, where kids don't have the opportunity of a job, and I've seen one, two and three generations that have been unemployed. It's very tough, because unless we give the youth of our nation the opportunity to work, to pick up a pay cheque rather than a dole cheque, we're not giving them much hope. So we have an obligation to ensure that there are jobs in Australia for people today.

So you definitely think there are rewards in work apart from the money you get?
Money is a byproduct of job satisfaction. If you're motivated by money, you won't get job satisfaction. You might accumulate money, money is always a byproduct. If you go after the money you'll lose sight of the real objective.

Do you think there is an acceptable level of unemployment?
No. Australia should have no unemployment.

So do we look at employment as being 40 hours a week, you know, in a particular job, or just the opportunity to work?
The opportunity to work. We've got to revise our tax system, we've got to revise the number of hours you work during the week. Lots of people in the workforce today work 50 or 60 hours a week. Maybe if the tax system was a bit different, and for 40 hours' work you only got taxed 20 percent, there might be an incentive then for an individual to only work 40 hours and those 20 extra that he is working at the moment might give somebody else a job.

Do you agree – in general – with the idea of some sort of national service or work-for-the-dole scheme?
I'm a great believer in national service. I went in on 7 August 1956 for three months and it was a turning point in my life. On the aspect of working for the dole, if you look at the great depressions and all the hard times that Australia has faced, we had people working in the botanical gardens, we had them working on the Great Ocean Road, the boulevards, and we finished up with something to show for the money that we paid them. Today we give people money for nothing, they're getting no

job satisfaction, and we're getting no useful outcome. It doesn't work. We need to have work programs in which at the end of the day the money given to people is reflected in something that the community benefits from.

Do you see any potential disadvantages to such a scheme?
No, none at all. It's taking a handout versus people working and getting money. Those things are a mile apart. And one of the issues that you look at is – take the lions at the zoo – they've been in captivity now for probably 10 or 20 years, they get fed two or three meals a day. Put them back in the wild, and they won't be able to get a feed. We have kids in our community today who have never had jobs. How are they going to face the world when there is the opportunity of a job? It will be very difficult. It will be the exact reverse psychology of the lions at the zoo who are fed and can no longer go out and feed for themselves. Kids today who have missed out on a job for three or more years are just about finished.

What do you think of the argument that government work-for-the-dole programs would make second-class citizens of the participants?
No, it can't be a disadvantage. As a kid I sold newspapers, I collected bottles at the football, I sold ice creams – they were all learning experiences that gave me the opportunity to move, as a truck-driver's son, into buying a truck. And from there on I learnt by practical experience. Now life is about practical experiences. If you can't get a job in the area that you want to, then you've got to make the best of whatever those opportunities are outside of that environment. My folks wanted me to be a lawyer. I was lucky – I didn't become one!

In your experience is Australia a racist nation?
Fundamentally, yes. But I think a lot of the racial prejudice is breaking down. Definitely, after years and years of the White Australia Policy, you can't turn from black to white overnight. There are elements of racial prejudice in Australia – there always have been, while we've never had the same problems as America or South Africa – but I think that is gradually breaking down.

Does education have to be in a classroom?
No, there are two forms of education. One's academic, one's practical experience. The academic is the kid that goes on from year six into high school and on to university. Practical education is the kid that doesn't go on but takes an apprenticeship or a course using his hands rather than his mouth, and either can take you all the way to wherever you want to go.

So, practical or academic, it doesn't matter. If you buy a new camera, the only reason you look at the instruction manual is when something that you play with doesn't work. That's the practical approach, where the academic approach would be to read the manual and then try and convert what you've read to the application of making the camera work. They complement one another, but I would prefer somebody who's had good practical experience and then rounded that off with additional education.

Are first-class educational institutions and good access to those facilities critical to Australia's future?
Education is critical to any nation. I'm 100 percent for the best possible facilities to pass education through to Australians going into the next century, yet I never went through it. Education never hurt anybody.

Do you feel that you would have been worse off or better off if at some stage you had had some yourself?
I think with an academic qualification – let's assume I had been an accountant or an economist – I could never have justified buying a second truck, let alone the first.

Do you believe the introduction of a significant increase in 'up-front' fees for university and other tertiary education is a step in the right direction?
Well, the American system, where you can take a loan from the government and pay it back over the next 10 years after you've finished your academic education – I'd be more inclined to look at a model like that than try and work out how kids can get enough money to put themselves through university. But at the end of the day, if you know that you've got to make that commitment, the initiatives that are required for you to earn that sort of money won't do you any harm.

If your child had a drug habit, would you want a society that viewed them as a criminal or as an ill person requiring treatment?
No, no, you can't look at a user as a criminal, you need to look at a user as someone that sort of ran off on the wrong path. The reality today is the whole process of drugs, the penalties for drug dealing, need to be of such consequence that people don't want to have anything to do with it. It should be the same penalty as murder. Because once you take a kid's mind and completely bend it, the chances are you're taking that kid out of his existence on this earth. So I think the penalties need to be related to the damage you do within the community. I'm more in favour of the Singapore or the Thai model, where they either shoot you or hang you if you are a drug lord, or a dealer, and if you're a trafficker chances are you're in jail for life.

Our approach to the drug issue over the last 20 years hasn't worked. Do you think it's time we had a fresh look at the problem and perhaps looked at new solutions 'outside the box'?
No, I think drugs have got to be stopped before they get into the country. People won't want to do the time, so they won't commit the crime. It has to be a more proactive approach rather than reactive. Eliminate as much as you can. You don't have drug problems in Singapore, you might in Thailand. Singapore is a drug-clean community. If you look at places like Zurich in Switzerland, and Amsterdam, places like that attract people from all over the world, to get themselves wiped out. From

a family point of view, there is no satisfaction whatsoever in helping to create that type of environment. What you've got to do is find out if kids are on drugs, how quickly you can get them off, what are the best, most appropriate methods of doing this – and initially concentrate on eliminating the process of drugs coming into the country and being available as they are today, in nightclubs, throughout the major cities in Australia, even in some schools.

So legalisation would not help?
No, legalisation is only creating an environment where you'd get people coming from other countries to get involved in the dope scene here. I don't believe the legalisation of drugs would be good for any country.

Do you think tax reform, and a consumption tax as part of that, is desirable?
I think a GST is probably what we need today, but on the basis they do the job completely. GST should impact on petrol – where currently about 90 percent of what you pay for petrol is tax. Take it back to the bare cost, and then add GST. But don't keep petrol out of it and bring all the other things in. I don't drink beer, but don't penalise the beer drinker by charging him 90 percent duty and excise today and then adding the tax, take it back to the nett costs and add the GST. If they're honest and want to bring in the GST, let them take all taxes off everything and just add the GST. Yes, I'm in favour of that.

Do you see it as part of a much bigger reform, capital gains, the whole tax structure?
Well, capital gains, capital losses, are separate situations to GST. But all of the elements of the general sales tax should relate to a base cost, not to an inflated cost that already has government duties and levies.

Is this a fundamental issue for Australia? Is it part of something you talked about earlier, requiring a bipartisan approach? Could you imagine the two parties sitting down and working it out?
Ultimately they've got to. If you look at the original Hewson model, which was probably followed by Keating ... if Keating was in power today we'd probably have a GST. And Howard is pushing forward and talking about it at the moment. Whether he's got the strength to carry it through, who knows? It's certainly in the interests of the nation to institute a tax that is applicable to all people, including all visitors.

Does the current tax system really encourage young people to grow their wealth?
One of the problems really relates to the worker who is working 60 hours a week and is taxed 30 percent, if she could earn enough working 40 hours, that would probably create a hell of a lot more jobs. Those extra 20 hours she is working are 50 percent of the work requirement for one of the unemployed. The tax system needs to be better balanced. Somebody should get three people to run around the world and look at what appears to be the best tax system, so we don't have to re-invent

the wheel – there is one already out there. At the moment we are heavily taxed, 50 percent of the revenue that you generate goes back to the government. It's stupid.

Finally, are there any real concerns in the tax reform agenda, GST, this argument that you shouldn't tax food, you shouldn't tax petrol, should it be just straight across the board?

I don't think you've got any alternative. You can't differentiate. Otherwise you aren't creating a level playing field. You must look at where you get your balance, and if you balance. You create a shopping list, say here's what the cost is today, which includes your food for the week, your clothes, your petrol, your beer or your alcohol, and here's the new shopping list with GST. Now the new shopping list is identical  to the one that is pre-GST, and there should be an advantage for the new one. If there's not, it's not going to work. It's as simple as that. People complicate these things. If your mum and your dad did a shopping list for the month, saw what the cost was, then analysed that to all of the other nett costs plus the GST and there was a difference in your favour, you would be pretty happy.

Will Australia ever be a republic? Do you think it will happen before 2000, and why would the average person care?

The republic is a big issue today for Australia. Not for ramifications of changing the Constitution but really the opportunity for Australia ultimately to be Australian. So that we stand on our own two feet, still having a relationship as a Commonwealth member, but being a nation that has responsibility for itself. All of the other issues about the Constitution, how a head of state is elected, they've got to be resolved. All we need to do is take the queen off the seat and put an Australian into that position, as an Australian at the top of the Australian political system. We can't do much else. Then, over time, if we need to make other changes, we can implement them.

Do you think that the average people on the street, with the other things they've got on their minds really see the republic as critical to their future?

Look, I don't think it's a critical issue, it's something that's been evolving for quite some time. The Americans did it with the Boston Tea Party. We have the opportunity to do it in a civilised manner, where all we do is make a simple change. If we complicate that process by talking about the Constitution and whether the appointment should be made by a popular election, we complicate it.

So we should leave it to the experts?

Really, the original Constitution took three years of negotiation in a more stable and more committed environment. We can't do it in three months. In this environment it might take five years for any rectification of the Constitution, and all those points would have to go to ballot to be accepted by the Australian people. But that shouldn't muddy the waters as to whether we have the queen as head of state or an Australian.

Could you imagine a situation where the option of voluntary euthanasia would be desirable?

I think voluntary euthanasia in the area of serious illness is probably desirable. But as for going through the process of legalising suicide, no. There's a difference between suicide and euthanasia. Euthanasia for medical reasons – yes. Euthanasia as an excuse to opt out – no.

Do you agree it's really critical to have strong checks and balances?

You're dealing with life, so there's always got to be checks and balances. Family and the individual and the doctors. You know, somebody with terminal cancer who is going through pain and only has maybe one week or a month. Why should they suffer? It's not hard to get ratification in that situation. Somebody with any sort of sustainable life – I don't think you could get people to sign off on that. But if somebody had a terminal cancer and they were fading away and in great pain ... if it was your dog, your cat or your horse, you'd shoot them.

Looking at the Howard Government's Ten Point Plan, do you think a plan that effectively alters the outcome of the High Court's Wik decision is necessarily in the interest of Australians?

I think the handling of the whole issue of native title and Aboriginal land rights leaves a lot to be desired.

Most businesses have a plan of where they might be in five years' time. As the government has a Ten Point Plan regarding Aboriginal land rights, would it be good if they had a clearly communicated vision for the country, perhaps in the form of a ten point plan?

Government comes back to leadership, departments led by ministers. In many cases those ministers responsible for maybe education, transport, Aboriginal rights and so on don't really understand the elements of what they've been given. As a result most of those ministers bring on board a number of advisors. But they're a mile off! You shouldn't have to convince the advisors, who are not appointed by the Australian people, you need to talk to the minister, but you're talking about things he doesn't understand. We need in Australia a model similar to the USA, where the president might ask up to 12 leaders of various industries to work in conjunction with a ministry, to help them become more commercial and more attuned to what's required in a specific portfolio.

There seem to be a couple of points you've made in terms of a bipartisan approach, with industry and leadership in general.

All of those points relate to a single person – I am, you are, we are Australians. That has to override the distinctions of whether we're Catholic, Protestant, Jew, black, white, Labor, Liberal or National Party.

Is that what good leadership is about?
A good leader is prepared to perform his job for the benefit of Australians. Very few politicians are prepared to perform their jobs for the benefit of Australians. They perform their jobs in the way that will get them re elected. But in business, my house is on the line, I live or die by the success of my decisions. A statesman, on the other hand, puts it all on the line every time, because he believes what he's doing is for the benefit of the community. If he fails at it, he's out of politics. So what? As long as his beliefs and his ideology are right, he'll get through.

So there is a dearth of good leadership in general? Not just in government but in industry?

At the moment Australia's leadership must be at an all-time low. An all-time low. The major companies in Australia today have recruited their chief executive from overseas. Leadership within the government, with the exception of Jeff Kennett in the State of Victoria, doesn't have the balls to take decisions and make things happen. The federal government doesn't have a clear-cut direction for a month, let alone the five years that you talked about. Now if a federal government takes a decision and changes it 24 hours later, where's your direction?

Thank you very much for your time.

The Right Hon.
Malcolm Fraser

Prime Minister of Australia 1975-1983

'Different times, different circumstances'

BRETT KELLY: *Is there an idea, person or event that has had the single most profound impact on your life?*

MALCOLM FRASER: I don't think you can mark it down to any one idea or any one person. It's more complex than that. A whole host of people would have had an influence on me and a great many ideas have had an influence on me.

So there wasn't anything in particular that sticks out?

I don't think any one person or any one idea. I suppose it depends on how you define idea, how narrowly or broadly, but life is complex and I think if somebody is dominated too much by one idea or one person then their own life is going to be unbalanced.

Is there a motto, quote or thought that you feel summarises your approach to life?

Well, you're asking the same question in a different way. You're asking is there one person or idea that has been dominant and then you're asking is there one set of three or four words that would govern everything. Again, that's oversimplifying it. Different times, different circumstances. You need to approach questions and problems in different ways, and a phrase or a motto, that's fine, but it's not really a definition of your approach to life.

The question I've asked the other former prime ministers who have contributed is which things that are reflected in Australia today do you think are a legacy of your time in government?

Well, again it's a great many things. My government was very active in environmental matters, was active in relations with Aboriginals and in policies relating to land rights in the Northern Territory. It was also active in promoting investment in Australian industry and I think in the late '70s investment was running higher than it's run at any time since. But we also had social influences. You can't get it down to one thing. How can you compare what must be a social issue with a tax deduction for a corporation? You can't say one is more important than the other. Each might be necessary to achieve a fair or balanced Australia.

What do you think are the most critical issues facing Australia in the next decade?

Probably unemployment would be one. Paying off foreign debt would be another. And I think that these two issues are related.

What do you think are the best things about Australia today?

Australia's freedom, tolerance, growing diversity. It *is* a multicultural Australia and Australians are much more tolerant than they would have been before the Second World War. That's come from the immigration program and refugee policies that have brought people to Australia from every part of the world including regions close to us in Asia. Basically we've achieved this transformation from an Anglo-Saxon community to a multicultural society rationally, reasonably, peacefully.

What are the things you think we, as a nation, could do better?

Probably we could do better at a lot of things. We could work more efficiently, we can address unemployment, we can save more and invest more. A whole lot of things we ought to do better.

What is unemployment? What I'm really trying to get at is whether it is less than 20 hours full-time paid work a week, or less than 40 hours, or whether it's some other sort of concept.

A formal definition of unemployment. If people work during the week they're not in the unemployment statistics. I think that's basically the only definition you can use.

So do you think there's an acceptable level of unemployment for a country like Australia?

Not at the moment, it's unacceptable.

The number should be less than what it is?

We went for 30 years after the war with unemployment under 2 percent, but no politician I believe can achieve anything like that again.

Can you suggest ways to alleviate the gap between what you consider a reasonable level of unemployment and what the level is today?

It's a very difficult world today. The government's programs are designed to help, but basically it's a question of getting more foreign investment and more investment from Australians. It's investment that really creates the jobs, so lifting the rate of investment in Australia, whether by Australians or by foreigners, would help. If it's by foreigners I much prefer them doing new things, creating new enterprise, rather than just buying out something that Australians have already created. And state governments, federal governments could all do more to attract investment.

Do you agree with some sort of work-for-the-dole or national service type scheme?

That's a current employment issue. I'm not going to comment. I think that with unemployment being severe as it is, all kinds of options ought to be pursued in order to be tested.

What role do you see voluntary euthanasia playing in the next decade?

I hope none. It will never hold the line. The Northern Territory legislation was designed to help people who currently had their wits about them but for one reason or another thought they had come to the end of the line. To qualify for euthanasia under that legislation you had to be conscious. You had to have your mind intact. And you would have to press a button.

Now if you accepted that legislation, people would have immediately pointed to 'what about *this* person?' He's not capable of making these decisions, he's not capable of pressing the button, not capable of rationally understanding what it's about. He's got a miserable life, he can't feed himself, he can't look after himself, he has to be watched. Wouldn't it be time to extend the access to euthanasia to such a person? And you'd have all sorts of very difficult cases put forth where people were not able to make their own decisions, and then those in favour of euthanasia would be saying that other people duly qualified should be entitled to make those decisions for them. That would extend, and it would extend. Philosophically, I'm against it. In practical terms I think it would be a totally retrograde step.

I also, incidentally, knew somebody who, after a stroke, was unconscious for 18 months and then recovered and continued to lead a very active and vigorous life. People have argued that somebody who is unconscious for 12 months or more should have the plug pulled on them. There are issues involved in euthanasia, both moral and practical.

Is Australia a racist nation?

Pauline Hanson has shown that there is some racism among quite a number of people. Pauline Hanson has tried to make it reasonable or acceptable to make the sort of comments that she makes. I don't think her comments are acceptable. I think racism is one of the greatest evils that the world has ever seen. More people have been killed in the name of racism than almost anything else, and I don't believe her racist comments are acceptable.

I adhere to the established general view that if people make racist comments about other people it diminishes the speaker. It degrades the speaker much more than the target. I think that in many ways that used to be the attitude that we have had in Australia. Policies should not be based on race – especially for a country like Australia.

Do you see any evidence at a national level that our policies are not inclusive? The feedback I'm getting is that there might be some racism but surely as a nation we can't be called 'a racist nation'. Do you agree with that view?

I don't think we can legitimately be called a racist nation. But there are racist beings – quite a lot of people. And I hope we will again achieve the circumstances in which those who *do* have racist feelings will know that to make racist comments is going to be to their own disadvantage – and then they will keep their comments to themselves.

I'm looking here at education, and with a view that it is fairly linked with employment prospects, I'm saying, well, what is education for today's young people?

Well, education at any time ought to be the preparing of people to participate fully in their community and the nation. To enable people to develop their own talents, to make proper and sensible judgements about their future direction, to make up their minds what they want to do. And to help them do it well.

What role has formal classroom education played in your life? Do you think that it would be or should be different if you were younger now?

Part of education is to have people understand themselves. Education doesn't end when school or university ends. It's a continuous process and people continue to learn. Formal education is critically important and one of the results to look for in education is that it teaches people how to continue to learn as they go through life.

Do you think educational opportunities are plentiful and well distributed in Australia?

The poorest people find it more difficult to get a good education. Probably a greater incentive is desirable to get a job or to try and get a job. By world standards Australia is an egalitarian society and education is very widely within reach of a great majority of Australians.

If your child or someone you knew had a drug habit, would you want a society that viewed them as a criminal or as an ill person requiring treatment? That is, is drug use a health issue or a legal issue?

Well, it's obviously a health issue. I don't think you can avoid it being a legal issue also. It's also a moral issue.

So, as a society, do you think we should be viewing people who are addicts – as opposed to dealers – as ill persons requiring treatment?

Addicts often become dealers, don't they? In many ways addicts *should* be regarded as ill people. But have they also been promoting drugs amongst other people? If so, it's inducing other people to become as ill as they themselves are. I'm not sure that you can draw a fine line.

I do think we need to be imaginative in trying to seek solutions to the drug problem. I also think that the people who have organised the drug trade – people who push drugs – probably ought to receive much, much more severe sentences.

We've been fighting the drug problem for 20 years. It hasn't worked. Should we be looking at a wider range of possible solutions?

Well, I don't believe we should look at legalised shooting galleries. But we should keep an open mind about the kinds of approach that we *are* prepared to try, and help addicts become free of drug dealers.

Is tax reform desirable? I'm looking specifically at consumption-based tax.

Well, tax reform is desirable and it is probably inevitable.

What are the primary concerns you'd have in any tax reform agenda that included a consumption-based tax?

I believe tax reform will include some form of broad-based consumption tax. I think it should. At the moment services are untaxed so you get too heavy a tax on goods.

Services certainly ought to be taxed just as other areas of economic activity are taxed. That's one argument for a broad based consumption tax.

Are there any dangers for our society or for particular groups?
I think the biggest danger is that it makes it very easy for a government to increase expenditure and just add another half a percent on consumption tax.

Will Australia ever be a republic and why should Australians care?
Australians are proud of their country and they obviously care about the system of government that we have. Therefore I think they care about whether it's a monarchy or a republic.

I should probably have put that better. I mean, care more for a change from a system that appears to work.
Well, the system works very well. One of the concerns a lot of people have in the rush for a change is that the changes will result in the system working less well. People will have to be convinced that that is not the case.

As there's a Ten Point Plan for Aboriginal land rights, should we have a ten-point plan that spells out a future direction for Australia?
Well, that's a question of governments setting up their ideas, their vision for the future. We should have a formal plan and we should certainly have a sense of direction, a sense of where we want to take the country.

So, whether it comes to a plan or whatever, so long as we've got a good sense of direction?
Yes, and that's up to political leaders. The way they run their parties, the policies they pursue.

Thank you very much for your time.

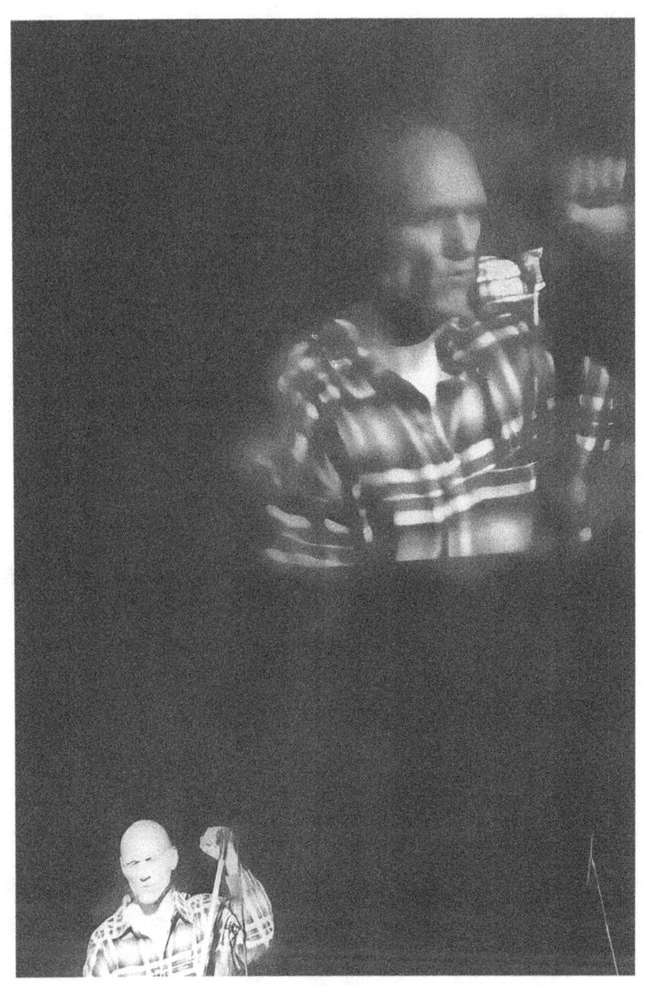

Peter Garrett

Lead Singer, Midnight Oil

*'Do what you do, do it well.
Never give in'*

BRETT KELLY: *Is there an idea, person or event that had the single most profound effect on your life?*

PETER GARRETT: In terms of explaining the kind of person you become, I think things like the nature of your family circumstances is probably the most important influence when you're young. Both my parents died when I was reasonably young, so that has had some effect on me, but I don't think an effect which explains the kind of person that I am. I think that is something which is set quite early and I don't have any profound or any momentous occasions which either changed the way I thought or confirmed for me things that I thought. I've always been pretty much the way that I am.

How would you describe yourself?

Basically an optimistic person. Open, hopefully, and positive about life and about engaging with people and engaging with issues and ideas that work. I'm somebody who doesn't set much store by material things or the trappings of success. Happiest when I'm with my family or sitting with a bunch of people around a kitchen table or under a tree, camping out or taking a wave with a few guys. To me that's as good as it gets.

Is there a motto, quote or thought that summarises your approach to life?

I don't have a particular motto that I get up every morning and say, this is the phrase that I have to repeat constantly. But there are two expressions that I carry around with me. One is, 'do what you do, do it well', and the other, 'never give in'. Those two things are a part of the way I approach life.

What are the most critical issues facing Australia in the next decade?

There are a number of critical issues which in some ways are interlinked, but which include moving our economy to a level of ecological sustainability so that we preserve and repair the natural systems that we rely on. The human systems.

We have to decide whether we want to buy into globalism in all its forms, and as a consequence of that relinquish a reasonable amount of say and control over our own lives in respect of things like media and delivery of services.

Allocation of tax income is another key issue. A small number of people are bearing the brunt of the taxation system while the rich are escaping tax. It's really a question for a country to choose either the American route of a low taxation environment – this is a form of social Darwinism, where some people do very well but a number of people do very poorly. Our alternative is to, in a sense, reconsider or buttress what I think is a more equitable approach to a distribution of resources, which spreads the tax burden more equitably and at the same time recognises and insists that there is a role for government. First, in making provision for those people that suffer under the system, and second, for the government to ensure that national social policy is reflected through private and public execution.

What are the best things about Australia?

There's a long list. I think probably the best thing about Australia is that it is a free, open, relatively healthy, stable democracy. That is not to say that it doesn't have its problems, but it's one of the few countries in the world to which those adjectives can be given. Added to that it has, by virtue of its distance from other parts of the world and its low population, a sense of natural beauty and space. Many people in many other countries never experience this, and I think that we should never take it for granted.

Are there things we should be doing better and what are they?

We have to decide as a country whether we want to value our cultural and natural heritage, and whether we are prepared to actually do that in a meaningful way, so that by the end of the 21st century Australia stands out very clearly not only as a country which has successfully managed all its ecosystems and its human resources but as well as that it is a tremendously attractive and desirable place with which to have a relationship.

What we don't do well, partly because of our federal system and partly because conservation is still in some people's minds at loggerheads with economics, is properly preserve the health of our own ecosystems. It is a national disgrace that Australia's soils should continue to erode at the rate they do. It's a national disgrace that our river systems should be so heavily polluted. It's a national disgrace that we treat the coastline as though it's just an adjunct of a suburban block. And it's a national disgrace that we haven't identified those biological riches that we have and properly set out to preserve and protect them. Given that we receive such an enormous amount of foreign income from tourism, given that a large percentage of that tourism is directed towards experiencing Australia's natural beauty, it makes good sense to conserve our natural resources. Also, we need to be prepared to draw lines around places and say, 'this is a national park – it is for that purpose, it's not a place where you can make a profit *and* experience beauty'. So that's one thing that we could do better.

The second thing that we could do is think, all of us, very clearly, about what our guiding principles for a 21st century republican Australia should be. I believe the republic is an inevitability, but we need to have some very obvious, cogent and poetic principles or expressions or sentiments, which we agree are those things which are valued in Australia, and which in a sense tie Australia and Australians together and give us a sense of where we can go in the future. I think that we need to reform the Constitution and the political system quite significantly on a number of issues and in a number of ways, of which there is a lot to say – I mean the duplication of powers between federal and state governments would be the obvious one.

We need to recognise the fundamental place that Aboriginal people and their history and their tradition play in Australia's historical and social and psychological make-up. They should have a pre-eminent place in the idea of what Australia is, and also be recognised in our foundation document – the Constitution.

Finally, we have to consider the interests of children. Children get a very raw deal in this country. I don't think they used to, but they are certainly getting a raw deal now. They are seen by many companies as being a pool of small consumers, they're exploited and manipulated, they're pressured enormously. They fall into terrible depression in their teens and it takes some kids many years to come out of that.

Underlining all these things is the idea that we see Australia as a community of joined individuals, not as a series of individuals on their own who simply make up a nation in name only.

Is there an experience of unemployment, your own or that of a friend or family member, that has really given you an insight into the issue?
I don't have a personal insight into unemployment from my own experience because I was lucky enough, I guess pesky enough, to always work, even if it meant scratch jobs to pay my way through uni or whatever. But subsequent to Midnight Oil starting we entered into relationships with various people working on the cutting edge of youth issues, particularly youth homelessness and unemployment. As a consequence of that we've done a series of benefit concerts, and we have ongoing relationships with different agencies, the Salvos and others. So I've met numbers of unemployed people and come to what I hope is a deeper understanding of what it actually means to be without work. And most serious projections of unemployment indicate that it's going to increase over time, not decrease, under current policies. So the issue of unemployment is something that we've got to face up to squarely, because its societal costs are very great.

What rewards do you get out of your work that aren't monetary?
For me it's the feeling of satisfaction of being with four or five other people basically in charge of your own destiny. Not beholden to anybody.

Able to work by creating something and not exploiting someone or something. Having the freedom to decide whether you will or won't go to work in the morning and what time you'll leave. I mean, the way we work is completely in contrast to the way that most people experience working. That's not to say we don't work hard, we just do it in a different way. The ability to direct some of our work towards social issues or interests. To be able to make a big noise that pleases people. They are certainly some of the good parts of the work we do.

Is there an acceptable level of unemployment? Can you put a figure on it?
I don't believe that there is. I can't really buy into a vision of society which says that any percentage of people are going to be put on some kind of scrap heap and left there. I think that we are failing enormously in the reorganising, reprioritising paths that are necessary to bring unemployment down. The burden falls not only on the government but also on the unions, on business, on other individuals. It's really a crisis of some proportion.

The country is in such a privileged situation with its work, with its opportunities and with things that need to be done. We need people, from replanting trees and getting our native forests back in order to looking after the elderly, to assisting the development of industries, to being involved in creative areas. There is a great deal that we could and should be doing and we need people to do those things. It's scandalous that we're not doing them.

The idea of a work-for-the-dole or national service scheme, can there be any merit in programs of this nature?
I instinctively feel that a payment for doing nothing at all is not good for society or for anybody involved. At the same time I'm very, very sceptical of the capacity of an institution like government to properly administer and drive schemes like work-for-the-dole. But I think that if implementation is devolved to regional community levels – given that taxpayers are funding this particular payment – there ought to be some provision to enhance and increase both the self-esteem of those who happen to be unemployed and also their possibility for re-employment.

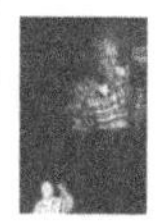

In your experience is Australia a racist nation?
My answer is, some generations in some places, yes. But as a nation, and generally for the majority of people, and particularly amongst the young, no.

I'm looking here at education and asking first, what is education?
Well, I see education first as a means of providing people with certain basic skills that will be necessary for them to enter the workforce and conduct themselves in a civil society. Second, it's a means of both regulating and grading people for employment and other purposes.

It's very clear that a well-educated, well-informed society is one that values democracy, that is productive, where human rights abuses are few, where creativity, imagination and expression rate highly. I think that we have a duty to invigorate and reinforce the education system. I'm not in favour at all of an American-style education system. At the same time I think there are some aspects of our education system which are lacking. An obvious point is the concentration, particularly the later years of high school, on both a simple benchmark figure that people need to achieve in order to go to college or university, while at the same time very little is given to those people who don't fall into that category, who are really just marking time.

To be a successful adult you need not only the ability to read and write and operate a computer – you need emotional intelligence, you need personal skills. You need to be able to apply your own common sense in situations and learn what it means to be self-disciplined and to respect others. There's a range of other important things which you have to learn somewhere along the way. You clearly don't learn very many of them from the media, and maybe they aren't always coming out of all people's homes. So I believe some focus on those elements of emotional intelligence ought to be considered in the curriculum.

Has formal classroom education had great importance in your life?
I have to say, not a huge amount. I mean I attended school and then went on to university, but in some ways I regret that I wasn't a more diligent student, particularly in university. I might have come away with some real knowledge instead of just a capacity to pass exams. So much depends on the student's interests and aptitude, and also on the sort of teachers you have. Where I had teachers whose personality and capacities met my interests I got a lot out of it, but mainly I found formal classes and the formal teaching experience to be … not unsatisfactory, but not to be my primary learning area.

The movement to significant 'up-front' fees for universities and other tertiary institutions – do you think that's likely to affect the quality and equity of opportunities around Australia for young people in education?
I can't answer that question – I don't feel that I have enough real knowledge. What I would say is that the very considerable challenges that governments face in trying to apply taxation revenues for a variety of public services means that it's inevitable that short-term policies like this will be considered. But I think it would be a very sad day if the eventual outcome of that was to atomise education to the extent that good education were only available to the wealthy and to the highly motivated and intelligent but very poor. Which is the situation in the USA – you buy your education pretty much. I think we have significant standards and equity issues in Australia, because it's very clear if you look at the percentages of kids that matriculate from private schools it is greater than those coming out of high schools; that's because their parents paid for their education and it's not desirable, it breeds a stratified society – even though I went to a private school myself.

If your child had a drug habit would you want society to view them as a criminal or as an ill person requiring treatment?
I don't see that viewing them as a criminal is particularly useful, even though certainly in relation to certain drugs, I think it should be made very clear, that they are dangerous, and also that there are penalties for use. But we are in the midst of a crazy hypocrisy where some drugs are legal and some are illegal. In the ones that are legal, addiction is viewed as a physical or medical problem. For illegal drugs, they're viewed as criminal or political problems.

If how we've been dealing with this issue for the last 20 years isn't working, should we be looking 'outside the box' for different solutions?
Well, I don't know that there is a long-term solution to drug abuse in historical terms, because I think that there is always within any society a level of drug abuse. It's just whether they're mandated or not and how they are ameliorated. You cannot wave a big stick in our society over people to the extent that some people would like to in order to restrict drug use.

At the same time I believe that our whole society, from politicians down to ordinary men and women in the street, need to decide that they want to address the issue and devise meaningful ways of taking on the question of drugs. This seems to me to require a multilayered, multidimensional approach, with physical resources, financial resources, which government would provide. Government already provides some. You would have to think through clearly issues of addiction and criminalisation, and you'd have to think about issues of actual counselling. Those are complex questions and to my way of thinking drug addiction itself and the scale of it – I mean it's terrifying, for example, the price of heroin. I think this is genuinely fearful and quite capable of destroying sections of society, the users themselves and families who are affected by it.

People can't sit back in their lounge rooms watching 'A Current Affair' and think it's just a set of cliches which require putting more people in gaol. It needs a much broader approach than that. Ultimately I think there is, if you like, a spiritual aspect to drug use in a society where people feel that they have to turn to these things anyway. Not enough love. Not enough creativity. Not enough community. And allowing a drug culture to actually exist, which we clearly do, means that we will have drug abuse for some time to come.

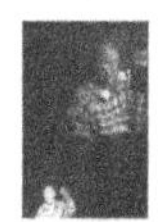

Is a tax regime based on consumption desirable?

A consumption-based tax clearly discriminates against those on a low income, the elderly and others on a fixed income. It's an easy way for governments to get hold of money. Most other countries have it. But I personally think that it's a secondary issue, it's not a threshold issue. A threshold issue is the way in which tax is collected and distributed. I think that there are three or four things which are so clearly wrong and out of whack that they need to be addressed as a matter of urgency. One is the way in which provision for interest is used right now by large companies, and the repatriation of monies to low tax entities. The fact is that we've got very large, successful corporations here who pay very low rates of tax.

The second thing is the fact that pay-as-you-earn salary taxpayers have no way of getting around tax except by setting up a trust or pouring money into their family home. Housing is way too expensive, and I don't believe that the family home should be capital gains tax free. I think that's just an anomaly in the system, along with things like negative gearing.

The third is the complexity of the system. It is way too complex, and it doesn't provide any incentive to small or medium-sized business. There's a whole set of complex interrelated taxation-bookkeeping issues. The way we work is a very good example of that. Ideally, I think a band like Midnight Oil, which has succeeded in setting itself up as an international recording band, would love to have built a recording studio here, to employ somebody and have people who are working on videos, producers and so on. But because the requirements for taxation are so complex here the first person you employ is the tax agent and accountant – they should be the last!

Should Australia be a republic and, more critically, why?

I've always believed Australia should be a republic. I think I was born a republican, to the extent that the monarchy means very little to me, and my sense of what Australia is has more to do with the future than a colonial past. Which isn't to say that I don't recognise the strength and merits of some of those institutions – it's just that I expect our head of state to represent us and us only. I think it's an anomalous situation. I don't think there are any good arguments for keeping us a constitutional monarchy. However, it's without doubt the most significant question Australians today will face – that is, the question of what's the future structure that we want going forward. I believe that it's not a process that should be hurried and I believe that it needs the most extensive and wide-ranging deliberation, consultation and education.

In terms of whether it happens before 2001 or not?

That's an artificial barrier, which I think is a red herring. We shouldn't move down the road of a republic until a very significant majority of Australians have an adequate grasp of what it is we have and what it is we're leading to.

Could you imagine a situation where voluntary euthanasia would be a desirable option?

I'm not in favour of voluntary euthanasia as it is described currently, because I don't believe it is going to have the consequences that its proponents argue it will. Whilst I recognise that there are rights and civil liberties issues that attach to people's capacity to have control over their own life, including ending it, I guess I have a residual concern and fear that the defenceless, the weak and the disempowered of the community may find themselves in a voluntary euthanasia web where they're not fully capable of recognising the consequences of their actions. And I think that would be a terrible road for society to take. So, as far as the debate currently sits, I haven't been convinced by the proponents that what they're proposing is something which I could find satisfactory.

Do you think there could be a role for it over the next decade?

Well, I think that we've got to revisit our ideas about death anyway. It seems to me that the idea of voluntary euthanasia is an extension of the idea of individual rights. I guess I may feel very differently when I'm crippled with cancer at the age of 66 and I want to go myself and I can't. But the compassion, in a sense the valuing of age and the valuing of dying, that to me isn't an isolated thing. It's something which happens in a family and community context. It should be appended by all of those things which give it dignity and which give it meaning. I'm not sure that voluntary euthanasia fulfils, if you like, that larger hope that I would have for the dying process.

I'm looking at native title. We've got a constitutional monarchy and, as I understand it, the idea is that the legislature and the judiciary should be separate and they should respect each other's role. Is it dangerous for anyone in government to denigrate the role of the High Court?

Yes, I think that one of the truly destabilising aspects of the native title debate over the last 18 months is that senior politicians from the conservative parties have attacked the High Court and the High Court has not been defended by the senior law officer. I think that is a matter of enormous regret. We are, I think, incredibly fortunate in Australia to have a non-corrupted and independent judiciary. That's the final gate, if you like, before you go in the mad paddock, and to have a few politicians kicking it down because they don't like the decisions that have been made by the High Court is fairly frightening – and I think not to Australia's ultimate good at all.

In terms of native title itself, what is your general feeling towards the debate? It seems awfully fuzzy to most people. 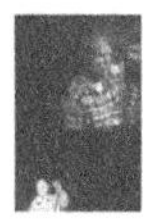

I think the debate has been conducted with an enormous amount of emotion, storm and fire and shouting and yelling. It's been conducted between people talking different types of language as well, overlaid upon which is actually a very technical issue of native title.

It seems to me that the question of Aboriginal people being given the common law right by the High Court goes a substantial way towards dealing with what is an aspect of Australia's legacy which requires repair and accommodation, and that is the fact that all the land here, with some exception, was taken illegally by the settlers when they arrived. It wasn't lawfully taken from Aboriginal people, it was illegally taken. I think that that is something that all Australians have got to come to terms with, and I'm not pretending that it is easy for people in the bush to do that. It's probably easier for people in cities to do it. But it can be worked through, it must be worked through. That right that the High Court has found, no Parliament should snuff out. Because that will, first, divide the country and second, breed increasing hostility and resentment by Aboriginal people – who were originally dispossessed and who, up to this point in time, I think have shown extraordinary magnanimity and patience.

Is it a good idea to have another ten point plan to communicate the future direction and aspirations of our nation?

I'm very much in favour of having clear, identifiable values that we all, in a sense, buy into. Some values deserve to be either restated or identified. At the same time its real purpose would be to serve as a signpost, that shows a direction through the fog of the years ahead and describes the kind of Australia we would like to be moving towards.

I think that is particularly necessary here because, despite our physical size, we are a small country. We don't count enormously on the world stage. We're likely to be buffeted about by world events, and certainly by the world economy, and if we don't have a sense of where we're going then our public life in many ways is simply going to consist of reacting to the things that happen to us. Reacting to currency crises, reacting to governments saying things, reacting to our history and economy and to things that happen in other places. I think that we should be proactive in developing our own history, not cut off from the rest of the world, with the shutters up. We are a nation in a global community, but one which is capable of choosing its own path to some extent. And to choose your own path you have to have thought about what you want your path to be.

Thank you very much for your time.

Sir John Gorton

Prime Minister of Australia 1968-1971

*'... always remaining capable of
laughing at yourself'*

BRETT KELLY: *Was there an idea, person, or event that had the single most profound impact on your life?*

JOHN GORTON: Yes, I think there was. The idea of democracy had an enormous influence on my life. You can either have a dictatorship or a democracy. If you have a dictatorship, sooner or later you get into trouble. If you have a democracy you may get into trouble, but you won't get into such bad trouble as you do with a dictatorship.

Sir John, do you have a motto, quote or thought that summarises your approach to life?

I don't think you should take it too seriously, but I think we should take it seriously enough, always remaining capable of laughing at yourself and other people.

What do you think were the achievements of your government that are reflected in the Australia of today?

I think that the universities were a great achievement – not so much by my government, but by the Menzies Government.

What do you think are the most critical issues for Australia in the next decade?

I don't know about computers – I'm computer illiterate – but they do such wonderful things now. This will be significant in Australia's future. There is also the question of unemployment which is going to be significant in Australia's future, but not as significant as some people think, because they talk about huge numbers of people unemployed now. But, you know, if you have five or six hundred thousand people unemployed, that's nothing much, because we've had that all the time. We have reached the stage where we've got too many people who want employment who simply cannot get it.

What do you think are the best things about Australia?

Sunshine, harbour, beaches and sea all around it, trees here and all around the coast and the hinterland. Australia is a delightful place to live and, talking about a wonderful place to live, it hasn't got anyone coming along such as terrorists opening fire on everybody around them. We don't have that in Australia so far.

What do you think the worst things are about Australia, or things we could do better?

Giving in to the Wik decision and handing the Aborigines over a whole lot of the mainland. I don't know what will happen when the Wik decision goes to the Senate but the whole thing started with Keating – he kept giving away a lot of Australia to people who are already equal with all Australians. They can buy land if they want to. Looking at the future, this could be one of the very bad things in Australia.

At a personal level, is there an experience of unemployment, not necessarily your own but that of a family member or friend, that has given you an insight into this issue?

No, there isn't anybody I know who is unemployed, so I don't know about unemployment. But I do know that when I was in my last year of school, in the Depression, we used to go out and carry around food parcels and we could see people who had fought in the war who didn't have enough food. They were looking for jobs but couldn't find them. This certainly made an impression on me.

Did you find rewards in the work you did, apart from the money that you got?

Oh yes, an enormous amount of rewards. Just the things that you could think of and could then see translated into being. Well, Siding Spring [the deep space observatory near Coonabarabran, NSW] ... I built that. That's just one example.

So was it the sense of contribution and something to do, a reason to get up and get into it?

Oh yes.

Is there an acceptable level of unemployment?

I think 5, 6, 7 percent would be acceptable – after that it is not acceptable.

Would some sort of national service or work-for-the-dole scheme have any merit?

It seems to have – I'm a bit mixed up, I don't know how it works.

Not the Howard Government's scheme in particular, but the idea in general?

Well, if you can find people you can make work for them ... picking up rubbish, anything at all.

OK, so do you think there are real advantages to that?

Well, great advantages compared to not doing anything and not being able to find anything. Yes.

Do you think Australia is a racist nation?

No, I don't. But the Aborigines are very racist. They're trying to drive the white people out from areas of Australia. They are already equal to all other Australians and they can do anything in that capacity they wish to do. But now they're demanding to have some land given to them and that means given to them for ever.

What do you see as education?

Oh, that's a very difficult question. Ordinary education is whatever it is you are interested in, you're educated up to a certain standard, but that is only one aspect of education. I don't really know how to answer that question at all.

What role has formal classroom education and training played in your life?
It played a big part in my life, but it wasn't the same as it is today. Things are much better than when I went to school.

Do you think the educational opportunities are plentiful and well distributed in Australia?
I think it depends. The private schools are much better than the public schools on the whole, but I think there are a number of good public schools that are as good as the private schools. But I read in the newspaper that teachers want to get rid of the selective, top-achieving public schools.

Introduction of substantial 'up-front' fees, do you think this is going to be a positive step in getting the best people into these universities?
If people apply to a university and the university takes them at a substantial 'up-front' fee, I don't think that matters. I believe that the ideal way of providing university education is for everybody to pass the examination and then receive Commonwealth scholarships, that are free for the people who are good enough to get them. Unfortunately that scheme was knocked out by Whitlam I think. I don't know what they're going to do now. It seems to me at the moment there are far too many overseas people coming to Australia to have an education which they are paying for.

If your child had a drug problem – and I'm not talking about drug dealers – would you want society to view them as an ill person requiring treatment or as a criminal?
I wouldn't want society to view them as a criminal. Not ever. What I would want is for them to stop this business of trying to stop any drugs coming into Australia because of the huge area – you can land anywhere and also get to any wharf, so it's ridiculous to say you're going to put money into stopping this. It will come in, in large quantities anyway. And if it does come in, it will be sold, because there is a hell of a lot of money to be made out of it. Therefore I believe the government should run a system by which it is not illegal to have any drugs that you like, because that way you would wipe out half the standover people. You'd stop a lot of money going into drugs, it would be far better all around. That is an approach that so far we haven't tried. I think that more people are coming around to that.

The second part of my question is, what do you think of the idea of looking 'outside the box' for new solutions to the drugs problem – as you mentioned, trying to stop the drugs coming in, drug programs and that sort of thing?
Yes, you have to have education for everybody. Education to convince them of the horror that drug taking can do to a person. Incidentally, one of the good things that would come out of legalisation would be if they did take a shot they would know that it was proper stuff and it wouldn't be mixed up with all sorts of other things that might easily kill them. I'm pretty sure that most people will agree that drug education is a good thing. It's a matter of driving it into politicians' heads, I suppose.

Do you think some sort of consumption-based tax would make sense for Australians?
I think it would. I think it would be a very satisfactory way to cut down the level of income tax, and just to be levied on things that people use, not for things they don't use. Yes, it would be a really good idea.

So you don't think that the current system serves us very well?
No, I don't.

What are your concerns in any tax reform agenda? In terms of having a consumption tax, are you concerned that people who earn less money will bear most of the burden and people who earn more won't?
Well, I don't see how that would happen.

Well, as a proportion of their income they'd be paying more tax.
You could say that a rich person would be paying far more tax at the moment than the man without much money, who would get to keep considerably more of his income. I can only speak in general about that, but it seems reasonable to me.

Will Australia ever be a republic and, if so, when?
I don't know. It shouldn't be a republic now, I don't think, because the people walking around screaming that they want a republic now haven't told us what the president they would appoint – what power he'd have. I wouldn't like a president to have any more power than a governor-general has got today. I wouldn't like that at all. I would like to see him elected by the Parliament, not by the public, though.

Do you see any benefits for Australia in being a republic?
No, I don't see any benefits. There are a number of Greeks, Italians and others who are good Australians and are quite happy with the present system. Why would we want to change when we're not told exactly what plan they have?

Could you imagine a situation where the option of voluntary euthanasia might be desirable?
Yes, I can. You hear about people with lesions all over their face and everywhere, who couldn't bear to live another minute, and I don't see any good in telling them, 'Pray to God and you'll be all right' or something like that. I think voluntary euthanasia should be introduced.

So do you see a role for voluntary euthanasia in the next decade?
I think so, yes. The thing they tried in the Northern Territory, which the federal government came in and told them they couldn't do, it seemed to me to operate all right up there.

And finally, we've already touched on Aboriginal land rights, but I'm not looking at that as the issue. I'm saying if the High Court makes a ruling do you think it's desirable that the legislature, as the government, then tries to turn around and change the effective impact of that?

I think it's a very effective way of going on, because it does make a ruling like that.

Traditionally people say that for a constitutional monarchy to work well you need that separation of powers between the High Court (the judiciary), the legislature, and your departments.

Yes, that's what they say. On the other hand, when you get people like Keating in who passes a law which he doesn't understand, and the High Court then has to say, we've got to apply this somewhere we've never thought of, to the rest of Australia, then there's no reason that I can see why another government can't then say, well we're going to withdraw that law.

Terrific. Thank you for your time.

Kathryn Greiner

Sydney Alliance, City of Sydney Council

'To thine own self be true'

BRETT KELLY: *Is there an idea, person or event that has had the single most profound impact on your life?*

KATHRYN GREINER: It's hard to pick one that had a singularly significant impact. I have had a life that is a series of chapters, with a whole lot of different experiences. I grew up in Washington DC, so I lived from 1954 to 1960 in a world where there was a natural exposure to politics, to the international dynamics, and living in a foreign city gives you a bigger breadth of vision. Back in Australia in 1960, I attended an Irish Catholic school, came to grips with very strong women who were at the cutting edge of encouraging women to have an education.

Certainly my father – who worked his way up from errand boy to managing director in the Commonwealth Bank – my father had a profound influence in terms of going out there and getting things done. He encouraged my sisters and me to get an education, and this background enabled me to have a tertiary education. That was obviously an important launching pad.

Then I had a variety of chapters of life with Nick in terms of political life and experiences, so if you had to name one ... it is often a cliche to say it's your father, but I think his lifestyle and his achievements reflected his attitude, which was loyalty to the company. He taught me the value of loyalty, of civic duty, of commitment to family and commitment to your community. There are sets of standards and values and behaviours that are important, and he was a man of great integrity. So those are pretty good building blocks.

So it is a 'can do' attitude you seem to have ended up with?

Yes, I think that came from both my parents. My mother was a strong supporter of my father and I suppose I was able to play that role in Nick's life, in terms of his political career. I think I have a very positive nature. I don't sit around wallowing in the cups of life – you have to get up and get on with it.

Is there a motto, quote or thought which really summarises your approach to life?

'To thine own self be true' – it's my favourite, out of *Hamlet*.

What are the most critical issues for Australia in the next decade?

I think there are some really critical issues. Understanding where Australia sits in the broader context of the world. The concept of nation states is breaking down. Boundaries are shrinking, rivalries in Europe, in some parts, are coming up again. But on the whole, Australia needs to compete in a world market that is not going to look after us just because we produce the best wool, but rather because we are very competitive. Our real future lies in South-East Asia. I think that is one of the key issues.

Another issue is that we can no longer afford the luxury of taking more and more from the employer and not giving a just and equitable day's work for a fair day's pay. You don't want to have exploitation of the workforce, and the union movement has helped us come to grips with that. But the excesses of the union movement have caused us to be uncompetitive and these are the same people now who are demanding that we don't reduce our tariffs. If we don't grow up, stand on our own two feet – we have gone from top five standard of living to seventeenth or eighteenth on the list – we will not continue the quality of life we take for granted.

Why do you think we can be so competitive in sport yet perhaps not transfer that same competitive attitude into business?

Two reasons. One is we began taking a very professional attitude to sport 10 to 20 years ago, and we also now have a generation of sports men and women who are wanting to give something back to the community – such as Tony Roach and John Newcombe, who were wonderful tennis players in their own time, have been able to use that sport to springboard themselves professionally, but also encourage young people along the way. People are seeing that there is actually a career in sport and I think that is why we are succeeding in sport. There has also been a lot of government money put into it; there are better training facilities. But the real question is, why aren't we doing this in terms of science or the arts? It is because we as a community don't value them.

Is there similar high-quality leadership in Australian business, in science, technology, the arts, to that in sport?

I think our actors, scientists *have* to go overseas – we are only 19 million in a land mass the same as the United States, which has more than 250 million people. Our artists and scientists have to go overseas to establish their credentials, and indeed most often they will stay overseas because the work is there. I think that that is a real dilemma for us.

The interesting issue when I say overseas is, look where they go – to the United States or the UK, as opposed to Japan or Malaysia. I think our scientists and our artists have got some problems. I actually support the view that we have given lip service to being part of Asia, and now we – our business community – have to understand cross-cultural communication very clearly, and understand what it means to do business in Japan as opposed to business in Malaysia. I know when we are in the UK they still refer to South-East Asia as the Far East and we say to them, don't use that term any more. There is a sort of colonial attitude, and we carry some of that, it is part of our heritage. But it must change.

What, as a nation, could we be doing better?

I think there are always things we can do better. One of our greatest mistakes has been developing a concept of rights, without a parallel concept of responsibility – that is a fundamental flaw in the Australian personality. People march in the streets for their rights, which is fair and just – I don't have a problem with that – but at the same time there are so many people out there all busily rotting the system.

In terms of people having access to jobs, this means that they need education and skills. Once they have got those, and I have to say to you that most people do, I think there are far too many people on the dole, far too many, where work is available. It may not be the job they want, but it's the job they have to have until they can get a job somewhere else. I see very intelligent people of all ages who just say, I haven't quite found the job I want yet – so they are on the dole. Well, sorry, that's not what I go to work for, to pay my taxes to support somebody who has the luxury of waiting for the job they want.

Can you be an extremely well qualified hamburger maker and perhaps use that, or any other job which may not be your first choice, as a stepping stone to the job of your dreams?

I think you can be an extremely well qualified hamburger maker! There are two issues there – one is, you may not want to make hamburgers for the rest of your life, so therefore go out and get some extra training – and if it means doing it part-time, as it did in our day, or over a number of years, then do it.

I have to tell you I have given the awards presentation for the University of Western Sydney, and it should be videoed and put on television. Here are the *real* people in our community, who are working night and day and doing their diplomas and courses bit by bit, and getting their degrees, moving themselves forward. And these people haven't had the educational opportunities that I have had, and many come from the ethnic community – they are unbelievably fantastic people and I just take my hat off to people like that. So be the very best hamburger maker you can, and do it all with a sense of pride and joy, because that radiates out.

Is unemployment a statistical phenomenon or is it also a social and attitudinal issue?

I think there are social issues around it – I'm just sorry we haven't picked up on a couple of programs floating around overseas. When I worked in the areas of children's services, I would have young graduates ring me in November or December each year and say, what are the jobs, can I get a job? Always I said to them, look, you may not be able to get a job, but let me suggest something – why don't you go and work in a cake shop for two days a week and volunteer at the local child-care centre three days a week. The cake shop gives you some income, and if you volunteer you will get the skills. When you go for a job interview, you have evidence of the fact that you have got some skills. So often, the kids that volunteered ended up with the jobs.

The oldest argument in the world – I don't have a job because I can't get experience, how the hell do I get experience?

Volunteer. We should be pushing this. I would be very happy for somebody to receive unemployment benefits knowing that they are volunteering to work in any trade, it doesn't matter what it is. You might go out there and learn the skills or if you are volunteering one day per week, it may be that you come into an office position, you may only be filing and photocopying, but look around, make yourself useful.

I read somewhere – somebody said that they got a job because they made themselves indispensable. Very clever. They wanted to work in that environment, there were no positions, so they volunteered their services, got to know the people, the routine, and when a job *did* become available they got it, they were already trained into it. So I think there could be a lot more of that.

You are suggesting that there is more in work than the pay cheque at the end of the week?

I think everybody needs a path, everybody needs a purpose to get out of bed every day, and I do empathise with people who are in the wrong job. From time to time we see people ... I was at a conference a couple of weeks ago when a very well known person spoke so eloquently, not in the area on which we would normally hear this person, and a colleague turned to me and said, this person is in the wrong job. Sometimes you *are* in the wrong job. And you have to say, OK, how do I change that, how do I get into the job I want? On the whole, I think work should be fulfilling you, it should not be confining you.

Would a work-for-the-dole or national service type scheme be a bad idea for those who are unemployed and want to take up the option?

No, it isn't a bad idea. There are two issues that have come up in the news over the last couple of months. One was a group of kids whose training program had fallen through and the comment from one young man on television was, we want to stay together, we are a team – because they had developed camaraderie, developed friendships. Out of that came a unity of purpose, a sense of moving forward with their lives, and it's the same for the people who work for the dole – similar comments on television, we have developed ourselves into a good working team. I thought, those are the key ingredients – getting the intrinsic values and skills that work brings.

In your experience is Australia a racist nation?

No, I have to say to you I don't think we are a racist nation. I think racist nations have laws that prevent people from participating if they are not of the nationality of that country. On the contrary, we have been proactive in creating community harmony. I think that if we had a magic wand and went back 20 years, we would have a much greater skilled migrant mix than we would have had a family reunion migrant mix. That's not to say that those people who have come here aren't contributing to the community, but a nation of 19 million people or less requires skills. This is a nation desperate for skills. It is always in my eye a strong argument that if we have enough people with enough skills in this country, we will be income generating, we will be job producing and we will in fact be able to compete. We will then provide enough of a support system for those who can't look after themselves. The logical sequence takes place.

I also have to say that I am passionate about Australian nationhood. I think people who choose to live here should take out Australian citizenship, and it is something that they should value and we should value. You never know what you've got till it is gone. You never know how lucky you are until you lose the value of what you have got. I think one of the reasons why we got the Olympics is that in New South Wales we have 150 different nationalities. We can speak just about every major language. No other country in the world can do that, and all of these people are equal – in the eyes of the law they are equal. We should note this with pride.

What is education?

As a child develops, there are physical, emotional, social building blocks upon which you constantly build. Education is a series of building blocks, and if you get them wrong, it's like a house if the foundations aren't right. So the building blocks are really important. It isn't about academic learning, but it is a springboard to learning about life, yourself, the community.

What role has formal classroom education or training played in your life?

Pretty high. Probably every five years I have gone off and done another course. As I said, I had a private Catholic girls' school education. My father paid one year's university fees, I picked up a Commonwealth scholarship after that. A couple of years later I moved back to the US, took a course in early childhood education at the local college, and did another one at Macquarie University for a year, a certificate in early childhood education. In the '80s I did a course at what was then the Ku-Ring-Gai College of Advanced Education on cross-cultural influences in communication, so probably every five or six years I have done some formal learning.

So when does it start and finish?

It never finishes. It's a lifelong process. One of the next chapters of my life will be some more formal learning. I just think that it is a bit like life, if you stop moving, you are dead. If you stop learning, you get dull. So yes, I think it is great to keep on learning, keep on doing courses, keep on doing things that keep the brain ticking over.

Educational opportunities – do you think they are plentiful and well distributed?

That is a hard one for me to answer. I'm urban based, I have two bright children who got themselves into the courses that they wanted to get into. One of them got a training scholarship, the other we paid the fees. I think in terms of tertiary education there are probably not enough spaces. In terms of school-based education – and I have taken some interest in distance education – the use of satellites is changing the face of rural and long-distance education. We should be the pioneers in the world in that – there is probably not a single other country where we couldn't export that. We should be at the cutting edge of long-distance education.

In terms of socio-economic distribution, do you think that the introduction of substantial 'up-front' fees in universities is a positive step, or a hurdle in the path of good access for all Australians?

I am actually a believer in up-front fees. Free advice is worth what you pay for it and the assumption that the community somehow owes these kids a free education leads many to take up a university place when they quite clearly could be doing other things, and it demeans TAFE education, which is an excellent component of the education system. So let's get this on the table very early. I think it is important that at the end of the day you have a system that assists. I don't know whether the existing system is fair or not on low-income families, but if you pay say $1500 per semester in fees, it does mean that you have to be working. Both my children had part-time jobs to help them pay their way through university, and in that sense you can actually manage to work through university vacations to earn the money to pay the fees.

In the US, though, there are colleges that are first class, with enormous up-front fees but, if you can get a place, there are government loan agencies that support the costs of tuition. Do you think, personally, that, to incur a debt for something you value is no problem? Or, in the situation where you have to cough up thousands of dollars up front, might it perhaps be a significant barrier?
It is a significant barrier. My husband went to the Harvard Business School in 1968. We were married in 1970 and, like all of our classmates, we probably spent the next five years paying off the Harvard loan.

But if that loan hadn't been available? If you had had to come up with $35,000 plus living costs per year, that would have been difficult?
That would have been a different ball game altogether. He had a Fulbright scholarship that covered airfares, and his father supported him while he was there living on campus, and then we got part of the loan when he lived off campus. So I think in the US ... the volume of numbers allows that to happen. We are a bit slow here in picking up on scholarships, traineeships, bursaries.

If your child had a drug habit, would you want society to view them as criminal or as an ill person requiring treatment?
People do drugs for a whole variety of reasons. Sometimes they get hooked on painkillers – perfectly normal sane sensible people of all ages, all walks of life. So no, they are not criminals by any stretch of the imagination. They are people who need help. Then again, a lot of people, whether they are drug dependent or alcohol dependent, they are still dependent personalities; they need to be part of a treatment facility. My worry about having shooting galleries and free access to heroin is that in fact it takes away the individual's responsibility.

I come to the table with a whole variety of things. I am the victim of somebody who destroyed the lower part of my house, who was a drug addict. I have sat on the board of Odyssey House, so I have seen people who have worked so hard in a therapeutic environment to find themselves. I think that is important. You can't take one without the other. I actually have a real values problem. If the community at large says, this is an OK thing to do, how on earth do you say to somebody that alcohol and speed don't mix? How do you say to a young person that drugs will kill you?

Is it time to look 'outside the square' – shooting galleries, other programs, legalisation – to find an answer?

The Wood Royal Commission identified for us that we have corrupt police. Have we done away with the police in our community? Yes, we have illicit drugs and yes, the question should be asked, why do we have so many illicit drugs in our community? That is not a Pollyanna statement, I recognise the inherent difficulties of working through corruption in high places. Smugglers are getting smarter and smarter. And there would be a voice in the community that would ask, why are we spending so much money on these resources? If we take the criminality out of it we wipe out the drug barons. I would say to you that those people would find opportunities for corruption somewhere else. So I don't see that that is the answer.

Is it time we looked at our tax system, evaluated whether it is doing well or could be better? Is now the time to do that?

I have always thought it was the time to do that – actually it was time to do that 10 years ago. Paul Keating was right. Nobody knows how much sales tax they pay because it is hidden. First thing I would do, if I ruled the world, is have the base cost and the sales tax shown on every docket – like the Americans – and shock people into understanding just how much hidden tax there is on every single thing they buy. *Then* you get to look at tax reforms sensibly.

Nine million taxpayers, 18 million people, and we don't need tax reform on our agenda? We have a big problem – an aging population that is not being replaced by the working group, 8 percent unemployed – the writing is on the wall. There is no debate in my mind – it is just a question of getting on with it.

Can tax reform be achieved in a 'sensible', perhaps even bipartisan manner?

I think it can be done in a sensible manner, but you have to understand that the community out there is tired of change. All it is looking for is a bit of rest and respite, some shreds of security. Everything they have grown up to believe has been challenged. Those who love bureaucracy grew up believing that they would get a job in the public service or the banks and stay in it all their working lives – that hasn't happened. Entrepreneurial people who are used to taking risks are discovering that it is harder and harder to maximise the return on their investment. They have to be more creative, they are constantly in that sense of, how can I beat the competition? and they are exhausted.

So the community out there wants stability and the prime minister has picked up on that straight away. He is so in tune with the real world of Australia that what he is trying to do is steady as she goes, gradually educate people and help them see the reality. Then, let's face it, people get to make wise decisions only when they are given good information. I think that is the way it is going, more power to him.

What are your primary concerns for any tax reform agenda?

I think we have covered them. One is educating the community that we can't go on the way we are. Two is to show how much sales tax they are actually paying at the moment. Three is to have a sensible and logical debate about what a consumption tax is actually all about and how it would work. People then get choices; and, if nothing else, people want a degree of control back in their lives, they want stability. I know, as having gone through the stages of married life, young couple on their own, young couple with two children, paying off the mortgage, choosing to pay off school fees, you want to be able to make some choices of where that money goes.

The republican issue – Australia will be a republic?
Yes.

In the near future?
I think it will. It is a question of when the prime minister wants to move the issue forward. He may – not to repeat what I have just said – be doing it at a slower pace.

Why would your average Australian care about whether Australia becomes a republic?

It will make no difference – not one iota. Not one skerrick in day-to-day life. The sun is going to rise in the east and set in the west. And I think the republic movement has not articulated that, that it will not make any difference but will give us a sense of mastery over our future.

What about the potential for political instability, as the result of a move to a republic?
I don't see that there would be, unless you went to a radical change of the Constitution – which is a separate issue. You may decide that the entire Australian community needs to be changed, get rid of the States, have regional councils.

All the complexities ... ?
Well, that becomes a constitutional agenda. OK, and I actually take the view that if the prime minister said tomorrow that on 1 January 2000 we are going to be a republic, the royal family would say, send us a note, tell us when you want us to go, we will be gone. I mean, they're not stupid, they understand the world is moving. It should be the governor-general who becomes the president. The governor-general, who is elected by the Parliament, or chosen by the government of the day. I presume it should be elected by both Houses of Parliament. And hopefully it will always be a bipartisan position.

It is really that simple?
To my way of thinking, it is as simple as that. There are constitutional changes that will come about because of the centenary of Federation and I think that they are more the working issues. I think there are broader issues, but we can deal with one without the other. Some people may believe that we should deal with constitutional issues first, before we deal with the republic.

Can you imagine a situation where the option of voluntary euthanasia would be desirable?
No. I think this is actually very interesting, there is a polarisation of the community. Those in favour are all under 40, those against are all over 40, and that comes about because we have witnessed people dying, as both positive and negative experiences. My answer is, I can never imagine that there should be an option of voluntary euthanasia. I am a great believer in developing palliative care, pain clinics that exist and are indeed taking people to a point where their final days or hours are often in a coma, sedated. It gives everybody a chance for the patient to go out quietly. I am not suggesting that people don't suffer pain, of course they do. And I have not had that experience -people that I have seen die, have died of heart attacks, have faded out. There is a problem in the medical care of any cancer patient who is not able to self-medicate, who is not able to be in control over their pain.

Is it too big a shift for a civilisation based on the value and protection of human life?
I find that view, that we can now be the controllers of life, untenable. It is a step backwards in our civilisation.

The Howard Government has a Ten Point Plan regarding Aboriginal land rights. Is the plan a desirable precedent for the relationship of the judiciary and legislature?
That's a complex one, and I don't know enough about it to give you a good and informed answer. My understanding is that the High Court has interpreted the legislation in quite a different way. I would rather that the government went back to the people at a Federal election than to have the issue reconstructed in such a way.

I don't see the High Court as setting policy, that's not their job at all. On the other hand, I think there is such strong emotional belief right throughout this country that the indigenous people have not progressed in their own self-esteem, not progressed in terms of perhaps your and my lifestyle, but particularly terms of their own sense of self-esteem.

The notion that a white Australian land owner, lease holder, whoever, would sit down at the same table as a black Australian and say, we will come to an adult agreement about this piece of land – it might be an inconvenience at the time, but in the context of the last 200 years is it a hassle worth bearing?
Absolutely. Absolutely. This is simply about saying to people, this is our land together. Now in saying that, it is a bit like Circular Quay where there were commercial property rights in play and the commercial developer had legal rights – lease holders have legal rights. Everybody has to understand both sides. But if we can't mediate our way through this, even if it is a step-by-step solution, then there is something wrong with us. We can put man on the moon, we can solve this problem!

So the notion that we can pay them off, that isn't really the issue?
No, it's not taking their needs into account. It does not recognise their needs as important. We've been throwing money at indigenous people for the last 200 years. Self-esteem and recognition of worth cannot be bought.

Should we have a clearly communicated national ten point plan outlining our goals for the next five or ten years?
Yes. Absolutely.

Thank you very much for your time.

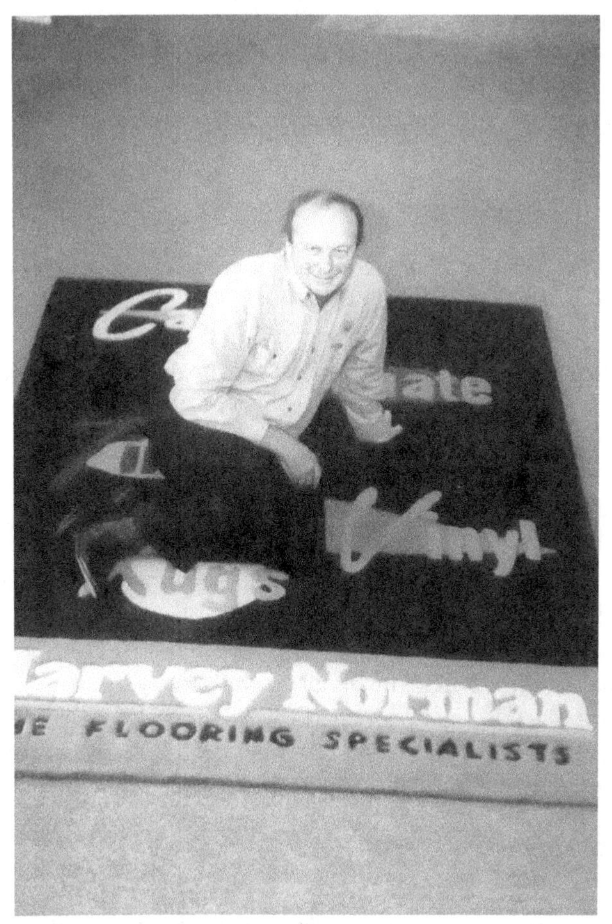

Gerry Harvey

CEO, Harvey Norman Holdings Limited

'Just be healthy and be happy'

BRETT KELLY: *What was the idea, person or event that had the single most profound impact on your life?*

GERRY HARVEY: Nothing in particular had such a huge impact on me that I would look back and remember it. Nothing.

Was there anything particularly that sort of spurred you into retailing?
No, I don't think so. I just ended up in it by accident.

How about Mr Bond – was he a significant figure?
Not really, he was an event – he wouldn't cross my mind once every three years, unless someone brings his name up.

Is there a motto, quote or thought that really summarises your approach to life?
Just be healthy and be happy, that's it.

What do you think are the most critical issues facing Australia in the next decade?
There is going to be an emerging 'haves versus have-nots' situation – there are going to be a lot more poorer people, unemployed people, and that will cause a major crisis. Also the fact that our country is being run so badly by our politicians that our debt is just growing all the time. We're heading further and further into the red. So those two things together will put a bit more pressure on Australia in the next 10 or 20 years. If you look at the results – the increases in crime, drugs, and hopelessness – people will see no future.

What do you see as the best things about Australia today?
The best things are our climate, our standard of living, the quality of food – Australia is as good a place as any in the world to live. It's traditionally been like that. Anyone I know in Australia who goes overseas always says that this is the best country to live in – very few of them ever think, I'd rather go and live in America, or Europe or somewhere else.

So what do you think are, not necessarily the worst things, but things we could do better?
Well, because politicians have stuffed up things, we've ended up with a country deep in debt, in trouble. And it shouldn't be, there shouldn't be anything wrong with it, it should be miles ahead of where it is. It is because we've had people who are not really business-minded – all politicians traditionally tend to be lawyers or trade union leaders or farmers or something – basically most are incapable of doing the job.

Do you think that's the thing we really need to do – get better people into Parliament, people who know how to run the country?

If we could somehow or other do like they do in America, employ the people that are successful in business. Maybe they don't want to be voted into Parliament because there's no money in it, there's no joy in it, it's a dreadful way to spend your time. But there is a way to do it, in that you can co-opt their help. A lot of them would do it for nothing. It's not a matter of paying them even. If you said to them, look, would you come into a certain government department, become involved, and try and either help sort out a department or help get government policy heading in the right direction in a specific area, I'm sure they would. Because every time you get involved with government, whether it's local or state government, you just walk away shaking your head. It's so inefficient, it's so bad, it's just dreadful.

OK, so as in the USA where they have a lot of industry councils where they get the top 10 guys in industry and stick them on a council and have them advising a department, even advising the president?

Yes, and you could bring them into many different areas, because the people who work for government and the public service, they're normally hopeless, there's a lot of them who are just not capable. If they came in here and wanted a job here I couldn't employ 90 percent of them. You know, they're just not very good at what they do. In addition to that, they think they are good at what they do, they've got this ego and it's just not justified. 

Is there a personal experience of unemployment, or that of a friend or family member, that has given you a particular insight into the issue?

Yeah, sure. I know lots of people who are unemployed. I interview lots of people who are unemployed. The biggest problem is, I look at all this and I think, what job can I give this person? There are a lot of cases where they're not educated enough, they're not skilled enough. You talk to young people sometimes and you think, there's just not a job for this person. The only sort of job this person could do is something very menial, they just haven't got the ability. You could put them on an assembly line maybe. So what job are you going to give that person in Australia? What are they going to do, be a gardener, work for the council? I mean, the problem is that they just haven't got the skills. They're nearly totally unemployable. But for someone with some skills, and if they're well presented, it's not hard to get a job at all. There's a big demand for that sort of person but there isn't for the others.

The notion of a work-for-the-dole or some type of national service scheme, do you think that could play a role in bridging the gap between somebody who might go in unemployable and come out, well, more employable?

Well, the thing is, if I had a kid, and he was 16 or 18 and he left school and couldn't get a job, I'd *pay* someone else to employ him. I'd do anything for that kid to get a job. Because while he's not working he's going downhill. Now you're 23, you've seen lots around you like that, girls who couldn't get a job at 16, had one for a little while at 18, nothing at 19, nothing at 20, and soon they're probably pregnant or unmarried with a couple of kids. They've lost all hope.

So any scheme – whether it's work-for-the-dole, national service – it's all a mile better than what we've currently got. But the problem is that politics comes into it then, because when one side brings it up, the other side says it's crook, it's exploiting kids and all this sort of thing. You know, if I was a kid I'd rather be exploited than have nothing happen to me. If I couldn't get a job, I'd go and work for someone for nothing, I wouldn't care. At least I wouldn't be going backwards.

So have you found rewards in work, apart from the monetary reward?
Well, I don't work for the money. You know, I'm a pretty wealthy bloke, I could have retired when I was 30, I'm worth over $300 million. Right, why do I work? OK, now let me assure you, I get on airplanes and I travel second class – I'm going down to Melbourne tomorrow. And the ones sitting in the first class seats are bloody public servants or something like that! OK?

I don't need a lot of money to live. I live very simply. But it's not money, it's all about achievement, making things happen, bringing people into jobs and businesses that they're doing well out of – you get satisfaction from that. The rewards have really got nothing to do with money at all, that disappeared 20, 30 years ago. But you can't be a complete hypocrite. You can't say, I don't do it for money. Money has to come into it somewhere. But if I said to you, 'You are now worth $300 million, you don't have to work tomorrow', would you work? A great percentage of people wouldn't. But what else are you going to do? What are the alternatives?

There might be no reason to get up in the morning.
Exactly! So if your reason to get up is to play bloody golf or tennis or cricket, to read books, go swimming, go hiking, things like that that you enjoy, you've got to like doing them. I like to do all those things, but I don't want to do them all the time. My greatest pleasures come from seeing other people do well. It's a more natural human pleasurable experience than anything else I can think of. I mean, there are other things, I guess, but if you've got a brother, father or a friend and you steer them into something that they do well at, do you feel good about that? Of course you do. It's just a natural human emotion. It's achieving. You know, you open shops, you build businesses, you see the things that work, you get a buzz out of it, you get satisfaction.

In your experience, is Australia a racist nation?
No. When I went to university, all my best friends there were Indians, Chinese, Indonesians, all sorts of people, and we used to live together and that sort of thing. There is an element of racism out there but it's a minority element, you know, that call the Chinese 'slopes', and that sort of thing. Unfortunately people like Pauline Hanson get up there and exploit that minority and by doing that she gets a lot of publicity. It would be better if the media just completely

ignored her and she'd probably run away. She'll fall over eventually because that sort of thing can't last.

Will we be a better country for having had a 'Hanson' jump up, spout off her views and sort of force everyone to deal with them?

No – but the country won't be any worse. It won't be any different. In the fullness of time, it will seem the slightest little bubble. When I say the fullness of time, I mean a 10 to 20 year period ... Hanson will be seen as just a little thing that happened once, then disappeared. Someone else will come up at some stage, very right-wing or racist or whatever – it happens in other countries, you know, whatever problems we've got here, they're not unique. America has got 20 percent of the population black people, and a much bigger problem than we've got here, ingrained racism. Racism in South Africa is a very big problem with black and white; if you mix yellow and white it's a lot easier than black and white.

But again, you know, public figures, people like Bob Hawke or me or plenty of others, you've got to be very careful what you say. People can say 'oh, he's a racist too'. So you can't just say what you think. Someone grabs it, twists it and turns it, and suddenly you're a racist. And you don't get open discussion on it, so that makes it very difficult. You and I could have an open discussion, in a pub or at home or wherever you like, and tell each other what we're thinking, but you don't tell  strangers what you think about Asians and Aboriginals or whatever – they've all got their opinions and they vary considerably.

Overall, though, Australia's a very interesting case because it's a mixture of so many races. There's no other country in the world with the mixture of races that Australia has. There wasn't so much when I went to school, there would have been some Asian kids there, not a lot probably but a few. And a lot of Italians. Chinese and other Asians who were born here, they're nearly as Australian as we are. You don't treat them any different. I mean, I've got friends, and you probably have too, who have been spat at in the street because they're Asian. But it doesn't happen a lot, and we're certainly not all walking down the streets spitting at Asians.

So over time even that racist minority should become smaller?

It all depends where your future immigration's going to come from. I have a view that in 50 years' time we'll probably be at least 50 percent Asian, maybe 70 percent. So that being the case, there won't be a problem ... well, a little bit, you know, like it is now only smaller. It's made out to be a big thing and it's not. You know that ... we haven't got a big racial problem here.

Now if you live in a country town – somewhere like Moree or Bourke, ... ever been there? – they have a lot of trouble with some blacks there because you know they run wild, they get drunk, throw bottles, thieve, they just run wild. How do you solve the black problem? Australia's got nowhere with solving it. You've got all these righteous people over the years, politicians and do-gooders, all going to solve the black problem – and it gets worse every year. They don't solve it, they're getting nowhere. Then you've got the black fellow who stands up and he wants all the land in Australia. And he's only half a black fellow, so is he a white fellow or is he a black fellow? In fact if he's got a tenth or an eighth of black fellow in him he says he's a black fellow. Bullshit! He's a white fellow. All right, so if he's half-black half-white, is he a black fellow or a white fellow? He's half of each. He's no bloody different to you and me! Why should he be treated any different to you or me? Most Australians think like that.

What is your reaction to the government's Ten Point Plan to deal with Aboriginal land rights?

You know, if you are a farmer – and I'm a farmer – and we think black fellows or white fellows are going to come onto our place and light a campfire and shoot the sheep and eat them – and not only does he do that, he leaves the gates open, he gets drunk and throws his beer bottles around the place, that's what he does when he comes onto your property, right? If he comes onto your property and he's not obtrusive, doesn't leave the gate open, his kids are all wonderfully well behaved and things like that – there's no problem. But that's bullshit, that doesn't happen. You know, I've lived in the country, I've got a farm. And white fellows, black fellows, reel fellows, I don't want *any* of them on my property. It's my property, right? You don't want them in your back yard where you live, either.

It's a very hard issue. Obviously the black fellow was treated very badly at some stage – but there aren't many black fellows left. There are a few black fellows left in this country. All the ones I see on television are more white than black. So I've got great sympathy for the black people, it's just very hard for me to come to grips with the fact that ... all the things that happened, I can't follow it. And all the country people on their farms, they can't follow it either. They don't understand it, they don't see that this is the way to solve the problem. As I've said before, we've got all these people that are not black fellows, not Chinese fellows, they're white fellows that aren't going to get jobs in the future. But the black fellows aren't either, they're not going to get jobs in the future either. If they're not educated by their family, how do you solve that problem? You'll never solve it.

What is education? Is it a matter of putting everyone through a good private school, or is it good vocational on-the-job training? How do we do it?

Look, you've got an education system that should be getting better and better as the years go on. When I left school I thought, kids are getting smarter all the time, you know, and I'll be overtaken. And what's happened is that I'm 58 and I'm better educated than 80 or 90 percent of the kids that come out of school at 17 or 18. They can't put sentences together, they can't spell, they can't do maths, they're just not well educated – I mean they can't speak properly. Their command of the English language is dreadful. I went to give a little talk one day – I've given a few talks at schools on occasion – and these were 12-year-olds. I was asking them questions that 12-year-old kids should be able to answer, general knowledge, maths, spelling. It was like 'this is going to be hard' and it was like fourth and fifth class in the one class as well, taught together. And they all come to school dressed however they like. All kids, in my book, should have uniforms and be regimented a little. I had a school uniform when I was a kid. It didn't hurt me to wear it. And if you had kids tomorrow, are you going to let them go to a school and do whatever they like? Or are you going to say, if I do the right thing by you as a father, you're going to have a better chance in life and you might have a happier life than if I just let you do whatever you like.

So what role do you see for formal education and how important is it in your life?
It is a most important thing. But saying that, I've had some very, very successful people working with me that are poorly educated – they're battling to put sentences together – but they've got this great desire to achieve. You see people that have left school at 14 or 15 with no education, didn't do well at school but did very well in life. There's lots of different areas to excel in.

OK, this sort of brings me to, what is this education – read, write, spell, speak? Or add a bit of drive to that?
Well, the thing is that you've got to have a foundation, and I would want any kid of mine to be able to read, write and spell – and to a reasonable degree too, not necessarily at university standard, but your good basics that kids had 100 years ago.  If you look at the lives, the backgrounds, of people that lived 100 years ago, they were very well educated in a lot of cases, and you wonder what education has come to now. They seem to just let them go through the system.

So is a university education a handy thing to have? And do you think increased emphasis on 'up-front' fees is necessarily the best way to get the best people in there?
No! We're talking about Australia going broke, we're talking about a country that hasn't got the resources to put all these people through university. And a lot of them are going through university from age 20 right up until the day they die. So knowing that, if you haven't got the money you can't do it. You've got to look for alternatives. Now we've got plenty of educated people in terms of doctors and lawyers – there is no shortage, we don't need more – so why would we go out and give them all a free education? If they want to do that, they should pay for it, because there are no jobs for most of them at the end of it anyway. So fees are probably the only way to go, and universities can start to make some money.

Should industry play a greater role in the operation of universities? Should they be paying more money to some universities?
I don't see why they should. They pay taxes, and those taxes are supposed to be used for things like education, that's what they're for. If it's insufficient then the government must find solutions. Why should industry have any affinity with the universities? Maybe the chemical industry or the drug industry might have

some sort of tie-in with graduates of universities, but the retail industry, why the hell would they care about universities?

Does our tax system work – do you think tax reform is desirable?
Look, we've got so many tax cheats in Australia, so much black money, drug money, everyone knows that.

So is the GST the way to go?
Sure. No one has thought up a better approach than the GST. They talk about other things, but where can they show you something that works? Practically every intelligent person that I know says that we've got to have a GST.

What are your primary concerns with GST?
The biggest problem with the GST is that if you put a GST on everything and put another 10 to 12 percent on its price, then the poor people are going to suffer more. You've got to give them some form of extra money so that when food becomes 12 percent more expensive – which it will – you have to then give them compensation so it doesn't cost them more. But at least you pick up a lot of the tax evaders.

The marginal tax rates are too high. The biggest problem with workers today is that the 50 percent rate comes in at a very low figure, $49,000 a year. And when you say to them, do you want to work a little bit extra, they earn $100 for the day and they've then got to pay out $35 in tax. So your tax rate is too high.

Do the marginal rates encourage young people to grow their wealth?
As you know, there are those on the dole who say, if I can only earn this, and there's not much difference, why would I work? I'd rather hang around than do something else! Work's got a dirty name.

If your child had a drug problem would you like them to be treated as a criminal, or as an ill person requiring treatment?
As an ill person requiring treatment.

Is it time, instead of the 'shoot them down, drag them out, protect our coastlines' type of approach to the drug problem, that we came up with some new solutions?
There's a lot more that could be done. You could double the police force in Australia. It wouldn't be hard to catch the people that distribute heroin, you just follow the trail back to Thailand or back to the source. It is not as difficult as people make out. If you *really* wanted to solve the problem, you could solve it, at least make it a lot better than it is now, and you could make it very difficult for people to pick up things like heroin in the streets. So it's not the drug takers you're after. You've got to get back to the source and get rid of the source. The sort of bloke that doesn't take drugs but makes money out of it and doesn't pay tax – you get rid of that bloke. And if you start getting rid of them at a rate of knots it will discourage others from coming in.

How about the argument of working backwards, say we had drug programs where an addict could go and get a controlled substance for free, which would mean that you wouldn't have people stealing for their drug habit and all the rest of it? There seem to be different ideas on this.

I am in favour of that because I think anything is better than what we've got. But again, if you have organisations giving people free heroin, this has got a lot of problems with it too, and for a government to bring that in is very difficult, because they'll lose a lot of votes on it – it's a very dicey political problem. But you know, I just wish that in politics you could go more for the common good rather than each side attacking each other. There are so many things discussed and then you hear the other side belting the shit out of them. The ALP under Keating in the early years wanted a GST, but now you've got Kim Beazley saying they'll never bring one in.

Offering nothing better. Not a solution, basically.

There's no alternative. He's got to suggest something else. *What*, then, Mr Beazley? I don't know. Bob Hawke didn't have the courage to bring it in. He should have brought it in – it was Hawke probably that stopped it. All this destructive criticism. One of the first things you learn when you're a little kid is, don't be destructive. You probably knew that at seven.

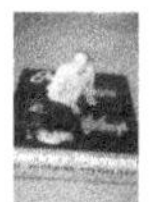

Should Australia be a republic, and why would we?

When I was your age I went to England and I thought, yeah, nice place. But I was very obviously treated as a colonial and I was not happy about that. Why the hell have we got some queen over here? We've got to be a republic, like America or something. Ever since I was 20 my view has been that we should be a republic.

An identity thing, symbolism thing?

A country like Australia now should have nothing to do with the Queen. Maybe in the beginning we were all white fellows from England, but now we're not, we've got people from practically every country in the world, Greeks, Chinese, Egyptians. And when you talk to people from all those countries, they say it's a lot of bullshit.

Will the republic be a reality before 2000?

Well, when I got my Constitutional Convention papers I didn't even open them, they went straight in the garbage. I said to the lady that does our house, what did you do with yours? I said I put mine in the garbage. And she said, as a matter of fact there are 21 people in our street and they all put them in the garbage.

I heard today they had a 34 percent return ballot rate in New South Wales.

Well, I listened to the radio the other day and they said it was 30 percent and they thought it might get to 45 percent. And I thought, gee that's very high, can't believe it. If it gets to 35 that would be high, because it's a bullshit thing. I mean, the very little I know about it, I'm not going to read all this, I've got other things to do, see you later.

So we should just have a referendum, yes or no, and then leave the experts to work it out? Spare us from the sort of big round-table two week convention.

It costs an awful lot of money to send out all those things, and at the end of the day the round-table conference is part of it, I suppose, to some degree.

Could you imagine a situation where you think it would be good to have the option of voluntary euthanasia?

You can't draw the line. Who's going to draw the line? That's the problem.

A lot of people have said to me, well I think you should be able to kill yourself, we just need to have a lot of checks and balances.

No one can draw the line, that's the problem. But there is a good argument ... if I get to a certain stage of pain and I'm useless, right, I can say, give me a needle, son. But by the same token I can go and sit in my car and gas myself, kill myself anyway. It's there if I want to use it. Or I can go and jump over the Gap – there's a number of ways I can do it. But what you're saying to me is, would I rather have the needle than the gas? It's there – voluntary euthanasia exists.

Will there be a growing push for it in the next decade?

For sure. But I don't see how it can ever get anywhere because no one will ever be able to draw the line. So you're better off not even talking about it.

Thank you very much for your time.

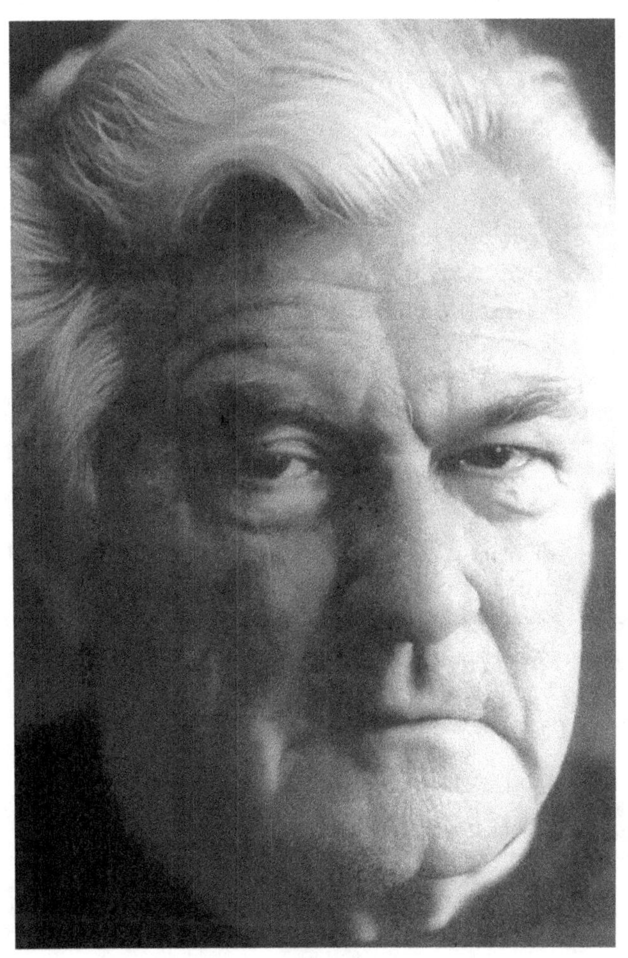

The Hon. Bob Hawke

Prime Minister of Australia 1983-1991

*'We have an obligation to be good
citizens, doing what we can to assist
those less fortunate than ourselves'*

BRETT KELLY: *Mr Hawke, was there an idea, person or event that had the single most profound influence on your life to date?*

BOB HAWKE: There was no *idea*, as such. The most influential people in my life have been my mother and my father. My mother first emphasised to me the importance of education and I was influenced very significantly by that. I stayed in the education system for a very long time and this education really equipped me for all the rest of my career.

My father was a minister of religion, and he engendered in me a sense of social responsibility – the idea that you had an obligation to your fellow men and women. He used a phrase in talking to me, and I heard him express it to others, that if you believe in God, as I did as a young man, then you must necessarily believe as a corollary in the brotherhood of man. The one follows from the other. Now, while I've ceased to have formal Christian beliefs, or involvement in the church, those ideas are still very much a part of me.

So my parents were more influential than anyone else. My father's brother, who lived in Western Australia where I grew up and was educated, was the leader of the Labor Party and then state premier. I was influenced to a considerable degree by him: while he didn't have the connection with the church that my parents had, he nevertheless was driven by similar principles.

The event I think influenced my life more than any other was when I was in my first year of university. I was in first year law and had just acquired a motor bike, and during the second term holiday I had a very serious accident where I ruptured my spleen. I was on the critically ill list for about a week, just hanging between life and death, and that influenced me very much. I felt that my life had been saved, and that I should make as much of it as I possibly could. I have really just tried to do that.

Is there a particular motto, quote or thought that summarises your approach to life?

There is not a particular motto. But as I said earlier, in respect of the influence of my father, I do believe that we have an obligation to be good citizens, doing what we can to assist those less fortunate than ourselves. That is not something bounded by national borders. The world is increasingly one place, and I think we have an obligation to do what we can to make it a better place.

Mr Hawke, what were the primary achievements of your time in government? Perhaps a lasting legacy?

When I was elected prime minister in 1983 Australia was a very, very divided place. We were unsure of one another, unsure of ourselves, unsure of our place in the world, and it was a very confrontationalist society. I set myself, in that election campaign and after being elected, to try to bring Australians together. Our theme for that election was the three Rs – Reconciliation, Recovery and Reconstruction. Within a month of being elected we had held a National Summit. I think Australians benefited from that. Predominantly they saw and understood, in a way they hadn't before, that organised workers and employer organisations could all have legitimate aims, aspirations to improve the position of the people they represented. But they were much more likely to achieve those legitimate aims if they cooperated rather than hated one another and confronted one another. And so I think, in a sense, we transformed the environment from a confrontationalist to a much more cooperative one.

While to some extent it is fractured today, I think we are still a more cohesive society than we were before. There is a greater preparedness to try and see the other points of view than perhaps there was before. That was reflected in a number of ways. On the industrial front, the level and seriousness of industrial disputation was dramatically reduced. We set the basis for changes in work practice that were not able to be achieved before, and that made Australia a more productive country.

As far as our ethnic composition is concerned, there was a greater understanding developed of the real importance of multiculturalism. It's a phrase that's perhaps been abused by some and not understood by others, but I think there is an acceptance that we are a richer country because we've had infused into our ethnic make-up people from all over the world. These people have brought new strengths to this country which are reflected in many ways. Regardless of the emergence of Hanson recently, which I hope is a passing phenomenon – and she certainly only represents a small minority – there is a greater positive appreciation  of – not just tolerance towards, but a *positive* understanding of – the values of the range of people that make up our nation.

We now have a better understanding of our place in the world. We previously tended to conduct our foreign policy vicariously, by which I mean we saw what Britain and the United States were doing and tended to just flow along with that position. The maintenance of the alliance relationship with the United States was important in that the 'Cold War' was still a reality; we had a Soviet Union bent on world domination, so it was important to be part of an alliance which would resist the spread of that hegemony.

But we expanded our foreign policy approach almost beyond measure, in that we started to give effect to what the future of Australia demanded of us – to become increasingly enmeshed with Asia. We have done that, we have become more and more an East Asian nation. This is reflected in the economic reality that more than 60 percent of our exports go to the East Asian region, and even now as East Asia is having somewhat of a fall back from its previous high rates of growth, it is still far and away the most significant economic area for us in the future. We are more sensibly related to the region than we were before. I've written that we tended in the past to look at Asia as a place for exotic holidays or as a source of threat to us. We see it in much more positive terms today.

What are the most critical issues for Australia in the next decade?
Well, there is a long list of them, of course, and I'm not necessarily putting them in order of importance. We need to achieve a real reconciliation with the Aboriginal people. I was very much dedicated to setting up a reconciliation process, and it

is still going on though it has had its ups and downs. I'm not sure if there's the same degree of commitment at all levels of government as there was before, but nevertheless it is still a reality of our life – we have got to transform the concept of reconciliation into a reality and it must be based upon mutual recognition. On the part of non-Aboriginal Australians, not something founded on guilt but a recognition of past injustices that must be rectified. And on the side of the Aboriginal people, recognition that we are serious and we want to have a society which is reconciled in the genuine sense of the word. Now I think that's a fundamentally important challenge still.

Second, a great challenge is to keep on with the enmeshment with Asia, not that we will be part of Asia, we are not ethnically Asian, although we have an increasing ethnically Asian population and that is a good thing. But while we are not ethnically part of Asia, economically our future increasingly depends upon good relations with Asia – economic, cultural, educational relations. And that is a continuing challenge.

Within Australia, there is the challenge of employment. We may not necessarily be able to return to a situation of full employment – that is, a market that can provide jobs for everybody. After all, if you look at the whole of human history we have only ever had very short periods where there's been full employment. And the fact is that we're getting smarter, humankind is getting smarter at making things and producing services; we don't need as many people to make a motor car now, we don't need as many people to provide banking and financial services.

I don't think we should be frightened about that, rather we should be proud of the fact that we are getting smarter. We don't want our children to have the back-breaking labour of the past. For instance 50 years ago working on the wharves was a physically debilitating thing, and it's much better now with containers, you can do things more efficiently. So we shouldn't be frightened of the fact that our technological genius is making it easier to produce things and provide services.

But if that means that the market is not going to be able to provide everyone with employment, then we must take the view that those who can't get a job in the market are not to be second-class citizens. I mean, you should not denigrate a group of people who pay the price for the fact that we are getting smarter. We've got to match our technological genius with sociological genius, so that if people cannot be fully employed in a market-supplied role, then we have to accept that the community will keep people in education longer, and that society will pay people to do environmentally useful things. Things that the market won't pay for, but which do not make second-class citizens of the people who do them. This may well be unreal, to talk about a 'market' full employment, but we've got to talk about full utilisation of the community's resources and be intelligent enough to make the fiscal adjustments that enable it to be done.

That's a huge challenge, but if we don't face up to it we will become a very divided community. We will have the privileged and the underclass, and that is a recipe for disaster – not just for the underclass but ultimately for the whole society.

What are the best things about Australia, and what are the things that we as a nation could do better?

Of the characteristics that we like to attribute to ourselves, the 'fair go' concept is still a reality, the view that everyone in the community is entitled to a fair go. And I think that's important. Another decent characteristic, one we mentioned earlier, is that we are in one sense a relatively classless society. I don't mean that there aren't the very rich and very poor, of course there are, I mean this in a class sense. We don't have embedded into Australian society the view that a person, because he comes from a particular background, is a better person than another. I think that's a very good thing.

Oddly enough, there is another side to this concept which at times has been disadvantageous, and that is the 'tall poppy' syndrome. So you can take an egalitarian view too far, in a sense, that high achievers should be knocked simply because they _are_ high achievers. To the extent that it merely is reflecting that Joe Blow is not better than Bill Smith because Joe Blow is very rich or powerful, that he is not _intrinsically_ better, I think that's good, but if it gets to the point of knocking achievement, that can be deleterious for the community.

Is there an experience, either your own or that of a close friend or relative, that you think really gave you a strong sense of what unemployment can be and what it means to people?

I grew up during the Depression and I can remember at times, in a country town in South Australia, the unemployed turning up looking for a feed. I can still  remember how many came to our place – and Dael didn't have any money, I mean Congregational ministers were not wealthy – but they were never turned away without something. So I'm old enough to remember how debilitating that sort of experience can be, and I've done a lot of reading about just how awful the Depression was. One fundamental aspect, for me, is the inequities that arise throughout life for people because of an initial lack of educational opportunity. When I went to the ACTU in 1958, I'd been fortunate enough to have spent the best part of 30 years of my life in education. I went there and I saw men – and I say men because officials then were _all_ men – I saw blokes that were forced to leave after primary school or not finish their secondary school, who if they had had the educational opportunities that were available to me could have been professional people of the highest calibre. They hadn't had the opportunity, but they weren't bitter, they were marvellous in the way they helped me. Here was this bright young bloke out of university, who they could have looked at and said, bugger him, he's had good luck and we haven't. But these people were unbelievably helpful to me. They seared into me the necessity for the equality of educational opportunity.

What we had to do when we came to government was to increase the equality of educational opportunity. When we came to office less than a third of kids completed Year 12, less than a third, which was one of the lowest rates in the Western world. So by a whole range of incentives and scholarships which related to financial assistance, which was means tested, we lifted that retention rate up to over three-quarters of children completing Year 12.

What will be the impact of the introduction of significant 'up-front' fees for university courses?

I don't have any problem with the concept of fees. In fact, one of the greatest stupidities was the proposition that the Whitlam Labor Government introduced of 'free' education. There is no such thing as free education, it's a question of who pays and how it's paid for.

Now kids that go to university – I'm speaking as one, I was fortunate, I had scholarships all the way through – but those kids have the best chances and if, as a result of the community investing money in their education, a boy or a girl comes out and has a better opportunity for higher income, then I see no problem in the concept of paying back this investment when they are in a financial position to do so. Provided the systems of fees is done the way we did it: they didn't have to start paying back until they earned a proportion of average weekly earnings and it wasn't a financial disadvantage to them. But you've got to get rid of the idea – it's absolute bullshit – that there is, ever has been or ever could be free education. The social democratic society is about equitable payment. And the beneficiaries, I believe, have an obligation to make a contribution towards the cost of it when they can.

Will the introduction of these 'up-front' fees be regressive in terms of educational equity?

The way we did it, with the HECS system, no one was disadvantaged because they didn't have to pay then. But any situation where having to meet a payment now may mean a person can't go there – that is objectionable.

Are there rewards in work other than monetary compensation? If so, what are they?

Oh yes, sure. I could have earned much more than I did by doing other things than those I did, but it was a deliberate choice on my part, and I got enormous non-financial satisfaction and reward out of what I did. Both as head of the trade union movement, and then as prime minister. If you've got the honour of leading the trade union movement, there is tremendous satisfaction – the opportunity to cooperate with governments and industries to try and create a better environment. Then as prime minister you get immeasurable satisfaction out of doing it – there's no question about that.

I went to the ACTU in 1958 and that was my first permanent job – as a university student, I'd always got labouring jobs and so on. But when I was doing my doctorate at Australian National University, I was 27, 28 then, and that was my first full-time employment. It was enormously satisfying, because I had the responsibility of preparing and presenting all the major cases for the Arbitration Court and doing all the research work which leaders of the ACTU used in negotiations with governments. Soon after I started as the ACTU's advocate I had some pretty large successes, and I had all sorts of financial approaches from industry and so on, but not for a moment would I consider them.

Do you think that part of your success was that you really had a passion for that area?

Yeah, if you don't have a passion for what you're doing, I don't think you're ever going to come anywhere near utilising your talents fully.

Looking forward, do you think that work-for-the-dole schemes, national service and so on, are worth looking at?

As I said earlier, I have the view that because we're getting smarter – it's not as though it's happening for bad reasons, it's happening for good reasons – if the market cannot provide the jobs, then you just don't pay a person the dole because that is an underclass-creating gesture. What you do is to pay people for doing things of value to the community. Now I mentioned keeping people in education longer, environmental work – there is so much work we can do to make a better environment which, by definition, it's not the job of the market to pay for, but the community will benefit from as a whole.

There are also things like ... our society is interesting compared to the Eastern societies, you don't have the bonding between generations in our society. Now if  you had a situation where younger people could be involved in caring for, creating a better environment for, the elderly and incapacitated ... that sort of work, which again the market may not pay for, but nevertheless it's something that makes for a happier, more cohesive community, and we should be intelligent enough to work out a way. Then we need systems which enable us to reward people who are doing those things.

So must these schemes be voluntary and have some skill component? Do you agree with that, or is there anything else that is critical to their effectiveness?

No, I'm prepared to be tough-minded about this. I would take the view that if a person can't get work and is able to do the sorts of things I've been talking about, these non-market things, then they should be required to do that. No person has got a right to be paid to do nothing, if the community is prepared to give them something worthwhile to do.

What is education itself? And further, what do you see as the role of the classroom in a formal training environment in the future?

The role of education is basically twofold. First, it is, if you like, talent development and vocation – to make people able to take their place in the community in one way or another, equip them with skills and knowledge and understanding to do that.

The other part of the role of education is wider than that, and it is to help young people to understand the world. Not simply how to be a good welder or mathematician or electrician or plumber, but how to live decently with other people. I take the view that every child has within him or her some talent or capacity. That's why, when I was prime minister, I'd go around talking to schools and I'd always say, don't make too early a judgement on yourself and don't allow your parents to make too early a judgement. It is remarkable as people stay on in education, the longer they do the more they find things that they have a talent for. I argue that kids should be kept in the education system as long as they can, for these two reasons. One, to find out and understand, to develop the intrinsic talents that I think lie within everyone in varying degrees. Second, the longer they stay in the education system – if it is a good education system – it's going to make them better citizens, it's going to help them understand the world better.

The second part of your question – what is the role of the classroom? I think it follows from what I've said, that good teachers matter and the classroom is nothing – just a physical place where education occurs. It's all about teachers, that they have both the capacity to do the didactic work of instruction and skill development, and that wider capacity to help kids understand this world in which we live. It's the most rapidly changing world in all of history and they won't make good decisions for themselves if they don't understand what it's all about.

Can education happen outside a classroom, can a manager in a workplace be a mentor and a teacher?

Of course they can – and so can a worker be a mentor to a manager, it is not a one-way thing. In fact one of the more interesting things said to me by the [then] head of BHP, John Prescott – he was trying to get a more cooperative approach between his managers and workers, and he said to me, one of the silliest things we used to do at BHP (and he started at the steelworks on the IR side) was to require our workers to 'leave their brains at the gate'. That's the way he put it. He said, we have found that those most likely to know the weakness of a particular way of doing things are those that are seeing it all the time. He said, we should look for input from the workers, and he said to them, if we're talking about making operations more efficient, that may mean some workers have to go, but it may mean some managers have to go as well.

If you look at the world today and compare it with 50 years ago, one thing that stands out is that most people 50 years ago had one job, and one job for the whole of their life, they went along one career path. Today, with the enormously rapid changes that are taking place in the way we make things and provide services, in every developed country we see people tend to have two or three or more changes. And that's going to be the case I think in the future, so there will have to be a continual learning process.

Mr Hawke, in your experience is Australia a racist nation?

I don't think Australia is a racist nation. But having said that, there is no doubt that we do have pockets, elements, amongst our 18 million people, who are racist. These people have this obscene and absurd view that a person is intrinsically better because they have one type of skin. I find it morally repugnant, but it's also intellectually absurd. What choice did a redneck racist here have, as to how he happens to be in the world? Does he happen to have white skin? He could just as easily have been born an Aboriginal, he had no control over it. It is just quite absurd to take the view that because a person has a different skin colour or slanted eyes rather than round eyes, a different religion – that they are inferior. There's no moral, biological or intellectual basis for that view.

It's very hard to have dialogue with the Hansons of this world, as they are very dogmatic, but I'd be more than happy to have dialogue with her. It could be argued that Hanson has made people more aware of the danger of that sort of attitude, and if that's the case it strengthens what I think is the basic 'fair go' attitude of the overwhelming majority of Australians, and you could see that as a plus. But she is doing a lot of damage in the process. I can tell you, as one who's spent a lot of time in Asia, I've never been in Asia, since she's been around, without seeing something in the papers about her, and she's already having an adverse impact on this country.

Most of the informed people you talk with in Asia recognise that Hanson represents a small minority. But I know of people in Asia who were going to send their kids to be educated in Australia and they are not doing it now because they're frightened, not that the overwhelming majority of Australians are like that, but that the kids will suffer unpleasant experiences. And that's a loss to Australia.

If your child had a drug habit, should we want a society that views them as a criminal or as an ill person requiring treatment?

Certainly, as needing treatment. I mean, there are all sorts of reasons why a young person would resort to drugs and they are not criminals. They may get involved in criminal activities to sustain their habit, but they are not essentially criminals, and obviously we should approach these people with as much compassion and understanding as we can, because they are capable of being rehabilitated with a lot of love and a fair bit of money. It ought to be done.

Our conventional tactics against illicit drug use have not been successful. Do you feel it is time to look for new solutions to this issue? What are your thoughts on programs that supply drugs to addicts?

Well, good question. I've obviously thought about this quite a bit and I had some problems with it too. I mean, part of the argument is that you decriminalise marijuana and so on. I understand that argument but, against that, I know the evidence about the way in which people move from the so-called 'lesser' drugs to the 'harder' drugs. I think that's a problem.

On the wider issue of heroin trials, again I've had genuine intellectual doubts about that, but I think on balance it's worth trying.

Is tax reform desirable?

Yes, of course we should be looking at tax reform. We haven't got a perfect tax system. I wrote as far back as 1979 in the Boyer lectures that we should get rid of the States. A part of our problem is that we've got three levels of government.

We've got the national government, we've got these overhangs from our colonial history – which we call States – and we've got municipal government. And there is this totally artificial division of power between the national government and the state governments. It is not based upon any rational consideration, the States just represent lines drawn on the map by British explorers wandering about this continent over 150 years ago – they drew a line here and that was a colony, and it became a State. If you were sitting down now to work out a rational basis for governing the country, you wouldn't tolerate what we've got. That's what is technically called vertical fiscal imbalance, which is economist jargon for a very simple proposition – that the States have expenditure responsibilities for a much higher percentage of revenue than they raise. They raise about 20 percent of revenue and spend, whatever – a much higher percentage. So always, not just about tax but in other matters such as education as well, you've got an artificial division between them.

My own view, expressed as far back as 1979, is that if you were really going to make the best contribution you could to dealing with Australia's problems, not only in the tax area but in a whole range of areas, you'd get rid of the States, you'd have one national government and then more relevant local government units. Well, that's a counsel of perfection, in my mind, because both parties have a vested interest in having as many seats and as many parliaments as possible to put their supporters' bums on. So you're not going to persuade either party, as far as I can see into the future, to accept this ideal solution.

OK, we've still got the States and the Commonwealth, so within that framework you need a system to get a better correlation between responsibility for revenue raising and responsibility for outlay. That's one aspect; the second aspect is the taxation system itself. I mean no one could argue that we've got the ideal mix. How could anyone possibly say that? I'm all in favour of having taxation reform on the agenda. I'd like to see the situation where both sides of politics could put aside their party differences and say, we're prepared for a period of time to cooperate with the community in sitting down and examining the whole tax mix. And ideally, if you get agreement for how it should be approached, that would be good. But you're not going to get that if you're not prepared to sit down together and talk. Now, within such an approach, a goods and services tax should be looked at.

When I was prime minister, when we looked at tax, I said we should examine a GST. My real problem was, and remains, that it is essentially an inequitable tax. It means that I, as a rich person, pay the same tax on a carton of milk as a poor person, and that's regressive and inequitable because it's a much greater burden on the poor than on the rich. I'm in favour of it if we can get a proper mechanism to offset the inequity which is inherent in it as it is usually applied. I wasn't satisfied back then that they'd come up with a system of compensation which would meet those concerns, but that doesn't mean it can't be done. I would be perfectly happy about a detailed examination, preferably on a bipartisan basis, of the concept of GST within a broader framework of tax reform – provided that an element of that examination was ensuring that it didn't impose an unduly harsh burden, or even a relatively harsh burden, upon the poor. That is surely not beyond the wit of man ...

Do you think we're currently at a state where our federal politicians could actually sit down round a table and say, we've got to work on this issue because it's in the national interest?

Well, the evidence is not too promising at the moment I would have to say, but at the same time it may be that recent events may make our politicians a bit more serious. Let me say I'm not a politician basher, because by and large I think they are committed people who try and do a good job, but they must understand that the population doesn't hold them in very high regard at the moment, and this was reflected to some extent in the recent South Australian election results – the non-major parties' vote really went up quite a bit. So I don't give up hope that it could happen – there's got to be a fair bit of sea change for it to occur, but I would certainly like to see it happen.

Do you think the current system encourages young people to grow their wealth?

Oh yes. I mean there is no doubt that enterprise can be well rewarded in this society, though maybe there are better ways of providing socially acceptable incentives. I don't think any young person should feel that the tax system that we've got at the moment is unduly punitive, and by international standards Australia is not a highly taxed country.

Australia as a republic – do you think it will ever happen?

Yes, it will happen, and may I say I'm not a Johnny-come-lately on this issue – most are catching up to me in a sense. Again, in the Boyer Lectures in 1979 I said I thought Australia should become a republic and I believed it would. But I didn't then, nor in a sense do I now, regard it as an issue of prime importance. If tomorrow morning, by me waving a magic wand (which I don't possess, but if I had it I *would* wave a magic wand) Australia could be a republic, it wouldn't affect these young people. The level of unemployment would not change one scrap. I think there are issues of higher importance than the republic. That doesn't mean I don't support it – I do – but I'm not in favour of investing an enormous amount of our intellectual capital and time and money on it.

I think it ought to be done in a way which is calculated to try and make it easier for people to understand that it's worthwhile, and done in a more cohesive way than it is at the moment. I mean, now it's still roughly speaking about half and half – pro-republican sentiment seems to be increasing a bit, but still the community's roughly divided on it. I'd cut all the bloody cackle and put a proposition in favour of Australia becoming a republic at the death or at the end of the reign of the present monarch. I reckon if you put that you'd get about 80 percent vote for it and it'd be a much more cohesive approach. There are a lot of people who have a respect for the reigning sovereign, which I can understand – I think she's got the worst job in the world – and they don't want to give her a kick in the butt. So if it was put in those terms, OK, we want to be a republic, it comes into effect when she finishes her reign, now you can have that referendum, get it out of the bloody way, make all the arrangements, and then get on with the things that matter.

The overwhelming sense I get is that it's not really an issue that is going to make any difference to anyone. Do you think it's a symbolic issue?
It is an important symbolic issue, but for God's sake, there are so many more important things. It's not as though we are not a sovereign independent nation, of course we are, if we weren't I'd have a different approach.

Mr Hawke, has there been a time in your life, someone you know, a friend or relative, or could you imagine a time when the option of voluntary euthanasia might be appealing?
I'm in favour of it ...

Do you see a problem in terms of it being a fundamental shift in Western values from a system that's really based on the value of human life?
Why don't we face up to the fact that it happens now, that it's hidden? I mean, people are taken off life support systems who could be kept alive longer, but it's a tacit agreement between the relatives, the sufferer, the doctor and the system. My simple requirement would be that it is legislated in a way which gives an absolute certainty that the sufferer is protected – that it's what the sufferer wants and that they are not the victim of rapacious bloody relatives who want to get them out of the way.

I'm looking here at Aboriginal land rights, Mr Hawke. Not specifically at the Howard Government's Ten Point Plan, but as I understand it, the Ten Point Plan is really a way to circumvent the separation between the judiciary and legislature and basically create an outcome that perhaps wasn't intended by the High Court. Do you believe that the High Court is sort of the umpire of the situation? Who should be making the law?
Of course it is the umpire, under the division of powers between the executive, the parliament and the judiciary – that's what the division of powers is all about. You must have an umpire who adjudicates on whether the constitutional powers have been properly exercised.

And let me make the point that there is a lot of ill-informed nonsense talked about the recent so-called 'judicial activism' of the High Court. It's bullshit. The High Court has been judicially active from day bloody one. Let me give you an example. I read all the Constitutional Convention debates, read them right through, when I was doing my PhD, and the Constitutional founders had quite definite views about what they intended. The High Court started to change that from day one, from day bloody one, and it continues to do it. If you want to address judicial activism, look at the period of Barwick's Chief Justiceship, when he interpreted the taxation laws in a way which was appalling, to protect the tax avoiders and rob the community – that was judicial activism at its worst. So when some judges interpret in a way which, it is said, is looking after the Aborigines or something like that, they're not doing anything that hasn't been done from day one. You'll always have to have a court to adjudicate whether the Constitution is being adhered to.

And on the question of land rights, I only wish it had been in my period of government that the Mabo decision had come, which said that *terra nullius* was bullshit. We would then, in my period, have had the opportunity of legislating on that basis. That was the good fortune of Keating and his government, to have that decision of the High Court. The important thing is now that, within the division of powers, the legislature should act in a way which will ensure the protection and the rights of the Aboriginal people, in a non-discriminatory way. And I have a fear that that's not being done.

Well, I understood the idea was that you had a High Court that protects you from politicians to some extent ...

It's not so much to protect you from politicians. For better or for worse we have a Constitution – given a federal system you've got to have a Constitution, it's not like Great Britain or New Zealand which are unitary states and don't have a Constitution – here, where you have a division of powers between the Commonwealth and States you've got to have the High Court, same as in the United  States, you've got to have an adjudicator. And what that means is that governments of both persuasions, when they're making appointments to the High Court, should try and get the best possible people they can.

Sure. Finally, Mr Hawke, it's a question that's fallen out of the questions I've asked people, and fundamentally what's come through is that a great leader can make a good cricket team a great cricket team, or a great team a super-team. Is leadership a fundamental issue for Australia looking forward, not just at a political level but throughout society in general?

Yes, I think leadership is very important, always has been and always will be. People need – not just want – leadership, and leaders can make a difference, as you say not only in politics but in our business community and our community organisations. Just take an example, say community organisations. I had the great good fortune when I was prime minister to have as president of the RSL, which is a significant community organisation and an important one, Sir William Keys. He was a man who was absolutely committed to advancing the interests of his constituency, and he did it well. He could see those issues within the broader framework and he didn't come to me and say I want this, this, this, and this. He'd say to me, 'Bob, this is important. I'd like that, but I know I can't have all of that, but if you could look at this I would appreciate it.' He could look at the broader picture, and that was great leadership on Bill's part.

So it's not just important in the political sphere, or the sporting sphere, but also in our community organisations and certainly in our business community. We've had – and still have – some bloody awful leaders in the business area, and we have some very good ones. For instance, relating it back to Aboriginal rights, there are some sectors of the mining community which have a very enlightened, cooperative and constructive approach in regard to Aboriginal rights, while others are, to say the least, not so far sighted.

Can we do more to foster that?
Well, we ought to, and I think the media's got a role here. I mean, I'm not a great fan of the Australian media – they are enormously good at handing out criticism and pontificating. They could do more to foster the question of the responsibilities of good leadership and acknowledge the fact that good leadership very often requires hard decisions, not simply to smack someone about the head all the time.

Terrific! Thank you very much for your time, Mr Hawke.
My pleasure.

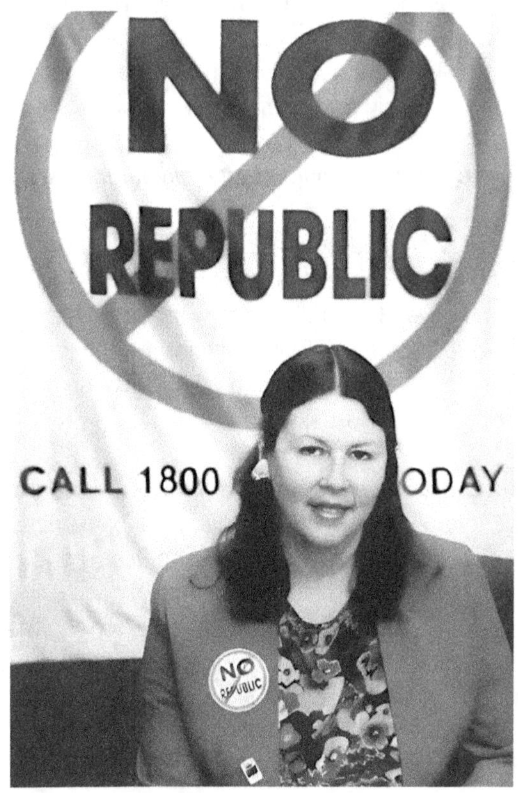

Kerry Jones

Executive Director,
Australians for Constitutional Monarchy

*'We should all strive for justice and
equality in whatever we're doing'*

BRETT KELLY: *Is there an idea, person or event that had the single most profound impact on your life?*

KERRY JONES: Well there's no doubt that schooling probably affects a person's attitude and development and opinions. I went to Loreto Normanhurst College, it is currently celebrating its centenary year, and a lot of the principles espoused in being brought up under the nuns have remained with me all my life. The founding person of the college, Mary Ward, her motto was 'Women in time to come will do much' (1609). I think that has stood me in very good stead in many different directions I've gone through in my career.

Do you have a motto, quote or thought that really summarises your approach to life?
Well, particularly in my work, and I suppose also in the way I hope I'm bringing up my children and coping with my life, it's that we should all strive for justice and equality in whatever we're doing, and overriding that, we should all do and contribute our best to whatever we're involved in. That is certainly what I've tried to do in each of the jobs I've had, as well as in my roles as a mother and a member of what I believe is a wonderful society here in Australia.

What are the most critical issues facing Australia in the next decade?
Obviously number one is keeping this wonderful nation a united working nation. That involves all society. I believe that we have a very proud and independent national identity in this country and that identity allows us to grow and move forward in a united and positive way. And I think all of us, whatever area we're working in, that should be the overall thought in our minds – unity, moving forward as a united Australia with a very strong national identity.

What do you see as the best things about Australia today?
Well, we're a peaceful nation and we are now recognised as the sixth oldest working democracy in the world. We've been able to maintain unity and stability for much longer than most countries in the world. Obviously when things go wrong in terms of the peace of a nation, in terms of civil unrest or obviously drastically war, that's what so often ruins a country and brings the worst out in a country. And so we must continue to recognise that the strength of our democracy is of course all about the system of government, the way that works, the way our legal system works, and all of the things that make us a united nation, and those things must be maintained.

What are the worst things about Australia today?
Criticism, by some elements of society, who say we don't have an identity, don't know who we are – criticism of our nationhood I find very disconcerting. Because it's overlooking the fact that we are, if not *the* best, probably *one* of the best working democracies in the world. And why is that so? We are able to live as a nation, if you like, a multicultural society, all living together, accepting each other for what

we are with our different cultural backgrounds – but living generally in peace and harmony. I'd be concerned at some of the minor but potentially serious issues that could come through if we don't continue to maintain this great standard we've achieved of racial tolerance, building on anti-discrimination programs, and obviously the critical areas of people's rights.

Do you think at the moment it looks like the pendulum has swung one way and might be swinging back the other way? Is that a natural process of finding a happy medium?

I think the general curve of harmony, peace and stability – if you like – as a nation that we've been able to achieve continues to move forwards and up. We have to recognise that there's always elements of society questioning, looking at, those sorts of areas. Our general record has been so good that if we all continue to work together in maintaining it, when we look back historically there'll be small ripples occasionally but I think our record is going to really go down as outstanding in world history. We are an outstanding nation with what we've achieved and what we're currently achieving.

What does euthanasia mean to you, and do you see that there will be a role for euthanasia in the 21st century?

That's a personal opinion. I believe absolutely in the right to life for every human being. So any part of a debate I would take would always be from that philosophy.

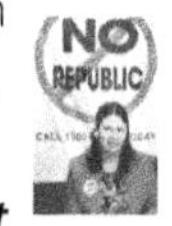

What is unemployment? What I'm really trying to get at here is the current debate that full-time employment be counted as 20 hours per week. Some might consider it's 40 hours a week. Does employment have anything to do with the hours you work, or more to do with the job you do? And when we're measuring unemployment, what should we be considering as unemployed and employed?

My attitude is that every human being is entitled to be leading a fulfilled and happy life. Now therefore anybody at all who is capable of being employed has the right to be employed – part of that fulfilment, part of their total wellbeing surely is going to be to have a job. So I believe that as a general philosophy we want as much employment as we can have, for people who feel fulfilled because they're doing something in their life, giving them some sort of purpose and satisfaction. Now I can't get into debate on how you achieve that. You need to be an economist.

Is full employment still a realistic target?

The problem here is that if there are people – and I don't know if there are – who genuinely don't want to be employed, and if they see that as part of their wellbeing and part of their fulfilment, and if there's good reason for it, perhaps they're not well mentally or physically, or perhaps there are personal motivational reasons associated with self-esteem ... There are certain people who really aren't physically, for whatever reason, able to undertake employment. I think society has got a role to look after these people.

You agree with there being some sort of safety net and unemployment benefits?
Without being expert in this field, I would assume that there's always going to be some people, for whatever reason in a particular stage in their life, who are really totally incapable of being employed. And we must be prepared to always look after them. People through different stages of their life may not quite be coping as well as the rest of society.

In terms of those young people who can't find jobs, what do you feel would make a difference in their searches?
Having three kids myself facing this issue of their futures, their careers, I'm very aware that young people need a lot of help and a lot of guidance. That's related to what we do at the educational level. I'm quite convinced that with the right support structures, most young people can be helped to move into a fulfilling career and employment. We as a society have got to be prepared to help, and to set up programs that can cope with the many problems that young people might be facing. I mean, we're aware from statistics that divorce is having a major effect on young people's self-esteem and how they can cope, so I believe as a society we have got to identify young people who might be having difficulty in focusing on career, focusing on where they're going, and offer support to them, in whatever ways we possibly can.

Do you find the idea of some type of national service or work-for-the-dole scheme repugnant, or could these schemes be useful?
Well, I'm a firm believer in freedom of choice, not compulsorily making anybody do anything at all. However, I believe there's room for programs for young people that are perhaps lost, not knowing where they're going. If they can be self-motivated to come into those sorts of programs they could provide a wonderful opportunity for them, and move them into that level of life where they're going to become a fulfilled person for the rest of their life. So anything that's going to help is worth a try, but certainly anything that is compulsory or forced – I think it's been proven time and time again, you can't absolutely force anybody to do anything.

Is Australia a racist nation?
We're certainly not a racist nation. The vast majority of Australians that I've met are aware of the wonderful principles that we've always had in this nation. That is, give everybody a fair go – tolerance and a fair go. There are some individuals who from time to time make racist comments and perhaps *are* racist. I think that's a great pity. It's one of the things we have to be proud of, that we are such a tolerant society, that we can live as a multicultural nation in great harmony, accepting the differences that come with people of different cultures. But we're certainly not a racist nation and the enormous effort we've put into developing harmony with people who've come from many different backgrounds, many different cultures, I think is something to be very, very proud of.

What is education, and what role did formal education and training play in your life?

I've done post-graduate studies in education. I'm also a firm believer in what's called 'life education' – that we learn new things every day and we move forward from what we've learnt. The moment we stop learning it probably means something is going wrong. But everybody must be given formal education, to the level they are motivated to achieve, and also of course to the level that they can cope with in what they choose. I believe we've got to continue to offer whatever educational opportunities our young people want, and this means that all young people that aspire to go to university should be given that opportunity, and obviously all young people need a formal school training – that's going to be critical.

So you believe that there's an inherent value in education that goes beyond what your next job might be, beyond the level of vocational training, to a level of developing your mind?

I'm a Plato-trained educationalist – and that of course means developing the whole person. Education is not just maths and English, it's the person's ability to cope with the whole life experience. Therefore it must be looked at as developing each individual as a whole person in all areas of their potential, which means, arts, sports, public speaking – all of the things that some people are very talented in. We must continue to expose our children to all those areas and then hopefully they can move into the areas of their choice as they mature and learn more about where they're going.

Are educational opportunities plentiful and well distributed to young Australians from all socio-economic backgrounds?

In my experience, yes. I've worked in schools in the country from K to Year 12, as well as in the city of Sydney, and I've seen wonderful opportunities offered to our children in the school system. I think problems do occur where perhaps home life is unstable or whatever, and that can affect a child's ability to cope in the school environment. We may have to continue to look at special programs and ways of helping children who are obviously having difficulty in their home environment.

If your child had a drug habit, would you like them treated as an ill person requiring treatment or as a criminal?

I would be appalled if they were looked at as criminals, because I believe we have to help all people who might be going through particular crises in whatever way we can. But I'm also conscious of the scarce resources. Just how far do you go in that assistance, particularly in monetary terms, and how do you justify the distribution of the scarce resources? I would be very much in favour, as a non-expert, of any program that's genuinely going to help people on drugs, in need. At the same time I'd be very conscious that you have to take the advice of the experts in the field, and really have a look at what resources are available, and at maximising the benefits of those resources. I do think it's probably one of the most difficult issues facing us right now.

Given that the current approaches that have been tried for the last 20 to 30 years quite clearly have failed, should we be looking at alternative approaches to the problem?

I think we've always in other areas relied on our experts. We've got some of the best experts in so many areas – watching that rescue at Thredbo – and we've got to rely on their advice. We should be talking to those experts and getting their advice. Then we should accept that advice and try it.

Is tax reform inevitable? Does the current tax system adequately serve Australia?

I do have a personal opinion on that. I believe that we've got to have a total overhaul of the tax system. In my previous job I was involved in the health industry, and it is very, very disadvantaged by the current tax regime. There's no doubt that in areas like the health industry a GST type tax structure would make things a lot more equitable. But I can only speak from that industry, and I believe that other industries complain that they would be worse off. Again we'd have to look to the experts and listen to what they advise, but my limited knowledge in the tax area is saying that we do need a major overhaul. It's not working, it's not as equitable as it should be.

Is it the sort of scenario where you would like to see a two-party approach, to really sit down and have a look at it in a non-political sense?

Absolutely. The big problem with tax is it's an issue where everybody is going to look at their own pocket, rather than the big picture. It is a weakness we Australians have, we vote for me, *us,* rather than the big picture. Probably the politicians and the experts have a lot of marketing to do in terms of achieving tax reform. I think most Australians would agree there's a need for it, but when they come to vote on it they're just going to look at it from their own point of view. So they'll need to have a pretty strong education campaign on the whole issue.

Will Australia ever be a republic, and if so when do you think this is likely?

Well, for all intents and purposes, as a number of experts, very eminent people, have said, we are already what we call a crowned republic. What we've got to get out to the Australian people is the educational process that lets them really know just how independent a nation we are. Now the debate is not about breaking emotional ties with the Queen, or England, or any of that. It's about the system of government here in Australia.

There are 116 republics in the world and they're all different. So far nobody has said which sort of republic they're going to give to Australia. What we do know is that we'll get another politician in the picture, we'll get a president – with any model of republic. Then you start to get into the details of the republic, which is not what we want to do today. So far in Australia, what we've seen is republicans becoming more and more divided about the nuts and bolts of their republic. Everyone you talk to, if you actually ask the question 'What sort of republic?', which is the real question, you'll get a surprisingly different answer. So until there is a united alternative model system of government and a real alternative Australian Constitution drawn up by the republicans, the whole debate is a nothing.

Where does changing the Australian flag fit into the republic debate?

The flag should be a separate debate, because the republic debate is about an alternative system of government – a very different system. The flag is a symbol.

Now let's look at the flag. OK, much as people would like to talk about the symbol of the Union Jack, you have to admit that one of the most significant events that has happened in our history is the settlement by the British – we would not be sitting here today if that had not happened. So the flag is a reminder of our history, and surely that's what symbols are meant to do. That flag's got not only the symbol of that part of our history, it's got the Southern Cross which represents all Australians who've been here in perpetuity, and of course the seven-pointed star represents the Federation. There's no other flag in the world that's got history, geography and Constitution on it. It's a pretty special flag. It's going to take a lot to change it and the will of the people should be listened to on that issue.

Now I started off by saying I believe we're already a crowned republic; our own governor-general exercises the power as head of state. The queen can do nothing unless told to or asked to by our government or prime minister. I believe we're already an absolutely independent nation, probably with the best system of government in the world, a crowned republic, with our own head of state, our governor-general. Why on earth would we risk a new system? We won't.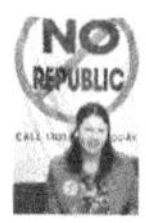

Who is the governor-general appointed by?

He is technically appointed really by the prime minister. The queen endorses that appointment but she absolutely respects the nomination of our prime minister.

So it would be unusual and unlikely to have a rift between what you could describe as 'best of mates', the prime minister and the governor-general?

It can't happen. When the Whitlam dismissal occurred, the governor-general at the time said, 'would the Queen offer advice?' and the Queen declined; she has absolutely no role at all in the constitutional affairs of this nation. Absolutely nothing to do with it. That's the wonderful thing about evolution not revolution!

Thank you very much for your time.

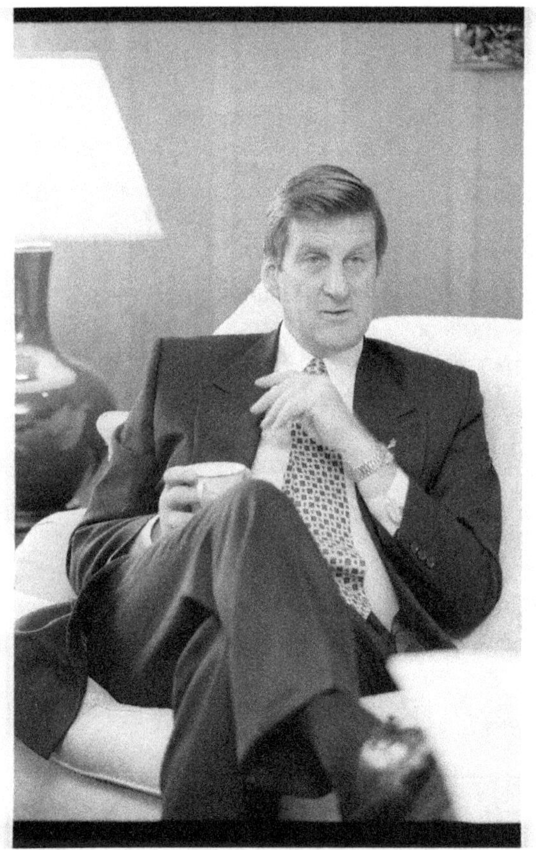

The Hon. Jeff Kennett

Premier of Victoria

'Everything happens for a reason and everything turns out for the best'

BRETT KELLY: *Mr Kennett, is there an idea, person or event that has had the single most profound influence on your life?*

JEFF KENNETT: If there was any individual it was my father, whom I continue to respect just for his incredible decency, his values. I think that he gave me, together with my mother, a very strong basis for living. I was fortunate that I was brought up in a very typical Australian middle-class family of mother and father, both whom worked to educate their children. So he was probably the most influential person in terms of both the theory and the practice of living.

I've had a number of experiences over my life which have been valuable. My army experiences were very valuable in terms of learning to relate to other people, chains of command, things of that nature, self-discipline. A car accident I had in 1976 had a profound effect. So there were a range of things.

Is there a motto, quote or thought that summarises your approach to life?
I think there are probably a couple. One is, 'Never give up'. Another would be, 'Everything happens for a reason and everything turns out for the best'. So both of those concepts I play up to the full.

What are the most critical issues facing Australia in the next decade?
I think the most critical issue right now is our very existence into the 21st century. And we've got to do better than exist, we've got to grow as a country. We've got to continually run faster, not stand still – we've got to sprint to do better. But the big issues for Australia right now for me are getting us into a competitive position so that we can employ and we can grow. Tax reform is very important. Further flexibility in the industrial relations system is important. The quality of education is fundamental in streaming people towards careers that are going to be relevant in the 21st century.

What are the best things about Australia?
I suppose the best thing about Australia is its democracy, its freedom. People have come from all parts of the world; they have elected to settle here, having left their own countries where they have seen their democratic rights eroded, threatened or in some cases totally obliterated. So we have a wonderful sense of freedom. Second, we have a magnificent rule of law where most of us understand the way in which to behave, to respect each other, respect each other's property, and that rule of law gives us certainty. That and the democratic process give us a great deal of security *per se.*

The environment in which we live is important. We have a wonderfully diverse environment right around this country – we've got all the diversity of the world here on one continent. We're very, very fortunate.

But it's also the mix of our people; we're a very multicultural society and to me that's a real asset. Our people are our greatest treasure, especially if we have those people living together harmoniously – as we do – and working together and enjoying each other's background and culture. There is a distinct Australian spirit, there is an 'ockerism' about Australia which I think is terribly friendly. We're a very embracing, forgiving people.

In what areas do you think we could, as a nation, do better?

I think we've got to do better at long-term planning. That is, we've got to clearly identify where we want Australia to be. We ought to articulate goals right into the middle of the next century. We've then got to develop strategies which will help us achieve those goals, and then within that there is a whole lot of subtext that becomes terribly important. But unless the community understands where we're going, what we're trying to achieve, unless people have some ownership in our destiny, then we're never going to maximise the opportunities that surround us.

We've got a Ten Point Plan at a federal level to deal with Aboriginal land rights. Would it be appropriate to have a ten point plan which addresses our future direction?

In my desk, in my top left-hand drawer, is a blue brochure on programs, which I will give you a copy of. We established, when we came to office in 1992, a program for execution from 1992 to 2001 – a 10-year framework which includes three elections. Normally most governments only think about the next election, we're thinking about the next three in terms of time.

We also have a set of goals which will take us out to 2050. We have established a set of priorities for this State based on goals for the year 2050 and strategies to get us there. I don't think there is anything similar at a federal level and there never has been. I mean, it's most unusual to get governments working like this. They're what I call our national goals – they're not Victorian goals because I think States will be less relevant by the year 2050 so you need to be thinking nationally.

Is there a personal experience of unemployment, or that of a friend or relative, that has given you an insight into this issue?

I have never myself experienced unemployment but I am obviously aware through family experiences of unemployment. I see unemployment as having a social consequence particularly on the psyche of the person who is unemployed.

But the answers to unemployment are some of the things we have already discussed – good education, not necessarily a university degree but a good rounded community education; also an economy that is growing so that it will create employment opportunities. The reality is that you cannot provide well for people socially if you don't have the economy there in the first place to do it. So economics are as important to an individual's opportunity as the other side of the equation, the social environment.

What rewards have you found in your working life that aren't monetary?

I guess the greatest reward is personal satisfaction. In my job as a politician money does not count as an incentive – it is the satisfaction of knowing that you are contributing as part of a team that delivers positive outcomes. It doesn't matter whether you're premier of the State or whether you're a finance person in a business or you're a tradesman, to do a job and do it well is very, very satisfying. And to me that is always and should always be more important than money.

The concept of work-for-the-dole or a national service type of scheme – do you see the advantages of these sorts of programs?
I think you're talking about two different things. A national service program is different from a work-for-the-dole program. A national service program ... one definition of it might be, where every male and female is called up for a period of national service for their country, probably over a span of years, when everyone might have to do one year's service, maybe two, between the ages of 18 and 24. You decide whether you do it before or after you go to trade school or university or whatever. But everyone has to do it, and there's no point in having a national service scheme unless every male and female is involved in it, because equality is important. Also the value of national service is that everyone has the opportunity of mixing with other people whom they may never have met otherwise. And I think you are enriched as a person by that.

A work-for-the-dole scheme is a program that attempts to make people earn their social welfare benefit. In other words, if you haven't got a job, you want the community to pay x amount of dollars a week for your upkeep for doing nothing. We believe you should be contributing to work. Again, there is nothing wrong with the principle – it's in the execution. Clearly there has to be a very strong training component and then it has to be matched with employment. If it's done well it can be very, very good. If it's done badly it can be just a joke.

Here in Victoria we don't have responsibility for national employment, but we do have a responsibility for employment in Victoria. We're putting in place a training program whereby people who wish to do so voluntarily, who are unemployed, can join this scheme. They will be given nine weeks' intensive full-time training to lift their skills, then they'll be matched with an employer. They'll go out into the workplace for 12 months and during that 12 months, four days a week they work with the employer, one day a week they go back for more training. At the end of that they are well positioned for employment for the rest of their lives.

The good thing about this program is it's voluntary, but also young people are seeing a re-igniting of their self-esteem, and the attention of young people to this program has just been enormous.

Is there a figure for an acceptable level of unemployment in Australia?
None is acceptable. However there are some people who unfortunately are always going to be unemployable, or else the economy is not big enough to employ them. There may be flat spots in the economy, and from time to time with the introduction of new technology we drop employment in some areas and create new jobs in other areas. So there's always a changing scene, and technology has imposed a great deal of change in recent times.

In your experience is Australia a racist nation?

No. I think history past and present clearly indicates that as Australians we live very well with one another. You don't find racial issues on the front page of the papers – you may get the odd claim – but even if people have less tolerant views they invariably respectfully keep them to themselves.

So if you look at the Pauline Hanson so-called arrival on the scene, here in Victoria, in all the polls, less than 1 percent of the public are attracted by her views. We are the most tolerant of all States because we are out there regularly promoting multiculturalism. We've never walked away from it. It's something we feel very strongly about and that is reflected in the way in which the public are dealing with the Hanson issue.

What do you view as education? Is there a particular view that you think is critical for young people looking to the future?

Yes, there are several aspects of education. The first one is to understand that it actually starts in the home. The most important education in a person's life is between birth and seven years, when their ideas and principles are established, not by what their parents tell them but how their parents act in front of them. So they pick up the good values or they pick up the bad.

Second is the more academic training, scholastic training, that comes through schools, which is designed to heighten the level of communication skills. To me, when you've finished your secondary school you should be able to communicate – write, read – excessively well. 

The third is what I would call post-secondary education, whether that be apprenticeship, TAFE or university, that is streaming for occupations. Streaming people for potential outcome.

The last area is what I would call education for life. There is no day when you won't be learning something. The important thing is how you use that education over a successive period of time. So in one sense education, either directly or indirectly, is the most important ingredient in determining the environment in which a person lives.

If your child had a drug habit would you want a society that viewed them as a criminal or as an ill person requiring treatment?

We have put into place a huge strategy, part of which I was releasing earlier today, called 'Turning the Tide'. I'm putting $100 million dollars over four years into a specific drug strategy to educate people. I've put out an education booklet. We're about to hit every cinema in Victoria for the next month, every showing of a film. We've got programs going left, right and centre. The basis is that people who are on drugs have a health problem. We don't seek to make criminals of them. If they continually reoffend, well that's slightly different. We also crack down very heavily on the traffickers of drugs. But fundamentally speaking it's a health problem, not a criminal position.

Is tax reform desirable? If so, what are your primary concerns for any tax-reform agenda?

It's not only desirable, it is 25 years too late. Therefore it is urgent and it must be addressed quickly and resolved quickly. Why? Because within two years the average weekly earnings here in Australia will be $50,000 a year. So an average wage earner will be in the highest tax bracket. That means there is no incentive for people to work harder. There's no reward – why do you do it?

That is not the environment in which you grow a country. You've got to grow a country in an environment in which there is quite obviously a reason for doing better. Second, you need it because you need to be internationally competitive. There's not much point having systems here that are so bloody complicated that you can't produce goods and services for export at a reasonable price. Third, the system we have at the moment in terms of taxation has so many different variables in it you can go and buy a product and you wouldn't have any idea of what tax you were paying. So you need something more transparent – a better system that will allow you to eliminate some of the dysfunctional taxes that currently exist.

Should Australia be a republic, and why would a young person care?

I think every Australian regardless of age should care about Australia and what happens to it. In terms of a republic, prior to the Constitutional Convention I was concerned that those who advocate change would not be able to present a single model. The Convention generated wide-ranging debate and canvassed a number of models but ultimately arrived at a decision. During that process I was able to declare my position, which would see a truly Australian head of state while preserving and strengthening the best elements of the Westminster system.

Could you imagine a situation where having the option of voluntary euthanasia would be desirable?

Yes, I strongly support it and believe in it. I don't see why, in this day and age, with medical science able to keep us alive – whether it be a use-by date for our brain or a use-by date for our physical capacities – why we should deny adults when in sound mind the opportunity to determine whether they wish to live or not. When I look around Australia at the moment, there is so much inhumanity as people are kept alive by good-intentioned people, but in my opinion in great pain and great loss of dignity.

Looking at Aboriginal land rights. The idea of a federal government using the legislature to effectively circumvent the intentions of the High Court, is this a precedent worth encouraging?

Questioning the High Court?

Yes.

I think there's two issues. If the High Court were able to consistently make commonsense judgements that interpret the law I don't think there'd be a hassle.

However, if judges make political comment they should not be surprised if a few politicians decide to put a counter point of view. So I think the High Court – the court systems around Australia – have got to decide how they see their role. We see it, as politicians, as interpreting the law that we make. They're meant to be above politics.

In terms of Wik, it's not as though the federal government is trying to reverse the decision of the High Court. What happened was, the High Court gave a judgement that was fundamentally fuzzy and none of the detail was there. So now Parliament is trying to work out the detail. John Howard has spent countless hours and hours trying to get a compromise together which is representative of the Wik outcome, but still there are some groups who won't agree to it.

Now at the end of the day you've either got to keep going on endlessly with all these talks or you've got to decide, enough is enough and we're just going to legislate and interpret as we see it, based on all the advice we've had. I think what he's come up with is a very fair package.

Thank you very much for your time.

Cheryl Kernot

Leader of the Democrats*

'Do unto others as you would have others do unto you and seize the day'

*at time of interview

BRETT KELLY: *Is there an idea, person or event that had the single most profound influence on your life to date?*

CHERYL KERNOT: It was not just one thing, it was an accumulation of things. Number one, moving to Queensland to live, number two, going to watch the Queensland Parliament and realising that there were just two women in the gallery listening to the debate that was happening at the time – a debate on abortion – and it was all men talking about an issue of profound personal significance to women. This is not to say that men don't have an interest in that, being part of the creation of another life, but they talked about it with an inability to actually even understand the physical aspects of the process of abortion. I mean, one man said 'don't know what all the fuss is about, it's just like a little spider thing hanging on in there and they suck it out with a kind of vacuum-cleaner-like thing'. And even though I knew there weren't many women in Parliament, it wasn't until I looked down and on the floor of the chamber saw what that physically meant, and then heard all these men talking for hours about abortion and nobody expressing what I thought was a pretty common woman's view, that I thought, I never knew it was like this. To me it said a woman's view, and particularly the view of a woman like me, seems to be entirely absent from this debate – and these people are making laws which affect my life. I think I'd rather have a say in it.

Do you have a motto, quote or thought that really summarises your approach to life?
No, there's not one.

Apart from 'keep the bastards honest'.
That's not mine. I don't like it, but not because of the word 'bastards' in it. What I don't like about it is that it says you're sitting in judgement on others and you don't have any ideas of your own. Like, 'oh *you're* honest today, *you're* dishonest' – it doesn't allow you to put forward your own agenda. So I don't like that. I like a combination of thoughts and sayings: 'Do unto others as you would have others do unto you'. Pretty hard to do in politics. I also like 'seize the day'.

What are the most critical issues for Australia in the next decade?
Jobs. How to share the amount of available work. How to meet the challenges of globalisation in a way that safeguards the things which we actually care about in this country. How to put the environment and social justice on an equal footing with the economy in political debate. Because we have been obsessed with the economy for over a decade now, and it's been at the expense of quality of life for people.

What are the things as a nation we do best, and what do you think we could do better?

In terms of the good things, we still have the most abundant luxury of space and a relatively clean living environment – and this is all relatively speaking, compared with the worst in the world – but fairly clean air and water and food production. We still have people whose life chances can be altered by education. If you're born in India and born into poverty you hardly ever rise above it. So we have some equality of opportunity … but these things are being eroded. I'm hesitating here because I believe this, but while I'm saying it I know that they are being eroded. I know we're not spending enough money as a country on things that matter. I know that some of our public schools are being allowed to run down, and education is so important. I know the debate we're having about the future funding of universities. You can't be a 'clever' country, and give young people the skills that they have to have in a really challenging globalised world, without investing in education.

So while I'm saying there are some great things about Australia, I think they're incredibly under threat. They've started to be eroded. I also think Australian people have a really likeable irreverence – but when it matters they still care enough.

Now I'm really worrying that this is going to be undermined too. Our egalitarianism, which I think has been really important, is under threat because we've got the gap between rich and poor growing larger, and those who _have_ are not necessarily coming into contact with those who have not. Because a lot of people who have plenty can send their kids to private schools and afford private hospitals, can live in estates where there are walls around them, have private security. Now no one's begrudging them that, but what it means is they never have to go down  to the public school down the road and see what conditions are like, so they don't have to care. It's not that they're opting out deliberately, it's that their life doesn't bring them into contact. That worries me about the way we're going in this country and I think it's the worst feature of what's facing us. The challenge is the threat to egalitarianism and the threat to the way we used to all care about each other.

No sense of community?

Community is really important, and it's under threat in this country.

Is that an Australian phenomenon, do you think, or are the forces of globalisation and technology taking people out of interaction with each other?

No, there's a resurgence of community around the world – I mean politicians discovering it here are just coming in on the coat-tail of the big communitarian movement in America. Tony Blair has talked about it a lot. Bill Clinton's talked about it a lot. But talking about it and actually making policies that enhance people's identification with community are different things. You can't have community if you cut away at the things that bind people together, and if you cut away at the social safety net people can't have jobs, then they don't share in the good things that society has and they get alienated from the processes and they don't make a contribution either. That's why I believe in a more interventionist government than we have.

There's two images that come out of what you've said on these issues, and they're unemployment and education. On a personal level, are there any experiences of unemployment, a close friend or a family member, that have really struck a chord with you and brought home some messages?

Well, my brother has been unemployed off and on, but that is probably because of his emotional mental illness, so I don't take him as a benchmark. I know the process you have to go through to get your unemployment benefit and I don't begrudge one cent of my taxes going to unemployed Australians. It's the role of the government to make jobs, and we haven't done it well enough. And I don't believe all the propaganda about 'dole bludgers'. There are some, but the real majority of Australians want to work because they know what flows from work, and it's not just money. Meaningful work is a defining reason a lot of people have for living.

Have you found rewards in work apart from the monetary compensation? If so, what are some of them?

While I don't like John Howard's compulsory work-for-the-dole, I do like Tony Blair's version of it, of welfare to work. I think the version we've got in this country is mean-spirited and unimaginative. In Britain you're given four options. Government gives money to business as an incentive to employ young people, or they can opt for training, or they can opt for work in the community sector, or they can do some environment work. Now if they can't match up with one of those things, then they lose at least 50 percent of their benefit and they get another chance.

But John Howard's scheme doesn't give any training along the way, doesn't give a guaranteed job outcome at the end; he's just trying to make people feel good that he's making young people turn up for 28 hours a week and calling it work. And I really object to that. We should be doing something like Tony Blair. And the reason we should be doing it is because we do have a generation of unemployment, we do have young people who don't have any purpose, structure, routine in their day, and they need the personal contact, they need the sense of achievement. But you won't get that under compulsory work-for-the-dole, for the majority of people who do it. For some lucky people, the people who take them on say they can provide some training, and the contact and the structure of the day will be good. But for the majority of them it won't work that way, you wait and see.

Do you agree with some kind of national service or work-for-the-dole scheme, not commenting on the current government's proposal?

I'm just trying to think – I've done an 'around Australia' stand in shopping centres for quite a few months now, and I've had people come and talk to me about unemployment. There have been some incredibly sad stories. Terribly sad stories.

People discriminated against because of their language, their ethnic origins, because their communication isn't as good as it ought to be, irrespective of their high-quality degrees. Or young people who have to go back to university, they've already got one degree, they have to go back because they can't find a job. Highly qualified, and they can't find a job. And the single parents, the young unemployed who just have no hope. I find it incredibly moving. In all of these conversations I had with people around the place, one thing I learnt is that the people who are in work are just as terrified of losing their jobs as the ones who've lost them. They are incredibly vulnerable because in this country we've had over a decade now of downsizing – lean, mean and efficient. We don't care about what happens to the people when they get put on the scrapheap – some of them never get a job again, aged 50 and over. That's the end of a purposeful working life, and I think we should be able to do a better job than just believing all the rhetoric that says, you know, a smaller company and smaller government is necessarily better. This government, by the time it finishes its privatisation of Telstra and the downsizing of the public service, will have contributed 180,000 jobs to the unemployment queues. And you wonder why people have no confidence! The fact is, they've had five interest rate cuts since this government came to power, and people aren't out there doing cartwheels in the street because of the extra money they're getting in their pocket, they don't want to spend it because they think they're going to lose their job tomorrow – because we have this ridiculous ideological pursuit of downsizing. And even the person in the USA who coined the term 'downsizing' said last year that it was a big mistake.

What do you think of the argument that a young person should start in whatever job is available, if they cannot gain employment in their area of choice, and gradually work themselves into the role they want?

Well it's tenable, but all the people who are telling other people to do it never did it themselves. We don't have a culture which ascribes dignity to everybody's work. We say, oh you're just a garbo, or just a cleaner, whatever. You can't blame people for thinking, this is a demeaning job if I have to do it with my hands. And we as a society need to stand back and say, everybody's labour makes a contribution, I'm able to live cleanly in my neighbourhood because I have a council who employs people to do these jobs, they're not particularly highly paid but I actually think they're important, they fit into the chain of contribution which is everybody's labour.

But we are a very status-oriented society when it comes to work, and we've got too many over-paid people. It is immoral that some people in this society can get $2 million for their skills, and they get $2 million a year while the company they're running is running into debt! We have to iron out the discrepancy between what a person who cleans the toilets at the airport earns and a person who minimises paying tax, earns all this money and bonuses in art, houses, cars, school fees, and so on. There's a huge discrepancy.

Is Australia a racist nation?

No, I don't think we are. We've just got pockets of it – the same right wing mentality that exists in most countries. Unfortunately there is a fair bit of focus on it because of Pauline Hanson, and I suppose in my view because our prime minister has been, to use Noel Pearson's term, 'dog whistling', which means sending out ambiguous signals, rather than definitively saying, 'the views of Pauline are not what this country is about – there's no place for these views in this country'. And saying things in an ambiguous way so they appeal just as much to the racists as to the people who aren't, because the words are crafted in that way. But we're not fundamentally racist, and our young people are not racist because they're the product of a multiracial, multicultural society.

The success of the blending of the many races that make up Australia is unmatched in the world, and when I've travelled elsewhere people have asked me, how do you do it? We do it because we're essentially a tolerant nation – that doesn't mean that there aren't pockets of problems, there are, and there are some big problems – but at a national level, as a nation, the way we regard ourselves and others regard us, we are not overtly or even covertly a racist nation.

Do you think that to have someone like Hanson is necessarily a bad thing in terms of the long-term interest of the country?

Yes, I think it's a very bad thing. I don't subscribe to the view which says, well it's lucky that she's there because she's drawn attention to the things that people are worried about. Yes, people are worried about jobs, yes they're worried about globalisation, yes they're worried about the plight of indigenous Australians. But you can highlight all of that without scape goating others.

So it's not good for this country; it's bad for the people who have been able to use the same language that she's been using; it's bad for Australians who've come here from other countries, who've suffered offensive abuse at the hands of people because now they think it's politically OK; it's bad for this country because of the attitude to us abroad and the cutback to the numbers of students who are coming here to study; and it's bad because it's going to take a long time to undo the damage.

You can have all the concerns that she has without seeking to blame Aborigines or migrants, and without telling absolutely blatant lies about the level of immigration, about the so-called benefits that indigenous people get. It's bad! I don't subscribe to it at all. I'm passionately opposed to anybody saying, oh it's a good thing she's popped up because she's drawn attention – it's *not* a good thing, the damage she's done can *never* be categorised as a good thing.

What is education?

It's being given the skills to learn to learn. Because you will need them. Because you will not necessarily have one job for your entire life, you will be mobile and there will be huge challenges thrown at you to cope with new technology, and the kind of learning that I had would not equip me for that.

Do you think that reading, writing, basic arithmetic and the ability to evaluate and solve a problem are useful skills, in terms of training?

Yes, but that doesn't mean that I'm a fanatic about basic skills and back to basics. Of course they're necessary building blocks. I think some of the education we've had in recent years, which hasn't taught kids any rules, has been made a little murkier and cloudier for kids in the basic skills area. But there have been fantastic other things that schools now do which they didn't do when we only concentrated on the basics, which give kids a greater appreciation of what's required to be a participating citizen in a much more complex world.

Is it a matter perhaps of just working on the balance?

Minister for Education David Kemp is talking about a crowded curriculum, so you're asking me what would you take out. Unfortunately, our young people have to cope with so much, they need so many different skills. They need to be able to analyse the media in a way we didn't have to, so that they're not victims of media manipulation – we didn't have that in our life. They need somehow to maintain all their reading and literacy skills in a technological society, which means they have to cope with all the computer literacy skills as well. Because of technology and a more sedentary lifestyle, they need, I think, to have an emphasis on recreation and leisure and sports to a greater degree, because they often need to rely on their own skills. And because of the changes that are happening in a society where people eat out all the time, I think it's important that they have a greater emphasis on nutrition and parenting skills. Now schools have to get all of this in, it's incredibly difficult for them. I think that teaching is a highly valuable but totally undervalued profession, and what we ask of our teachers is extraordinary – I have a professional interest in this, because I was a teacher. 

We have to encourage young people to believe that teaching is a worthwhile profession to go into. I just met a student that I taught twenty-two years ago, and he told me that he and his brother are both teachers. And he said, 'I love it'. I said, 'Do you feel valued?' and he said, 'Oh, in my school I do, but I know as a professional you're not particularly valued.' You've got to say to young people that pursuit of the information technology-based jobs for the future is not the be-all and end-all. *Someone* has to teach our children, it's an investment in the future. We as a society have to start saying to teachers, what you do is important, you have de facto custodianship of our children for all these hours a day and that's important, and it's vital that we have really good people. I think teachers are underpaid, and I think we've lowered the entry standards over the years far too much, we've had to do that because we can't get enough people to do it anyway. It's one of the vicious cycles.

What role has formal classroom education and training played in your life?

It's been very important for me, because two female teachers I had were incredibly influential in shaping my life opportunities for me through education. I couldn't have gone to university if there were no scholarships or if it were not free. My parents were not wealthy, they weren't poverty stricken either, they just had four children, and I had a good education, a good state school education of which I am proud. I got access to university on a scholarship and really I had a good education in infants, primary and secondary school – in those days you did. Now it's very patchy whether you can be guaranteed a good education in public education, and I think that is wrong, because a lot of people in this society do not have the economic choice to send their kids to a private school where, in most instances, the range of subjects is better, extracurricular activities, sporting, coaching, all those things are good.

There is a lot of competition about funding for public and private schools, it's about saying 70 percent of our children still go to public schools, it's the responsibility of government to make sure that in those schools they get the best opportunity to develop their talent and skills. I'm a product of the '60s and what good public education could do for people's life chances, and I don't have confidence that young people today have that same opportunity as I had. In my book, that is wrong.

I had inspiring teachers, they worked hard, they taught me to think, they were provocative – two women in particular, one of whom's dead, but when I was 14 she was my teacher in English and the other one was my history teacher for the last two years of my senior schooling, and they were incredibly influential. I look back at them now and I know they taught me to think, because I didn't come from a home where either of my parents had a university education, though this is not unusual for the time we're talking about. I was the first person to go to university from my family, but those teachers gave me a belief in myself and the ability to think beyond the narrow confines of what was in the textbooks; that has been crucial for me.

Are educational opportunities plentiful and well distributed in Australia, and are substantial 'up-front' fees in universities a positive or negative step?
Education is an investment in the future, but I still find it hard to accept HECS. I don't accept the argument that because you get benefit out of university education you pay for it. The fact of the matter is, we have a progressive income tax system. If you earn a higher salary as a result of your tertiary education, you pay more tax.

So do you think the introduction of fees is a step in the wrong direction? It seems that you may not have had the opportunity to go to university in a fee-paying environment?
No, I wouldn't have had the opportunity because my parents could never have afforded that. But things are different now. A lot of people are saying, middle-class families can afford to pay for their children to go to uni, but some of them have two or three kids at uni, and how do you give each one of them equal opportunities? It's also a shame that mature aged students don't find it easy to get there, and some females don't find it as easy, but you know they manipulate the data on this – you can't be sure what's happening. The government has only just introduced the 'up-front' fees, it will be interesting to keep an eye on it. Education should not be the province of the wealthy.

Is there a role for government in providing deferred loans and the like? It is a big part of the system in the USA, and we had it in HECS but it appears to be being gradually walked away from here. Are loans potentially a better approach?

Yes, we're looking at that too. If you want to tinker with it, what's worse: up-front fees, HECS set at particular rates according to the subjects you take or the degree course you take, or a loan that you pay back? They're all variations on a theme. Probably the loans don't have the same regressive impact as up-front fees, so I'd go for loans first, graded HECS second, and up-front fees third.

If your child had a drug habit should he or she be treated as a criminal, or as an ill person requiring treatment?

I hope my daughter does not ever have a drug habit. I don't think she has an addictive personality and I hope she'll have sufficient self-esteem. Who knows why people try their first joint or heroin or whatever? I don't see that as criminal, I see that as a personality, emotional, chemical issue. I don't want them to be treated as criminals. I hate it when I go to the chemist and see the methadone addicts, it is pathetically sad. Because I think when people lose control of their lives, it's really hard to cope with. But I'd much rather them do that, I'd much rather have supervised access than the crime rate, the breaking and entering, the theft, the black market in drugs. I didn't have this view once. I do have this view now.

I think our prime minister is out of touch with where most progressive, and even not so progressive, Australians are on this issue. Because they look around at all the other options and they know they've failed – what can be wrong with a supervised heroin trial? The cost of doing nothing, going on as we've been going, is too huge. I don't find it easy to say that. I hate the thought of shooting galleries and I would never go to one and watch people shooting up, it makes me feel physically ill. But they're somebody's children and they're doing it for a whole range of complex psychological and chemical reasons ultimately, and we've got to find a way to deal with it which is humane. It would be just fantastic if we could find some rehabilitation-based solutions. 

Is tax reform desirable?

Tax reform is desirable, a consumption tax in not inevitable. There are a lot of things that we don't look at in our tax system which we should be looking at. The way people use family trusts to minimise the payment of tax – legally – they do it and we don't crack down on that. The way companies minimise their tax is wrong. We should have a minimum company tax as they do in America. The way in which our tax system favours speculation, for example negative gearing – you get all kinds of higher rates of return for speculating in real estate than you do for investing in plant and equipment in a productive factory. There's a huge bias in our tax system in favour of the speculative and against the productive which we need to address.

I have not yet seen the design of a consumption tax which doesn't hit lower income Australians, and when things are tough, to raise money governments just keep putting up the base rate. Calculations are that at the moment it would have to be between 10 and 15 percent, and there is only to be a one-off compensation for low-income earners for food and other essential items. The Democrats think food should be exempted from any consumption tax, and the whole issue is a long way from being adequately resolved – there is a long way to go.

But we haven't closed the door on discussion about tax reform. Australia can't go on for ever cutting expenditure, talking about balancing budgets, and trying to do it only by cutting and not by raising the revenue side of the ledger. You can't have a decent level of services and all the things that citizens expect and want in a civilised society, and have no money, and not have the guts to talk about how you raise money fairly. You can raise money fairly without having to hit middle Australia's income tax. Politicians and the media are so immature in this country – every time anybody talks about tax, everybody says they're going to put the tax up, and then we don't get anywhere.

So it's time for a mature approach and round-table discussion?

But I don't think we're capable of doing that. Because when the High Court just recently said that the States could no longer have the power to raise excise on petrol, alcohol and tobacco, the shadow treasurer was asked on a television program, well what is that going to do? And he said, 'Well it's a bit of a blow to them because they've been raising a lot of money on this', but he said, 'of course they still have the Constitutional right to have inheritance taxes and death duties if they want to'. He didn't say they should do it, but all the next week in Parliament Peter Costello totally manipulated that and twisted it around as saying the Labor Party and Shadow Treasurer say we should have death duties and inheritance taxes. We are incapable, while ever those people run the show, of having a mature tax debate in this country. It's very frustrating, it's also very masculine and juvenile in my view. That is not a sexist comment, that is based on my experience in this place.

Will Australia ever be a republic?

Yes, it will. I don't know when – I hope it's before the Olympic Games because I don't want John Howard to open the Olympic Games as the face of Australia to the world. We will be a republic because it's the next step in our nation's maturity. We are geographically, and now I think emotionally, divorced from the British royal family. We can remain a member of the Commonwealth of Nations, I don't have any objection to that. Young people support a republic overwhelmingly. We're stuck on how the president should be elected or appointed.

The benefits – you can't say when we turn into a republic we'll have to spend $5 million on changing the coat of arms and the letterheads of everything so it's too expensive – the benefits are psychological, emotional, and they are tangible in the respect that we're a multicultural nation and a whole heap of our citizens object to swearing an open allegiance to a foreign head of state. So I just think there are a lot of nation-building symbolic things that will flow from us being an independent nation, standing on our own feet, with a more secure identity as Australia.

Is it critical that any republic debate focuses on coming up with a form of republic that can be as stable as our constitutional monarchy?

Well, this convention in February is going to be hard, but it may come up with some models. You're going to put all these talking heads together for two weeks and they're asked to come up with consensus when the nation hasn't even had a discussion about what kind of models. I think people care a lot about stable government, they don't like politicians much, and they don't like elections much. They kind of begrudgingly accept what we've got, and democracy is a pretty imperfect thing but it's better than dictatorship in the main. I think we've got the cart before the horse – we should have had a vote of whether we want an Australian head of state and we should have had a convention on the details, what kind of republic do we want to be, and then have another vote. But we're not going to have it like that. It's going to be very confusing unfortunately, but Australia will not be an unstable republic simply because it's a republic, just as Germany is not an unstable republic. I don't think you can automatically say that a republic brings instability.

At a personal level, has there been, or could you imagine, a situation where the option of voluntary euthanasia might be acceptable?

There hasn't been one in my life, but I'm a strong supporter of voluntary euthanasia. I was in the Senate, and the Senate voted very closely in numbers when the Parliament instigated the Private Member's Bill, Mr Andrews's bill, to overturn the right of people in the Northern Territory to access legislation which gave them that right. It's not about compulsion, it's about choice, it's voluntary. You don't have to do it because you're dying, you can still choose, providing you are not hung up on a religious approach of a particular kind.

For example, Max Bell, the person who went all the way to the NT and he had to go home again, that was incredibly tragic. That really made you cry: the pain and the suffering and his desire to end his life. He had nothing else to live for. I'm really aware of all the arguments about the sanctity of life but I don't believe that any of us has the right to impose a Christian code or a moral code on others. You can say, this is what I believe, but you don't have the right of the Parliament, you don't have the right to use my vote to say to Max Bell, you can't do it because I say so, because I have a certain moral code. I just don't think that is our right.

What of the argument that Western civilisations are built on the belief that human life is inherently valuable?

Only where Christianity counts for anything is that true, and if you look at the number of people who don't go to church, I'm not sure those values are true. I think there's a respect for life and I think the final result of a number of things that are different in the last 20 years is a reassessment of the difference between respect for life, sanctity of life and the individual's right.

***Finally, the Howard's Government's Ten Point Plan on Aboriginal land rights
appears to be a plan that skirts the umpire's decision, if that's how you view the
role of the High Court in a constitutional monarchy. Do you see that as desirable?***
No, you've got to have respect for the High Court. There have been decisions they
have made which I didn't like or agree with. One I didn't like most of all was their
decision on political advertising. But the High Court is a very important pillar in
respect of the law in the country, and I don't think this is an overtly political decision.
The Democrats believe there should be a different way of making appointments to
the High Court, that there should be a more rigorous selection progress. I think that
people like Justice Brennan are outstanding Australians, and so is Sir William Deane
who was on the High Court then, so Paul Keating got some appointments right.

This government is now talking about stacking the High Court with 'capital
C' conservatives. That is an overtly political statement. I think you've got to try as
much as possible to keep the High Court free from that overtly political faction –
people have confidence in the High Court because it *isn't* overtly political. It's the
final arbiter and if politicians undermine the authority of this judgement then I think
you're in danger as a democracy. And if the National Party and the Liberal Party
don't like what they said on Wik, that's too bad. All they said was, 'where there's
pastoralist's rights and Aboriginal rights you should go for co-existence, they should
be able to evolve together, but if there's any conflict over existing land usage, the
pastoralist's rights prevail'. I can't see why that is so difficult.

To turn around and attack the High Court about it, saying that they have
caused 'massive uncertainty', I think has been a smoke-screen by Tim Fischer, simply
a political smoke-screen, because he's in strife over the legislation and he needed
to get some passion and vehemence back into his message to Parliament. The
problem is, in doing that you are very divisive – you are saying that the rights of one
part of Australia, that is farmers, are more important than those of another bunch
of Australians, that is our Aboriginal people – and you can't do that any more in
this country, in my view. It is a dangerous principle to continue to attack the High
Court, it is so dangerous that both chief justices had to speak out twice about what
it's doing.

If you can't have confidence in the final umpire, then your democracy is in
trouble because life shows, and history shows, and my experience here shows, that
politicians in the main will do what they can get away with for their own constituency.
In the main they're not motivated by the common good – occasionally they will all
join together in the national interest – but they want to win the next election and
they've got to appeal to their constituency first.

***There is a Ten Point Plan on Aboriginal land rights, should we have a ten point plan
for Australia?***
I don't know about ten, but it would be great to have a plan that everybody knows
about, yes. Jeff Kennett's got one for Victoria, he was very keen to tell me and show
me. While I don't agree with it all, I thought it was very useful to have – saying this is
what we're aiming for in the next 20 or 30 years. He's got two plans – the first goes

up to 2005 and the other goes up to 2050. Now I think it is helpful to people to have shared goals. I'm not sure whether all Victorians had a say in what those goals ought to be, but it's better to have goals than to be drifting aimlessly, flotsam and jetsam on some international global sea, and have no control over life.

Thank you very much for your time.

Poppy King

CEO, Poppy Industries Pty Limited

*'The glass is half empty
rather than half full'*

BRETT KELLY: *Now, this is the company you started when you were 19. Can you tell us your story briefly?*

POPPY KING: Basically I started it because I identified a gap in the market for a particular type of matte lipstick ... Once I found the finance and manufacturers to make the product I then decided to go ahead and start the business and get it onto the market. My first range of product came onto the market in March 1992 and it has been extremely successful since then.

Is there an idea, person or event that you can say had a really significant effect on who you are and where you are today?

I guess there have been a number of seminal moments in my life, but probably one event that had an enormous impact on me was when my father died. I was very young – actually a bit too young to be able to think cognitively about what impact that had on me at the time. I was expelled from school when I was about 12 or 13, and that had an enormous impact on me in terms of learning about the pros and cons of standing up for yourself.

What actually happened? Is it an interesting story?

It was a combination of events. It wasn't really one event. It's just that I didn't fit in and it was a very rigid girls' school.

Is there a motto, quote or thought that sums up your approach to life?

'The glass is half empty rather than half full.' I think I am someone who always feels I can do better, I can get better, I can think better, I can get the business stronger. I guess I am someone who is constantly shifting my goal posts.

What do you see as the critical issues for Australia in the next decade?

There are a number of issues. Certainly women's issues are going to become more critical. Especially when currently women are actually going backwards in this country in a lot of ways. Also the republic is obviously an important issue that is going to be talked about in the next decade. Industrial relations is another area that is undergoing massive changes and is going to be at the forefront for Australia as a whole. What other issues? Aboriginal reconciliation and multiculturalism are certainly going to be critical issues.

What do you see as the best things about Australia, and what things could we do better?

I think the best thing about Australia is that it is a relatively young country and so it doesn't have a lot of historical baggage. So we can actually write the rule book as we go along – we don't have years and years of established traditions which make it very difficult to change. We can be nimble and really keep up with the rest of the world. So I think that is a fantastic thing about Australia. But I am worried that we are not going to reach our potential as a very sophisticated, free-thinking, cohesive, multicultural society. We really could be a role model for other countries around the world and we have the ability to be unique in that way. I think that is under threat at the moment, and it concerns me.

What was your first job? Did you enjoy it or was it a bit tough?

Well, I waitressed a lot when I was younger and even though ... I mean, it is certainly not a glamorous job, but I enjoyed it. Even when I was at school I always had part-time jobs, and I have always enjoyed working, but I have never done anything that I thought was completely and utterly soul destroying or beneath me. You know, I mean, I have done mundane jobs but I don't mind that.

Do you think that a young Australian should probably be prepared to start at something hard, not their ideal job?

I think whether you are young or old you have got to be able to roll with the punches and you have to be able to take the good with the bad. But it is very hard to take bad or mundane positions if you feel as though there is never going to be any upside to it. I always felt that I would end up doing something that I wanted to do. I never thought that I was stuck in any dead end, so it is very easy for me to sit on my high horse and say that you should just enjoy, just do, whatever you have to do and never complain about it. I mean, if you feel like that through your entire life it is very difficult to do it.

Do you feel that Australians, and Australia as a nation, are racist?

I don't think that Australians are so much racist, but they are afraid of difference, and there is actually a distinction. I don't so much see this as racist but what I do see is that we have a tendency to be frightened of people that are different to us, frightened of ideas that are different to ours. Which is quite a normal human failing, if you like, or quite a normal characteristic of human nature. I think that that exists all  around the world, but it is something that can often hold us back – particularly in Australia, with this idea of just trying to maintain the status quo and stick on familiar ground rather than taking the risk to change or the risk of having difference around us. And I think that that is really what is threatening us at the moment, this fear of what is different.

What is your experience of formal classroom education and training? Did you finish school and/or go to university?

No, I didn't go to university. I finished high school, did my HSC, and ended up starting this business when I left school. So I didn't go to university, but I really think that education is vital. And as far as life opportunities go, I don't necessarily think you have to be a doctor and therefore get higher marks. I just mean that the more that you open yourself up to learning, and the more that you learn in whatever fields or whatever areas, the more opportunities you give yourself to find direction and inspiration and interest. And so I think that education is vital in opening up those opportunities.

So you see it as self-directed and not necessarily confined to the classroom?
No, I think that it has to be formalised and I believe that a combination of both is better, but certainly when you are younger formal education is imperative.

Do you think that a drug user should be viewed as somebody who is sick and in need of a cure, or as a criminal? And, given that what has been tried over the last 20 years hasn't necessarily worked, do we now look 'outside the box' for a solution?
I think that it is now time to look at different ways of coping and trying to address the problem of drugs. Again, I am not an expert in this area and I haven't really thought it through well enough to be able to give you a formal opinion. I do think that it isn't something that you can just sweep under the rug and pretend that it is not there. It really does require some analysis and a new way of looking at it, to perhaps come up with some different ideas.

Is tax reform, some type of GST, desirable?
As a country we should never stand still and say that things are absolutely rigid and we are never going to change or explore other options. So obviously, there is a need to look at tax reform in this country and it is something that a lot of people have felt for a long time. As far as a GST goes, again I feel that it is something that I don't really know intricately enough to be able to make a very informed opinion. I can certainly say that I am open to it and I am interested to hear the debates surrounding it. I would definitely like to see what the pros and cons of a GST are, as long as this debate doesn't get hijacked by politics. If it is actually presented without either the fear campaign or, on the other side, without making out that it is going to be *the* answer from now on. Hopefully – I don't know whether this is possible or not – but if it *could* be put forward just in a bipartisan debate, an honest, mature approach.

Do you think that we are at a point where we could have a bipartisan debate on a topic of such national significance?
No. I mean, it is very innocent to think that we could, because realistically it is a political issue, and there is always going to be politics in politics.

Will Australia ever be a republic? If so, when? And then, further, why would an Australian care?
Well first, will Australia become a republic? I still do believe that it will at some point. It is just a logical progression. As far as when, I think that that is really in question now because it depends on the government of the day pushing this through. It is not something that is going to happen by itself. It is an esoteric issue; it is not something that is going to solve particular problems or improve anybody's quality of life and I would never suggest that it will. But it is something that I think is important, even though it is not as important as health care and education and unemployment and welfare and all these issues that are obviously fundamentally central to our quality of life.

I think the republic is actually a very important symbolic issue about moving forward, having a vision, having direction, realising that we are a country unto ourselves that doesn't still need an umbilical cord or an apron string attached to the UK. That was something to do with the past, and we are now in control of our own destiny. It is very much a symbolic gesture, and symbols are important in a society. To someone in the street it is not going to mean that his or her life is in any way remarkably different. But it is an important symbol of us taking control of our own destiny. Which I think we have every right and every reason to do now.

If we become a republic ... well, what sort of republic?

I am not a constitutional expert, so again I don't really have a strong sense of how it would actually be structured. I have my views on popular election versus parliamentary election and president and all that. I do feel that the president should be elected by the Parliament. And as far as the actual structuring of a republic, I don't think we should just put something aside because it is a bit hard or we can't really be bothered. That apathy is very dangerous.

Is that the challenge, though, to come up with a model that can really match the existing system?

The challenge first of all is to get the issue back in the forefront of debate, because I think it is quite obvious that the current government is not behind it and certainly would like to push it off to the side of the agenda. So, to get it back being debated. From that point, to make sure that we seriously examine what structure will be put in place to go forward, but not in a way that is necessarily populist. By that I mean having the right people, the experts, do it rather than Ray Martin and so forth.

Could you see a situation where voluntary euthanasia may be justified, where it might or should be an option?

I think that it should be an option. I realise that it is a very difficult issue, that it is very complicated, riddled with potential problems. From watching my father die from a degenerative disease like cancer I certainly have a personal feeling that it should be an option. It is just a matter of how you ensure ... put the checks and balances on it to make sure that it actually works. And that it is beyond any criminal or negligent activity.

What is your view on the issue of Aboriginal land rights, and particularly of the situation as it currently stands?

I personally support the Mabo decision and I am now very concerned. I thought that that was a very important step forward in Australian history. I think it was a very important foundation, that was put in place to move us forward as a nation. And I am very concerned that now we are trying to step backwards, that the issue has been completely hijacked by politics, and there is a lot of emotion involved in it. People have exploited the issue a lot. It has been exploited in both directions, not just by our current government but by our previous government as well, for their own purposes. It is a very emotive issue, and so it is difficult to ask people to think rationally about it. It is something symbolic.

Thank you very much for your time.

Hugh Mackay

Author, Psychologist & Social Researcher

'Recognise the value in everyone'

BRETT KELLY: *Is there an idea, person or event that has had the single most profound influence on your life?*

HUGH MACKAY: Because I grew up in a Christian household, it would be unfair not to acknowledge that. Although my present position is very different from the position of my youth, Christianity was certainly a significant early influence on the shaping of my moral universe.

Another key figure – almost the antithesis of the first – was Bertrand Russell. Russell was significant in introducing me to a more sceptical view of the world. His great example to me was of a man having the courage of his convictions, a man prepared to live in ways that were consistent with what he believed. There was plenty of hypocrisy in Russell's life, but at least in terms of his public persona he was an impressive figure to me. The third powerful influence came from an American psychologist, Carl Rogers, who reshaped my whole approach to research. He was a psychotherapist who developed the so-called 'client-centred' school of therapy (based on empathic listening: letting people clarify their own difficulties and reach their own solutions by listening to them with understanding and affirming what they're saying). I'm not a therapist, of course, but I found Rogers' approach to therapeutic psychology enormously helpful in developing a research philosophy. In response to that, I adopted a research approach which was quite revolutionary when I began developing it. (It's not at all revolutionary now.) It was an approach that encouraged people to talk, without imposing questions on them – letting them ruminate and then trying to analyse and interpret what they've said.

There are many other individuals – direct contacts as opposed to those remote figures – who have been highly influential on my career.

One of the most significant was a man called Peter Kenny – a prominent psychologist and researcher who died about two years ago. Kenny was an eccentric and disreputable figure with an appalling personal reputation, but he really did inspire me, rather in the way that Russell's writing did. I worked with Kenny for about three years, and he encouraged me to push myself, to work in ways that were consistent with what I really believed, to be unconventional. He wasn't a pioneer in qualitative research but he strongly urged me to be one, and throughout my working life, until he died, he would appear periodically and check up on me to make sure I was being true to myself! I greatly valued that. Another significant person, also now dead, was Keith Cousins who, for many years, ran the George Patterson advertising agency. I was running a research company owned by Pattersons, and Cousins was a mentor in the sense that, as a hard-nosed commercial operator, he saw value in the kind of research I was doing and created a commercial framework for me. So I received professional encouragement from Kenny and commercial support from Cousins.

Is there a motto, quote, or thought that summarises your approach to life?
I haven't ever tried to distil my approach into something you'd recognise as a motto, but it has something to do with attaching appropriate value to the other person,

I suppose – sensitivity to the other. I think what I aspire to, both professionally and personally, is to 'recognise the value in everyone'. If I could exert an influence, it would be in the direction of encouraging people to adopt that approach. If you attach value to every human person, it follows that any human person with a need is entitled to have that need met. I'd have to say I fall far short of that, but that would be a sort of a guiding framework for me. People don't have to justify why they're needy. If they're needy, that's all the justification that's required.

What are the most critical issues you see facing Australia in the next decade?

Number one, undoubtedly, is the distribution of work and therefore the distribution of wealth. One of the disappointing features of the present political landscape is that we are talking as though unemployment is a short-term issue: we're going to lick it, and everyone's going to have a job. Now it seems to me most likely that unemployment is *not* a short-term problem, that in fact the period of full employment post the Second World War was an aberration and that what we're looking at now is the beginning of a trend towards even greater unemployment. We're getting very good at doing what the Industrial Revolution made possible for us, that is, replacing people with machines.

So the real issue is not what we are going to do with all of these unemployed people. The issue is, how are we going to distribute the available work among the available people? (And are we going to allow people to be free to decide whether they want paid employment or not?)

I suspect that in a couple of generations' time we won't use words like taxation, or welfare, or unemployment, or part-time work. I suspect that we will have developed a new vocabulary for dealing with our central problem, which is: we have this much paid work available; we have all these people who need to be financially supported through work or in some other way. What creative and  imaginative strategy can we develop so the people who want work can have it, no one will have to work too hard, and those who either can't or won't work, or for whom it's just impossible to find work, will not be pariahs – will not be made to feel as though they have somehow failed – but will be carried along with the rest of us? So we need a radically different view of how the available work will be distributed and, in turn, how the wealth generated by work will be distributed.

What are the best things about Australia? And are there things we should really be doing better?

We are an example to the world of a hybrid culture that works. We have a genuinely multicultural society, and I don't just mean multi-ethnic (although of course that's a big factor). We're a dramatic example to the world of how people from different cultural backgrounds can coexist in a spirit of something better than tolerance – tolerance is a pretty cold word – but exist in a spirit of harmonious cooperation.

Obviously there are some dark sides to this. One is our history of appalling treatment of the people who were here before we got here, the indigenous Australians. Not just the fact that we acted like invaders, with massacres and such awful treatment as the 'stolen children'; not just things that we now see as embarrassing and possibly shameful, but also that even our finest efforts were a bit paternalistic. It's appropriate to rethink a lot of that. We can't be too smug, too proud of our hybrid culture and our multicultural, tolerant, harmonious society, until we have effectively reconciled black and white Australians. So that's a problem for us – as it should be – and we're a long way from solving it.

Another issue: I find it surprising that it's taken us almost 100 years since Federation to get around to acknowledging that for an independent nation there's something very weird about sharing our head of state with a number of other countries. So I think the republic is important; my research would say Australians at large don't think this is an urgent problem, and maybe it isn't. But I think, symbolically, it is very important. And there's a third issue we must address: the fact that we have lived and are living with such widespread poverty in Australia. About 30 percent of households are living on combined annual household incomes of less than $20,000, and about half of those are living on an average income of about $9,000 per annum. We've got to face that. We can't talk about social justice until we've tackled the problem of poverty. We can't talk about being an egalitarian society until we tackle the problem of poverty.

Is there a personal experience that has given you an insight into unemployment?
I come across it in research all the time. Obviously, money is a problem if you're unemployed. But there are two other things that strike me as most disturbing, most bleak, about being unemployed. First, it does seem to be harder for unemployed people to define their own identities. In a utopian world we wouldn't use our job as a source of identity, we'd all be rounded personalities; we'd be sure of who we are, regardless of what job we were doing. But that will take a while to happen. In our culture it's such a tradition to pin occupational labels on ourselves as part of our identity that that loss of identity is a serious psychological blow to someone who has been retrenched or suffers long-term unemployment.

The second thing I notice about people who are unemployed is the great difficulty they have in structuring their day, their time, so that they can create what the rest of us would call leisure. Employed people assume that unemployed people lead a life of leisure, but leisure, as a concept, depends on work. Leisure is time off. So if you don't have time on, you don't have time off. In a way, the most insidious effect of unemployment is that it robs people of leisure because there's never the sense that I've achieved something and I'm entitled to time off. I think that's one reason why unemployment is so stressful for people, and why there are so many health problems associated with unemployment.

What rewards do you find in your work that aren't monetary?
They are very rich rewards. For a start, the regular completion of tasks is a highly gratifying experience. That doesn't mean that the tasks have to be grand or deeply significant tasks; it's just the business of completing things that's gratifying.

Sometimes my work has been stressful, but I do like the challenge of trying to do things that at first glance may appear too hard. I start a research project and, early on, I sometimes think, this is too vast, too enormous, too complicated, too mysterious; I'm never going to be able to penetrate this. Coming to the end of that and feeling that I actually got some clarity, some insight, and made some sense of it – that's enormously satisfying to me.

As I have begun to do more creative writing, I have found that that work does create a real opportunity for expression of the self. I can really 'let myself out' through my writing. For some people, recreation lets them do that, they let themselves out through golf or writing poetry or taking photographs. But I've never been a hobbyist, so I've always looked to my work for that kind of satisfaction.

Do you see any merit in work-for-the-dole or national service type schemes?

As a general rule I accept the principle of mutual obligation. I think it's fundamental to a civil society that when you receive you also give. The question is, how do you implement the principle? And without getting into the specifics of a particular scheme, I would say that when young people are being trained and acquiring some experience – and perhaps finding it hard to get paid employment and needing social security support – I don't necessarily think that the moment when they have to give back is *then*. I agree that they've got to give back *later*.

Through history we've often indulged generations – for a long time we've given Australians free education at the primary, secondary and tertiary level and we haven't said, while you're receiving your tertiary education, you've got to work weekends and pay the money to the government. We've said, 'We're doing this for you; we believe that as you move into maturity and become fully functional members of the community we'll get a pay-off.' I believe we've got to say the same thing to people who are unemployed: 'We're carrying you with us for a while but eventually, of course, we want you to be able to fly solo – and not just fly solo, but contribute.' So I'm all in favour of the idea of reciprocity and mutual obligation, but I think it's very harsh when we expect it all to happen at once.

That's part of the larger question we talked about earlier: we must find more creative ways of relating the work that has to be done to the money that's available to be paid for it. There's going to have to be an expansion of voluntary work in the community, particularly in the welfare sector. How is that going to be funded? Maybe we will have to find ways of paying people to do what we've traditionally thought of as voluntary work – in which case it would no longer be quite the same concept.

In the short term, I fear we're going to go through a period of blaming unemployed young people for being unemployed and imposing on them the burden of some obligation to pay back now, rather than thinking that this is an investment in their potential to pay back eventually.

In your experience is Australia a racist nation?

The only truthful answer I can give is very unsatisfactory: yes and no. There is a contradiction here, as there always is when you're talking about human societies and human beings. The fact is that we have built a brilliantly complex culture out of immigrants from 200 countries – it's an amazing thing, and we're making it work. Yet it's still the case that we are naturally tribal and territorial creatures, so when some new tribe emerges – like Greek and Italian immigrants after the Second World War or Vietnamese immigrants in the last decade – there is always a natural resistance. People often express that resistance in remarks which are outrageously racist. But, gradually, we come to terms with each other.

Racism also springs from guilt, and the extreme racist attitudes still existing towards Aborigines are a textbook case of that.

I don't think it's true to say that Australians are more racist than human beings anywhere else; it's just that our tribal urges and our sense of tribal identity have been more constantly challenged, because we're a nation of immigrants. If you go out now and look for signs of racism in this community in 1998 you'll find them, and they'll be focused most particularly on Asians, on Muslims and on Aborigines. This is both ugly and natural and, generally speaking, in this society it's under control.

What is education as a concept for our future?

I have two answers to that. The conceptual one is based on the idea of education as a process of encouraging people to fulfil their own potential. The goal is to draw out of them whatever they are capable of – in terms of work, in terms of their ability to be responsible citizens, to enter into personal, intimate relationships with integrity, with compassion – and also to unleash their creative potential. We use various vehicles for getting there but in the end it's got to be about *this* person, and *this* person, and *this* person being encouraged to release their full potential.

In practical terms, I believe we must put increasing emphasis on education processes which don't just teach us things we need to know. (Of course there *are* a lot of things like that: we need to know about mathematics, about our literary heritage, our historical heritage, our geography; we need to know about scientific principles and all those things which will help us to unlock our potential.) But we've also got to find ways of developing an education process which prepares people to be more flexible and to lead richer lives when perhaps work will play a lesser role or a changing role. We must avoid educating people exclusively to be this or that occupational group, and to prepare them to lead more satisfying lives, even when they're *not* working.

Ideally, we should use education to create a society in which boredom ceases to exist.

If your child had a drug habit would you want society to view them as an ill person requiring treatment or as a criminal? And beyond that, if what we've done for the last 20 years hasn't worked, should we rethink our approach to illicit drugs?

On this issue, my position is classic liberal. That is, I think we should, almost without exception, regard people with a drug problem as ill and in need of rehabilitation and support. I'm in favour of decriminalisation of drugs in general because there is clearly a criminal aspect to drug traffic which is not to do with the victim, the addict, but to do with the suppliers, the exploiters, the pushers. There is a new criminal class in our society with whom we should be prepared to deal, but the starting point is to get rid of that criminal class by decriminalisation of drug use, so the whole thing becomes more transparent.

But there's no point in talking about any of that unless we are also embracing a broader understanding of education. Part of educating people to release their full potential is to acquaint them with ways in which they may _diminish_ their potential, and you'd have to say drugs are one of those ways. The nonsense that's sometimes talked about drugs liberating people and stimulating the imagination and so on – there might, of course, be isolated cases where that's true. But we know that the impact of almost any mind-altering substance is to reduce our potential, so we don't perform as well as we otherwise might.

Is tax reform desirable? What would be your primary concerns with any tax-reform agenda?

I'm at a disadvantage here because I've done so much research on this subject that I can't easily separate myself from the research. (This is one of the problems of being a researcher!) It seems to me the community is, generally speaking, in favour of a goods and services tax on three conditions.

One is that the tax is implemented in such a way that it will catch current tax avoiders. That's the central issue in the community's mind: let's snare the people who are managing to accumulate a substantial income without paying tax on  it. That's either 'the big end of town' or people working in the so-called cash economy. Here's a way of ensuring tax revenue from people who haven't paid their fair share at the point of making the money: let's get them when they spend the money. That's the number one factor in community support for the GST.

The second factor is this: if we can do that, it will presumably increase the tax revenue and create the possibility of an offset. (In fact, most people would say not _maybe_ but _definitely_ there should be offsets in personal income tax.) So there's a trade-off: lower the tax when we get the money, increase the tax when we spend it. It seems an appropriate trade-off, because we pick up more tax at the point of spending by catching the cheats.

The third factor in all this is that a GST will only be supported if we have a compassionate attitude towards people who are not earning substantial income, those who are perhaps on fixed incomes or relying on welfare payments. It's rather crazy to say people at the very bottom of the economic heap are going to be paying the same kind of goods and services tax as everyone else. So concessions for the poor and the disadvantaged and the welfare-dependent are fundamental.

That's one of the things about this society that I really like – on an issue like this, you do find that ordinary people are compassionate. They actually recognise that this is an issue. They aren't ruthless. They don't just shrug and say, 'It will be tough for people who can't afford their milk'. We're not like that.

Should Australia be a republic, and why?

I'm in favour of the move to a republic and a change in the flag, but I don't see them as necessarily linked. If we weren't going to become a republic I'd still want the flag changed, and if we weren't going to change the flag I'd still want to become a republic. I happen to be in favour of both.

I think it is simply crazy, when in fact we are not beholden to the British monarch, that we should retain any symbolic link with the crown. The monarchists will say – in fact John Howard has said – we're a 'crowned republic'. That seems to me to be the very argument in favour of becoming an uncrowned republic. If you're saying the monarchy has no significance, surely that's a ground for saying, give it the flick. Why hang on to something that has no significance?

Otherwise, it looks as if we're not prepared to take the final step in becoming an independent nation – like an adolescent pausing on the threshold of adulthood and saying, 'Look, I can go on like this for ever; don't give me the vote; I like being not quite fully independent.'

The move to a republic, whenever it comes, will be a symbol of our absolute independence as a nation, which doesn't deny our heritage – our heritage can never be denied. (Anyone born before 1948, myself included, was a British subject before we became Australian citizens, so we all know what our heritage is.)

There's another issue here, of course. Since the Second World War, there has been a gradual change in the ethnic composition of our society because of waves of immigrants from other countries for whom the British heritage doesn't mean what it means to me. I can see their point when they say that it doesn't make sense to them, on becoming Australian citizens, to swear allegiance to the Queen of England as our head of state. I agree with John Howard when he says it is essentially symbolic. That seems to me to be grounds for change. Symbolism is very important to us.

Can you imagine a situation where it would be good to have the option of voluntary euthanasia?

My view on this might strike you as inconsistent. There is voluntary euthanasia in the sense that any of us is free to arrange for someone to help us bump ourselves off at any time, and we know the medical profession is complicit in this. We know that, all over Australia, people's lives are being effectively terminated by an overdose of morphine because their pain has become uncontrollable and a compassionate doctor, probably in consultation with the family, possibly in consultation with the patient, has said, in order to manage the pain, we will increase the dose although we know it will become lethal.

I'm perfectly comfortable with voluntary euthanasia, as a completely informal arrangement. However, I become uncomfortable when we try to legalise that and give the State a role in it. Because then I have all the problems I have with capital punishment. I don't think the State has a role in terminating the lives of its citizens. I don't think we should kill people as punishment and I don't think as a State we should formalise, legalise, the killing of people because they desire their physical release from pain. Of course, I believe that they are entitled to death as a relief from pain and that people should be allowed to die with dignity. (And my understanding is that, generally speaking, they can.)

I just have a terrible feeling that if the State stepped in, over time the situation could be handled less compassionately and could ultimately be abused. I'd like to leave that one up to the individual.

Looking at the native title issue. Is the idea that the government would use the legislature to effectively circumvent the outcome intended by the High Court, is this a good precedent?

It was unfortunate that this particular High Court decision was a split decision. That has given people grounds for complaining that 'it was only one vote that determined it'. But a lot of historical decisions have been determined by one vote. (America adopted English rather than German as its national language on the basis of one vote in Congress. There are a lot of historical precedents for one vote being crucial, so that doesn't bother me at all.) In fact, in a democracy, we acknowledge that the majority determines the outcome and the minority lives with it because that's the contract. So the objection based on the *narrowness* of the High Court's decision is not justified.

I think it's outrageous that the spirit of that decision would not be implemented  and I think also it's outrageous to limit the decision by talking about the need for certainty. The claim is that the legislation will give the pastoralists certainty and Aborigines certainty. The Aborigines' certainty is a diminished right to negotiate. In effect we'd be saying, 'Now you've got certainty. You're certain about the diminished rights that you have.' I find that unacceptable.

Why certainty? Who of us has certainty about what? The thing that is least certain in all our lives is the thing that's most precious, our personal relationships. Death, divorce, sickness, all these things are uncertain, so it seems to me that certainty is a peculiar criterion to introduce.

Rather I think we should be saying, there's a lot of uncertainty about this, therefore there's a lot of need for negotiation. There are, particularly in South Australia, wonderful examples of pastoralists and Aboriginal groups who have negotiated and who have learned to coexist. And on leasehold land, leaseholders have known from the beginning that this was not freehold; they understood they were coming in on a lease. Many of those leases have been profitable, historically, because of the exploitation of Aboriginal labour. So now to say, 'I want certainty', seems to me outrageous.

The two groups involved, the pastoralists and the Aborigines, have a completely different view of the land, and a different sense of land use. Land as an economic resource and land as a source of identity and ceremonial occasion – these are so different that it's hard to understand how they could *not* be compatible, how you couldn't coexist. The answer is negotiation, not ruthless legislation. Certainty is the wrong goal. Coexistence is the right goal.

Thank you very much for your time.

Ray Martin

TV Journalist

'Life is not a dress rehearsal'

BRETT KELLY: *Was there an idea, person or event that has had a profound influence on your life?*

RAY MARTIN: Professor Fred Hollows was probably the most remarkable bloke I ever met, in energy and vision and humanity. He was almost a Renaissance man in the sense of being a man of good works and poetry, great at fixing eyes, a Leftie, committed to the women's movement, committed to racial equality, and much more. So it was very hard not to have some of that rub off on you when you met him. But everyone I've met has seemed to leave a mark, from Don Bradman to Hollows.

My upbringing is really working-class Catholic Australian, and as the Jesuits say, once they've got you for the first seven years, they have got you for life. So probably the real morality of Ray Martin was formed in the first seven years by my mother.

She was a strict disciplinarian?

No. I was the only son of four children, the last child with three sisters, and so obviously the chosen son in my mother's eyes. And as I say, she set the family morals and she set mine. Other people just added to them.

Is there a motto, quote or thought that summarises your approach to life?

I guess 'Life is not a dress rehearsal'. That's a quick one. I'm basically a hedonist – I do things I enjoy, whether it be work or other things; the moment it is not enjoyable I stop doing it. But I'm not sure we come around a second time. So you really ought to do it now.

What do you see as the most critical issues facing Australia in the next decade?

Unemployment is a factor in all our social problems, from crime to the economy. It doesn't necessarily dominate, but our national ethos is based on having a job and that is a fairly recent thing. Unemployment is critical.

Clearly the environment is critical. Race relations are critical. Cyberspace is critical. If we don't jump on that information technology express, we are going to be left at the station, and that will influence our jobs, the Australia that my children grow up in. So I say, jobs first up, the Aboriginal problem, then the environment and information technology.

What do you see as the best things about Australia today, and what should we be working harder at?

The best thing is our decency. We are almost childlike in our decency. The old line of 'Everything I know I learnt at kindergarten' is probably right for Australia, but we are very decent in terms of our relationships with other people. The fact that a murder or the abuse of a child can dominate the front pages of our newspapers and our television news is indicative of the fact we care.

We have traditionally been strong in the union movement, the women's movement, from the earliest days ... perhaps with some exceptions – I can't quite explain our treatment of Aborigines. I think we have been decent in our treatment of immigrants – people are taken at face value, as against the tribal biases that many other people have.

We are down to earth and there is a lack of pretence in Australia (and New Zealand) that is healthy. It's almost the 'tall poppy' syndrome, but there is something healthy about keeping our high fliers' feet on the ground.

On the down side, I think we have an anti-intellectual attitude, we're a bit frightened by those who are able to express their thoughts. That's something we should get rid of – I think we should encourage our thinkers. In recent years we perhaps don't nurture our eccentrics as well as we might. We tend to try to make people fit the mainstream, certainly in the bush. We have had wonderful people who are inventors and fliers and sailors, and we've had wonderful eccentrics and adventurers, but we don't encourage them as much as we should.

Is there a personal experience of unemployment, perhaps a friend or family member or a story you have done, that has given you real insight to the impact unemployment can have?

I would quickly say the Paxtons. That started a media 'feeding frenzy'. It began as a story about the dangers of 'institutionalised' unemployment, where you have two – maybe three – generations of unemployed people. Now that's catastrophic.

It starts to become a problem in society when people no longer get out and look for a job, which I think was the problem in that family. It was meant to be a sympathetic story about a family that simply couldn't find a job, but as the story unfolded, it was a family that wanted the employment situation to fit their lifestyle rather than make a true effort to jump on board. In a situation where mum is unemployed for 20 years – can't get a job for 20 years – the kids grow up in that  environment and they start to think that is the norm. That is the danger, and if we don't break that cycle and get the next generation to work, it's deadly for them, let  alone for the rest of us.

In the nine years I spent in New York, as the American correspondent for the ABC, time after time I saw black families where two and three generations had never worked. And the debilitation, the erosion of any confidence in the whole family is just unacceptable.

That's why I said it is the greatest problem we face, and it's a problem that especially hits young people and young black and ethnic people. So I've got a job, have had for 34 years, and am overpaid. Do I appreciate what they are going through? Absolutely. Having come from a working class family, I know what they are going through. And we have to change it.

Are there rewards in work, apart from the money?

The rewards are not just the comfort of being part of a tribe going to work with everybody else, which is of course supportive. It's also the satisfaction of doing something that you enjoy, something productive. The satisfaction, at the end of the day, of having actually achieved something. Time after time. It varies with the job you do, but it is that sense of putting your hand out for a pay packet, having done a fair day's work.

That sounds silly until you don't have it. You talk to men or women who worked all their lives and now are suddenly on the scrap heap at 45, try to tell them they have a superannuation scheme and can live at least comfortably – and they are shot to pieces. It is the cliche of people dying of a heart attack – having suddenly stopped work, getting bored, losing their sense of still being part of human nature.

The big reward is not about the salary. That might give us an extra thrill, but it's got to be more than that. It sounds easy for me to say that, but I mean it.

How do you see the idea of national service or a work-for-the-dole scheme?

It's a tricky situation when someone who's got ability and energy says to someone who perhaps doesn't have the same ability and is lacking in energy or self-confidence, get off your bum and do something. Some people find that easy to say, but they ignore the fact that when you are unemployed you are basically depressed, your self-confidence is shot to pieces.

It's also easy to say, because we are paying you the dole, go and paint park benches, clean up the park and plant some flowers in it, be productive. That's fine in theory, but it immediately brands those people who can't get a job. Like the old labour teams. Once you get in that routine, you are not available to front up for a job that might become vacant. So in a sense, I've got serious doubts about a dole force that goes out and does public work.

I know people who do things on a voluntary basis, who work for the Hollows Foundation, Red Cross, Meals on Wheels, who get immense satisfaction out of it. So I don't think there should be a rule that says that if you are on the dole, after six weeks or six months, you have to do public service. For a lot of people that sort of work is fantastic, but with other people it alienates them more and more and makes them feel as if they are targets.

For me the ideal thing would be to have a setup whereby you could convince people that actually getting up at 6:30 in the morning and going to work, doing something productive, getting into a routine, is a valuable and positive experience. At the end of the day, you've got to solve the problem, not alienate people who happen to be at the bottom of the totem pole.

In your experience, is Australia a racist nation?

No, I don't think we are, compared with other places I have seen – I don't think racism is entrenched. There is a problem with people who are different, but that is the same anywhere in the world – especially Asian countries. Here it's more a problem of looking for scapegoats – and the scapegoats can be Italian, Chinese, Muslim, dress differently, have a different religion, or happen to be black.

For me the line about Aborigines getting 'too much' is ridiculous. My retort is always, would you swap places? And I don't know anyone who sensibly would, despite the crap from the Pauline Hansons about how much better off they are and people should be given an equal go. If we could give people an equal go in health, education, employment, housing and basics like running water, that would be fine. And that's basically what those who want to help Aborigines are after.

Oddly enough, so much of the racism in this country has come from working class Australians, from unions, from others who are also at the bottom of the heap, which amazes me. I can't understand why it took so long for the union movement to get active in the reconciliation process. I can't understand why Senator Neville Bonner and Ms Scott of ATSIC had to go to the Liberal Party or the National Party to run for pre-selection. Why did Neville Bonner become a Liberal Party senator from Queensland? The reason was the Labor Party at that time and the unions wouldn't accept him. That beats me.

What is education for young people, and what should it be?

Education is what we learn at home and what we learn from our friends, from our school. It is not simply what we learn in school. Education is affected by what your mum and dad say and what your family says.

So what should you learn? Obviously you've got to learn the three Rs, the basics to help you navigate through our society. Do you need a degree? Probably – a degree of some kind, whether it is a degree in carpentry or a degree in computers. It depends on the individual. I think we all need to have some basic skills in reading, writing and arithmetic.

Beyond that, because of the shortage of jobs, we will expect people to do things that are productive or creative or provide a service. Too often, the kid who was good at maths and science was the dux of the school, while one who was good at languages, art and music, or sport, was a lesser being. That is stupid. I mean in real life, you find later on that a Paul Keating leaves school at 14, or a Bill Gates leaves school not long after, or an Alan Bond. Yet in the areas that they go into they are outstandingly successful – though some fall over, like Bondy. 

But clearly the piece of paper that says 'I was a university medal winner' doesn't make you more relevant than someone who works with street kids or someone who paints marvellous paintings. The idea that success means living in a big house worth $10 million is not the full story. It may equally well be the person who works on the ground keeping the national parks together and never even gets a pat on the back. This computer age is showing us that someone who couldn't do history or languages at school is now designing software that can change our lives. So education is about learning, but learning is not about books – or not only about books.

If your child had a drug habit, would you want society to view them as a criminal or as an ill person requiring treatment?

I'm determined to get more radical as I get older, rather than more conservative, so my response is, has it worked?

To throw someone who is an addict in jail is senseless, expensive, and a waste of time and effort. But I'm not convinced that a 'soft' system that allows people to do what they want to do is the way to go either. At the risk of sitting on the fence, if the problems were easy to solve, we would have solved them. They are not easy to solve. The belief that politicians of either colour actually bring in laws just to make life more difficult is rubbish. If John Howard could solve the drug problem tomorrow, of course he would do it.

At the end of the day, they are tough problems. And the jury is still out on how to treat our drug criminals

I am looking at figures that suggest that what we are doing isn't working... Clearly, the figures on those in jail for a drug-related crime indicate that it is not working – some say 60 plus, some say 80 percent. It doesn't work to make it illegal to smoke dope and give someone a criminal record as a result of being found with dope.

Judges and magistrates, who we think of as the squarest of the lot, are coming around to the belief that it simply has to be decriminalised for some drugs, maybe even for all drugs.

But I'm not convinced, as I get older, that by loosening the reins, by making the boundaries a little wavy, you help the majority of people. I think you need to have some rules and for most people these rules work. We need to be flexible.

Given that what we've been doing about drugs for the last 20 years hasn't worked, should we be looking 'outside the square' for more innovative ways to deal with the problem?
The people I think are enlightened, David Suzuki for example, and the current governor-general, and a lot of what Paul Keating was talking about, and a lot of people who work on the ground with addicts and criminals, they are saying that putting people behind bars doesn't help, stigmatising people doesn't help. What you need to solve is the problem. You need to solve the environment that you are working in. I can't understand why any Australian would use heroin – I just can't understand it. We live in this extraordinary country. If you are a young Australian, if you don't have a job we look after you, if you do have a job we look after you, and there's sunshine, beaches, a great lifestyle, freedom.

I just don't understand why people do it. But they do. So you have to change the environment which encourages them. You have to deal with self-esteem and all those airy fairy things. You can't keep building bigger and bigger prisons to put drug addicts in – you actually have to solve the problems.

Is tax reform desirable?
I know almost as much about nuclear physics and brain surgery as I know about tax reform. Almost. I read a lot about it and I hear people talking about it, but I could trot in an expert who would tell you that we must have a GST. And then I could trot one in who says we must never have it. And I'm confused by what they say. Those I listen

to and respect convince me that we should have some form of GST, some form of tax across that area, that we need tax reform certainly as an incentive to businesses and the economy.

I have heard Paul Keating and the Labor Party go from yes to no. I have heard Australians reject Hewson on this. Those I trust, who don't have an axe to grind and who appear to be knowledgeable, seem to say that we are badly in need of tax reform, that we have one of the most archaic tax systems in the world.

So I am really for reform. I am in favour of taxing those who earn a lot of money far more than those who don't. I think if you earn $100,000, there is enough incentive to have $10,000 more than the bloke down the road to keep you going, no matter what you are taxed. The fact that these people can earn millions of dollars and pay less tax than someone who earns less than $50,000 is obscene. So a scheme that taxes those who make money out of society, I am in favour of – I think that's fair enough. But how we do a GST so it doesn't affect people who are genuinely struggling, and so rich people can't use the system to evade and avoid it, I don't know. Still, we need to find an answer.

Should Australia be a republic, and why would a young Australian be interested?

There is no discussion about the republic or the flag! It is absurd to have the Union Jack stuck up in the corner of our flag. It is a colonial trapping we should have scrapped 100 years ago. It is apron string stuff. The historical connection with Britain is there and it is always going to be there, thankfully, but we don't need that mistake in the corner of the flag.

As a republican, I believe the head of state should be Australian and there should be no link with some foreign queen or king. That is just absurd, the republic is beyond dispute. The present governor-general, Patrick Dodson, or Janet Holmes a Court, Dick Smith, would all be candidates for head of state, along with another half dozen we could think of – eminent and admirable men and women who could do the job admirably and fantastically. 

If the South Africans, for example, can change their flag and their Constitution  and their whole society almost overnight, it is ridiculous to say that the considerable brain power in this country couldn't get together to work out a formula to make a Constitution that doesn't throw it all up in the air, that just allows Australia to keep functioning, keeps the checks and balances in place and cuts those apron strings that are colonial and ridiculous.

I can't believe they actually need to have conventions. It is so obvious that we need to change to a republic, and I also think we have reached the point that Bob Hawke used to talk about – he said, it will happen one day and why upset people unnecessarily.

Could you imagine a situation where the option of voluntary euthanasia might be desirable?

Absolutely. These questions you ask, they are ... unlike Alan Jones, I don't have all the answers to all the problems of Australian society and I could be wrong in every answer I have given you. I could be wrong, but I would like to think that if I got terminally ill and was in pain, that someone would pull the plug. I would have done it for my mother if I had been in that situation, and I would do it for my wife or children if I was able to do it.

We have a freedom of choice, and that is part of the freedom of choice. It's like abortion for women. It is the freedom of choice that you have, to live or die, and we have got carried away with church morality on these things.

This is an area where life has changed. It doesn't mean that you have any less respect for human life, but there are moments in life ... my mother was very ill at the end, I saw her hang on to life way beyond what I would have expected. She wasn't in pain, but real life had gone for her in the last couple of months, yet she hung on.

I can't imagine people on the spur of the moment really seriously saying, kill me, because there is something in the gene that always says, I will hang on for another minute.

In cases where people are in terminal pain and need relief, we should have the right to help from caring professionals, apart from the family. I think that the problem at the moment, not having that power, is greater than the prospect of someone abusing it.

I'm looking at native title. We've got a constitutional monarchy and, as I understand it, the idea is that the legislature and the judiciary should be separate and they should respect each other's role. Is it dangerous for anyone in government to denigrate the role or members of the High Court?

In practice, there is something good about electing judges and police chiefs – the American system. They finally have to be responsible to the society and that's a good thing. We have too many judges, police chiefs, magistrates, who believe that they are a power unto themselves and that they have a right to say things and take stances that don't relate to the rest of us. I think that's dangerous. And that includes, perhaps, changes that John Howard's going to make to the High Court, that will make it so conservative that it may well come down and make decisions that I don't think are healthy for the country. You could say the same thing for Labor leaders' appointments.

What's interesting and healthy is that judges have shown over the years, once they get onto the High Court, that they're not quite so predictable. In fact they start to become more ethical or have different ethics. Given the fact that judges live in a rarefied world, I think our High Court's very honourable and decent. So even though a political leader might stack the court, when they finally get up there and can't be removed, they do the decent thing. I think that that's been proven.

So should politicians slag judges? No. And they generally get rapped across the knuckles when they do, as has happened recently. Because if we don't have respect for these institutions we start to fall over. So we have to show respect. But there have also been judges, through the history of the High Court, who have taken outrageous stands individually, and they should be reprimanded too. Or told they are being dorks or dinosaurs, if they are. That's what politicians could do, but they should do it sparingly.

As for comments made about the High Court recently, and people like William Deane since he became governor-general being criticised by politicians, I tend to think the politicians lose out in the end. Certainly the position of the High Court has to be protected, even more than the position of a prime minister or a politician, because judges are – or until they prove themselves otherwise they are – an honourable institution, an institution I would protect far more than I would protect a politician.

Earlier, I listed reconciliation as a key issue facing Australia today. Until we work out a reconciliation with the indigenous people, the original owners of this place, we cannot be a truly decent or great nation. We really have to work this out, give land back where we can, and we have got to say we are sorry – which is or should be easy.

I also said earlier that one Australian characteristic is that we are inherently decent as a race, and not cruel, but I think that we are being cruel and indecent by not fixing this Aboriginal problem. It cannot be fixed with money – it has to be fixed by changing the conditions and changing the society, and to do this you have to be grown up and generous. And I don't think we have been generous under this government – certainly not generous when it comes to reconciliation. The previous government was generous but didn't achieve too much, so it is not about hugging and feeling warm and fuzzy, as Labor did for 13 years. You have to fix health and education, housing and unemployment.

The focus of the world is going to be on us in 2000. When they come here for the Games, visitors are going to look at Sydney and say, what a beautiful city. And what else is there? And they are going to look across the mountains and see degradation of a kind that the rest of the world doesn't realise is happening here. And if we don't start to do something about that between now and then we are going to look what we are – neglectful.

Thank you very much for your time.

Rod McGeoch

Chairman, Corrs Chambers Westgarth

*'Leave things better than
you found them'*

BRETT KELLY: *Is there a motto, quote or thought that really summarises your approach to life?*

ROD MCGEOCH: Yes, for me it is 'leave things better than you found them'.

What do you see as the most critical issues for Australia in the next decade?
The challenge is going to be to regain and then maintain our position as a leader in terms of standard of living, economic output and level of opportunity for our people. We were number one in 1900 and now we're 19th or 20th. The world has become an extremely competitive place and it is going to be even more so in the years ahead. It is going to be very difficult but we must improve our position, as others themselves endeavour to move forward.

My motto 'leave things better than you found them' is really my response to this challenge. I think many Australians are of the view that our generation is not going to leave the next generation in a more fortunate position than we found ourselves. We may be the first generation to have produced such a negative outcome. I find that particularly disappointing as we do have the ability and the capacity in this country to provide a positive outcome for the next generation, but it will require fundamental change in a number of our policy settings.

I recently asked a secondary school group were they happy to leave our mineral wealth in the ground and watch our own mining companies employ people and make profits in other countries of the world. Our companies presently provide large employment opportunities in Chile and Argentina for local communities and the profits remain in those countries. Is this what we want? I asked them, or do we need to get some balance back into the debate about issues such as protection of the environment and native title rights?

We have the minerals in this country that we are mining in other countries, so the situation of forcing these companies to leave in order to progress their business is a very troubling outcome for our economic future. It should not be cheaper and easier to go elsewhere and the answers do not just lie in reforming the taxation system.

Is this because big business maybe is perceived as bad – that to have a huge company that's monstrously profitable ... ?
The rich versus the poor or the strong versus the weak is only part of such a perception. The message about economic fortune and growth producing high standards of living is just not well enough understood as a priority in the running of the country. So there is a major educative and selling task to be undertaken by both government and business.

The perception is also exacerbated by companies having worked in an era where being 'a good corporate citizen' has been found to be a notion that competes with producing profits for shareholders. Proposed corporate sponsorships and donations are often challenged at board level by the view that it is the shareholders' money and a company should not give it away for such purposes. In a sense, modern notions of corporate governance have driven companies into being less charitable and forced the government to undertake a greater welfare role. The popularity of business has suffered as a consequence.

We've got a Ten Point Plan to deal with the Aborigines. Do you think we should have a ten point plan for taking the country forward?

I don't think there is any doubt about it. You often hear a cry for a plan, a vision, an industry policy. It is extremely difficult in any organisation, let alone a country, to orchestrate change for the better unless the changes are understood in a larger framework. Strategy always needs to be placed in a context to be understood and that is another reason for having a plan. It isn't easy to formulate an agreed plan when you don't have a majority in both Houses of Parliament, but where that situation exists we have seen people rise up in support of the signs of leadership and the evidence of vision that then unfolds.

We can build Snowy Mountains schemes, we can win the Olympics, we have world class athletes in practically every discipline, with a country of only 18 million people, surely we can sort out native title ...

Everyone says it's too hard, and it *is* hard. However, it was hard to win the Games too. It isn't a question of the most money or the biggest country, it's all about attitude and commitment. I recently witnessed John Elliott, former president of the Liberal Party, question a current official on what he intended to do in terms of policy. No reply was forthcoming other than the person was going to administer the organisation. Elliott responded that he understood that answer but what was he going to *do*, what was his *plan?* No plan was forthcoming. I have to say, I thought it was a perfectly reasonable question. If you take positions of leadership, then, so far as I am concerned, it must be because you intend to *lead* somewhere. Those that hold positions of leadership without some agenda are really caretakers who are not going to take an organisation anywhere.

You can have, in effect, a passive plan in which your goals are to provide people with 'a comfortable living zone' but I actually think people are looking for more than a passive plan.

People do want goals and benchmarks and a sense of achievement, and they expect some of the difficult things to be done. When I look at Sydney Airport I cannot believe that we haven't got the political will to stand up for that airport, argue for its continuance and declare that noise will be shared equitably. It is Sydney's most important piece of infrastructure and it has become captive to the agendas of a number of interest groups, which is a tragedy.

If you're unemployed you're unlikely to be feeling comfortable ...

Critics of strong leadership would argue that it causes anxiety in people, but the same anxiety can occur when people feel they are in an environment where there is no direction and leadership. In my view, as Hugh McKay continually argues, there is a high level of anxiety in our people regarding their future. It seems to me the church has failed to provide the answers and to some extent those in politics have clearly not provided the answer either. When that happens you get the secondary effects of an aimlessness in youth, which then leads to drug use and violence. The challenge for leaders is to make themselves relevant, so that there is good communication, and messages regarding agendas, directions and plans are understood and accepted.

Is it important that people get involved, get their hands dirty, in politics and their community in general?

Well, I think it's important. People want to contribute somewhere in the time they're on the planet, and you can make a contribution lots of ways other than as a politician. So I don't advocate that we should stand up and be counted on one side of the political fence or the other.

I think our politicians, by and large, are underpaid and overworked, but you know the art of politics is in the compromise and a lot of people don't want that, they want adherence to principle. But when you haven't got control of both Houses of Parliament then compromise becomes essential if you are endeavouring to get at least part of your agenda completed. The sale of Telstra is a perfect example of this kind of compromise, and as an example of the art of politics it is in Olympic class.

Can you see any potential benefits in a work-for-the-dole or national service type of scheme?

I don't think you can conscript people into doing something they don't want to do, this is a democracy. But anything that helps these people get back on track, I'm encouraged to support. I think these things are peripheral to the real issue though. You know the Americans have shown with their economy, which is unbelievably strong, that the answer lies in these last couple of steps of deregulating the labour market. The Reserve Bank says it every time. We can't get past 3 to 4 percent growth without deregulation of the labour market. And if as part of that we've got to fix the wharves and we've got to fix the mining unions, I think that's got to be done.

I also think that governments have misunderstood the community's view. The community will support the government strongly that makes those changes. Now there is going to be a generation which suffers and they need to be looked after – no question about that. I mean, we are talking about deregulation of labour markets to help Australians in the next 100 years, we've got to be big enough to face it.

I think what it highlights is that we've reached a defining moment in Australia. We're not the only country to do it. Where people *have* made the changes they're finding out the government can't deliver everything and, in fact, government is going to get smaller. The countries that made the changes have undoubtedly improved their standard of living. One of the incidental consequences has been smaller government. Less regulation necessarily means less government departments but, at the same time, it has emerged that the government is only one partner in producing a positive outcome for the country. People are soon realising that it is the combination of the contribution of individuals, business organisations and government that produces the best outcome. Government was dominating the partnership, but that won't be so in the years ahead.

Looking at tax reform, is there adequate incentive for young Australians to build and create wealth?

Certainly I am an example of a number in the 45 to 55 age group who have been able to acquire assets within the current taxation system. I would have to acknowledge, however, that inflation and the odd boom time saw many of us benefit from huge rises in real estate values. Now that inflation is not a factor in the economy there may not be the opportunity to make these gains. Additionally, it wasn't until 1985 that capital gains tax was levied on these increases in asset values. Nonetheless, for many people there probably isn't sufficient incentive in the tax system – certainly a number believe that we now have an environment in which the rich are getting richer and the poor are getting nowhere at all.

The other side of the issue is for Australians to form a view on how much free education, health and other government services are they prepared to pay for. Because of our small tax base there may be a limit; indeed, there might be an issue as to whether we want to give up services rather than raise more revenue. If there was a feeling that some services could be forgone then there might even be the prospect of lower taxation which would increase incentive levels.

All of this tends to lead you towards the introduction of a GST, even though it means more regulation and more paperwork for business. I think we will see a GST which will raise more money and there will be an attempt by government to continue to provide basic services which, ultimately, will then be means tested. I am firmly of the view, however, that we do not need another debate or another summit as there has been more than enough work done on what are the options. The government should select its options and enact them as soon as possible.

If tax reform is an issue of national importance, is it time that there was a bipartisan approach to the issue?

If you can get that done, let's get another few things on the agenda – like the Aborigines. But the opposition political process is a healthy process. The problem for us is that with independents and one thing after another we get our Parliaments tied up these days – except Jeff Kennett, who's having a dream run because he controls both Houses.

I think Treasury has more than enough research and statistics to say to government, 'here are your options'. And government can say, 'well all right, we're taking that one'. And go. If you get thrown out of office you get thrown out, but you can't tell me there's another idea in this whole debate, I just don't believe it.

Somebody must stand up then?

The prime minister promised no change in the first term, and I think he'll probably stick to his promise. So I don't really quite understand why he decided to have a tax reform debate. I would've just kept doing other things in this term and next election say, this is what we are changing.

Australia as a republic, do you see that happening in the near future?
Well, near future I'm not so sure about. I am a republican, but I'm a due process person, and I think that taking a minimalist view is a facile solution. You must do it properly, so people are comfortable that it has been properly. The resolutions at the Constitutional Convention are not minimalist but are liable to attract strong opposition from some sections of the community which might defeat any referendum. I've got a feeling that the Howard Government will certainly get a second term, and it probably won't happen under that government. So if your 'near future' thing is three to five years, the answer is no.

Is it critical that we get a system that can at least match the system we've got now, in terms of stability and effectiveness?
Absolutely. I mean, that's why due process should take place. One of the great strengths of this country is the stability, it's why people invest here, want to live here and so on. I don't think for a minute that having a president will put that at risk. I think whether both Houses elect the president or the people elect him or her, whatever, I think Australia will be fine. I'm really bewildered that people can't see that the head of state ought to be an Australian. I just can't understand why people say, keep the Queen of England, it's sound, it's well proven. I would have thought we were at the point where we need to make the changes.

Is Australia a racist nation in your experience?
On the broad front no, because we're a combination of over 150 or 160 different nationalities all here living together, and by and large we get on. At my daughter's school, Ascham, the girl elected head girl is from India. Yet you get the comment in similar private schools that the Asian students don't play sport, don't participate at all in the extracurricular activities, and just want to get 100 out of 100 and not join in the school community.

So we're still growing and coming to terms with it. I mean, to me a racist is a person who intentionally wants to segregate and doesn't like anybody else. I think that a lot of Australians are in the 'I'm getting used to it' mode, and I don't believe that's being a racist. It's not saying 'build a fence and put them all over there', it's saying, 'I'm getting used to it and I think it's all right'. I believe that's a reasonable response at this time.

So is an influence like Hanson a bad thing, long term?
It's noticed overseas. I think that the answer will be known after the election. If they just throw her out, well there's the answer. But if there's a respectable level of support for her, then we've got a problem. The politicians need to be careful because a lot of Australians are not ready to fully agree with immigration when there's a lot of Asian crime and unemployment here. I mean you've got to be very careful how you

manage the debate, because there *is* a group of Australians – and they're the less fortunate – who believe someone's got their job, and they are very easily persuaded by a Hanson, and a long way from convinced yet that it's OK.

There's too much political rhetoric at the moment that says multiculturalism is a fantastic answer and look what a perfect solution it is. It's not perfect yet, we're still all learning. And you know I have days where I vacillate – it is a good thing that we encourage every person's type of music and every person's type of dress. I think a lot of us are like that. No, I don't believe we are racist, we are just uncertain.

If your child had a drug habit, would you want a society that viewed them as a criminal or as an ill person requiring treatment? And further on that theme, at the moment we clearly have a situation where drug abuse is a huge problem.

It is a disaster that the drug problem appears to have beaten us. I have read articles in the paper recently that said that heroin trafficking has defeated us. So we've got to find other solutions. It's just unbelievable that that's happened in Australia. I don't know whether it's the police or Customs or what, but it is a great shame that we seem to have descended to that point.

I'm not judgemental about the victim and I've never taken an illegal drug, so what I think is the reason they're taking them might be wrong. But it seems to me that a lot of young Australians look about them and say, well what's here for me? That view is too prevalent – kids driven out of employment, lack of parental love and so on.

The desperation, the looking for escape, is a sign we failed and they've gone looking for the solution. I think that's why people take drugs to start with – and then of course there's the habit.

So I am annoyed with people who sell it for gain. I'd be very annoyed with youngsters who encouraged other youngsters. I'm not into the 'they're all criminals', however I'd love to see them not doing it. I'd be terribly disappointed if I found my own children taking drugs. I'm not the best father in the world by any means but I think they know that I'd be disappointed. But if it happened and they needed me, they've got me – I'd be there, I'm not going to turn my back on them.

Is voluntary euthanasia something you see as an option, and do you think over the next decade that it is likely to gain support?

I'm actually opposed to euthanasia and my wife's not – her mother died in great pain, and I think her reasons stem from there. My reasons I think come from my legal training, that it's a life and you can't take a life. Also while I'm not a person that worships, although I got very intrigued by religion in my late teens, and I get intrigued by other people's worship of religion, somewhere in me I've got a sanctity-of-life issue as well as the legal issue, so I just find it hard to take the step that says euthanasia should be permitted.

I'm not critical of people who support it. My wife's driven by the pain issue – you know, when people are under unbearable difficulty and they're terminally ill, why not, that would be her view. I'm still struggling, I'm not there yet. You asked me will we get there. I wouldn't be too sure. It's a bit like the republic – I don't think we're going to get there as quick as people think we are ...

Change is like that, isn't it?
Well, these are very crucial changes, you know – it's not like changing your shirt and tie. Once you change them you've made a fundamental difference in values that I think troubles people, and I have difficulty with it. I mean, I have good discussions with our kids about things like that. They see it as very easy. And when I say, 'Are you sure?', they go, *er* ...

It was put to me that our whole Western civilisation is built on the sanctity of human life, and if you change that then you're left in a form of no-man's-land?
Yeah, that's a very important reference point. It is inherent in the abortion debate and in the whole issue of capital punishment. It's a very important reference point to change. I'm still uncomfortable about making the change.

Thank you very much for your time.

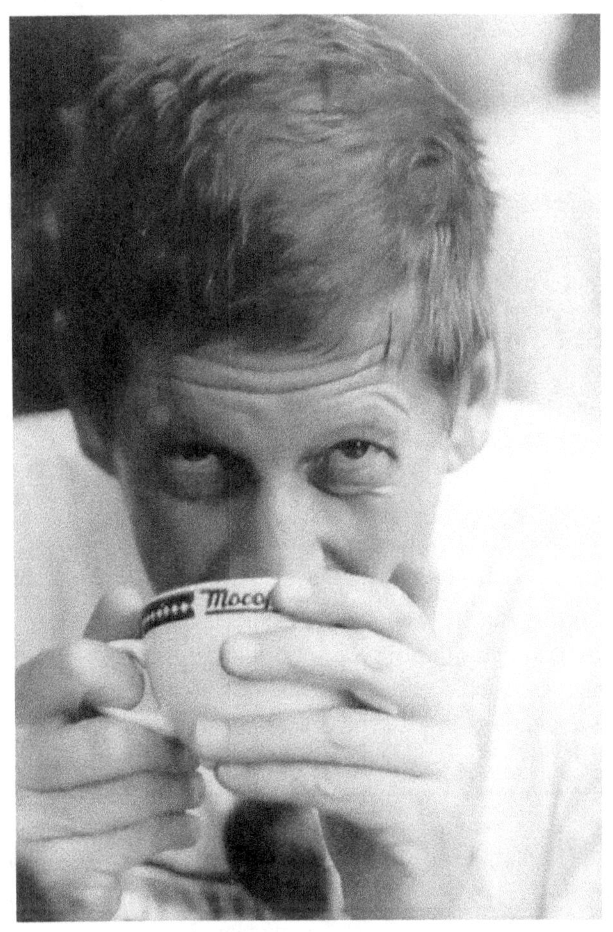

H.G. Nelson

Sports/Social Commentator

'Go in hard, early and often'

H.G. NELSON: A lot of people ask me what I do! I'm just an old boof-head who has spent his life hacking away at the coal-face. There are two edges to the coal-face – I work at both veins at once, sports commentary and social criticism. This isn't a mine that many other people get into. Most people just stay in either sports commentary *or* social criticism, but I thought, bloody hell! I'll try something new with my life – I'll dig both tunnels at once – and so far so good! There's no light at the end of the tunnel. If anybody wants to follow me, get the pick out of the shed and come on down. But you won't be seeing a lot of light once you get down here, so bring your peepers.

I grew up in the fabulous Barossa Valley of South Australia. People forget the Barossa Valley had the F1 in 1950. There's a rich tradition of great sporting events and great activities in the Barossa Valley.

I had a simple idea, I wanted to go down and fish out St Vincents Gulf. St Vincents Gulf is an area of water which has just held Adelaide back. I believe it's held South Australia back. People have been able to catch fish in it, and once you get rid of the fish ... it's open to the sea so the buggers are always charging up there when you least expect it, overnight, on king tides, on the full moon. Up they come, those bloody tommy rough and snook and garfish. I just hope that South Australian kiddies, if they want to do something with their life, will take up my challenge and fish the bloody thing out. So at least we could have an area of Australia where there are no ish, there's no life, nothing going on, so we could see if it worked. If we are going to ruin the planet we want to start somewhere, have a bit of a test strip, and get people from all around the world coming to St Vincents Gulf, put it on the map and say, c'mon down and have a look at 'bugger-all'. And if people like what they see when they see 'bugger-all' then it could work for the whole planet.

Adelaide (most people reading this would know) is the centre of the universe, and here we would have this dead bit of water out the front. It is a terrific idea.

There's so many, many personalities that have influenced me. A lot of them are South Australian personalities, people like Adriana Xanides, what a tremendous personality she is, she can do everything. People would probably remember the great Les Favell, South Australian cricketer and commentator of many years. He was a tremendous leader, opening bat for South Australia and a feisty commentator, and when he played the Victorians, in particular, he really rose to the occasion. Didn't care much about Western Australians, or Queenslanders but Victorians really got under his wick and he gave it the best.

Obviously, Don Dunstan was a tremendous influence on everybody who has met him. Dean Brown, in more recent times, and Johnny Olsen are very fine figures and they've done so much to turn South Australia around. They've sold off the water. Isn't Brown a tremendous name for a person who is selling South Australian water? Obviously, the water's pretty brown and Browney got rid of it!

Events. Well, there's so many great events in South Australian history. As you're growing up, of course you look to your own patch. I'll never forget the time the big tsunami was going to sweep up St Vincents Gulf and flood Adelaide. Don Dunstan had to go down to the Glenelg jetty and stand there and calm people down by saying, 'No, it's not going to happen'. It's that sort of place. Wild ideas can sweep through Adelaide at a great rate.

Is there a motto, quote or thought that summarises your approach to life?
Many. So many. 'Go in hard, early and often'. If we could just write that on the front of say the _Herald Sun_ every so often. 'Go in hard, early and often', says Jeff Kennett. Who cares whether Jeff Kennett said it or not.

'One in, all in'. That's another terrific one. 'Win the fight, win the match'. They're simple ideas. They're football ideas. I don't think there's enough use of them out in the broader world ... I remember years ago, there used to be a bloke go around and just write 'eternity' on the footpaths. He might have been a bloke called Bliss. People should get a box of chalk and just go around and write, 'One in, all in', 'Win the fight, win the match', simple things like this. Australia would be a better place. Just imagine the tourists coming for the year 2000, going to see 'Go in hard, early and often'. Or on official documents: Australia, coat of arms, simply written underneath, 'Go in hard, early and often' in various languages, depending where the letter is going to.

What are the most critical issues facing Australia?
I don't want to bore people stupid, but pig shooting. When are we going to get a decent program on Australian television that does for pig shooting what Rex Hunt has done for fishing? Roy and I have put this up to management after management over the years. People would love the romance of getting a couple of pigs at dusk, running across the hilltops and then taking a bead and pulling one down, ripping its guts out and pulling its skin off (which you save for later) and then grilling it slowly over the hot coals of a couple of red gum stumps. That's the sort of Australia that's gone. It's a romantic idea which unfortunately no television management in Australia can see the wisdom of making a show about.

There's some really confronting issues. The big hope is the Olympic Games. I have been disappointed with the development of the Olympic Games but they turned the corner recently when it was announced that we are $500 million over budget. People won't come to the Olympics unless they realise that they're going to a place called Sydney, Australia, which said, let's spend a billion and a half more than we budgeted for on this shemozzle. People _love_ to see money spent foolishly and this is going to lure people in.

I like the idea that alarm bells didn't ring at SOCOG headquarters when they were $100 million out. (Personally speaking, I would've felt worried about it slightly.) The gong didn't go off when they got to $200 million, or $250 million, no! $500 million! Then I think, bloody hell, how did they manage to keep that secret for so long? I think it's just a _tremendous_ credit to all concerned. Let's hope they go past the $750 million mark. I'd like to think that the whispering campaign and the leaked documents could demonstrate that we are a billion and a half in the hole by the end of 1999.

Then I'd like to see what we're going to miss out on because of that budget blowout. The government may not be able to improve the road between, say,

Newcastle and Cloncurry as much as they'd like or they mightn't be able to have anaesthetics in hospitals, or people may have to go in for home birth a lot more often. Kiddies mightn't be able to get a hole in the heart fixed up quite as neatly. It's tremendous that people do have to make sacrifices. People think the Olympics is all beer and skittles, but it's not.

Other issues confronting Australia. Obviously, people are looking forward to some of the problems created by global warming and whether we should clear more of Australia. Clear the bloody lot off. How will we know if the temperature's going up unless we get it all off? This mamby-pamby middle position which suggests we can have our cake and eat it too! There's no future in that. People *want* to see people do really silly things, and then they'll come for a shufti. Just imagine a Queenstown all over Australia. That would look sensational. People travel all the way to Tasmania just to have a look at a place that's got no trees. We've just got to get on with it.

Those three problems, the Olympic blow-out, a pig-shooting show and clearing Australia of every blade of grass and lawn, and then you'd be able to see something of the future. People are working on these things all the time. But are they doing any good? Is Roundup the best we can come up with? Is Zero weeding-wands the best we can do? Surely to goodness we can get out and shake things up and get the drop on Nature. If I look hard enough I'll find grass growing up through the cracks of pavements. People will come and laugh in the year 2000. They'll go home and say, 'Did you see that bloody grass growing up through the cracks in the pavements?'

These I believe are the hidden issues in Australia. They're so hidden. When you hear talk-back radio and when you read the *Daily Telegraph*, they're not mentioned. They're not tackling the issues and it disappoints me. Roy and I do our best at getting issues promoted, but no one's listening.

What are the best things about Australia?

It's a tremendous place. If I could just point out Australia has Panthers' World of Entertainment at Penrith in Sydney. For those who haven't been there – and people might be reading this interstate – you'd be idiots if you didn't think to yourselves, I've got a few days at Easter, what I'm going to do is just make a bee-line to Panthers' World of Entertainment. Once you've been there you can be absolutely content with the knowledge that you have had a fulfilled life. You don't have to go anywhere else, it's got everything you need. It's got aqua golf which is a sort of golf played from the edge of a putrid, stagnant lake into a lot of targets set out at 100 metres, 200 metres and so on. It's got cable-ski where you don't need a boat – and that's the future of skiing for mine. It's got a TAB. It's got a bottle shop. It's got a travel agency ... not that you'd need to travel. It's got a motel attached. It's got three or four restaurants – you could not hope to eat your way through in a lifetime, because you'd have favourites and return maybe for bacon and eggs more than once. And it's got lots of different levels of entertainment. That's a tremendous thing that Australia's created.

The Hills Hoist. I just hope that we can see a display of the history of the Hills Hoist at the time of the Olympics, so that people can come along and have a look at a photograph of the bloke who invented the Hills Hoist and then maybe his backyard, and the first Hills Hoist that he made, and the improvements that they've made.

The stump-jump plough. That's always been a favourite of mine. I'd love to see people have a look at the variety of wheat that we've created. Have a look at some of the problems that rust can cause in wheat and have a look at the strains that are rust resistant – simple ideas like that. Brilliant!

And your grape. People still think that wine comes out of a bottle. There's no relationship to that purple round thing in the vineyard and that whole wine-making process.

All these ideas are what makes Australia great. The fact that a lot of these ideas float up and aren't taken up by the SOCOG powers, that doesn't mean they're not good ideas. At the moment we're trying to be like somewhere else, like America, or Bhutan or Uruguay. These traditional Australian inventions and icons are the things that we should be celebrating. They're what make Australia a great place.

What are the worst things about Australia?

Well, I can't think of anything bad about Australia. I mean, let's take the problem of 1997 being the hottest year on record. A lot of people might have their hands up in horror, but I'd love to see the temperature go up in leaps and bounds by say five degrees every year, not just a paltry one degree. One degree! That's hardly an effort at all. We really should get out there and give it a red-hot go, see how hot we could get the joint before people started complaining and really sort of saying, 'I think we've gone too far, it's going to be curtains from here on in'. The only thing I dislike about Australia is that the wisdom of ordinary people, pig-shooting Australians, shark-fishing Australians, isn't taken more seriously.

Your personal experience of unemployment?

I've been unemployed more often than I've had a job. What we do have a problem with is how to put in the time when you don't have a job. The government has come up with this work-for-the-dole, which is obviously exciting a lot of people,  but I feel it's not solving the problem of jobs. Getting people to do jobs for nothing doesn't help people feel confident at all about the jobs that they are in. I introduced myself as somebody who has been working at the coal-face of sports and social criticism. If work experience people want to come in and have a go at that sort of thing, well I'll understandably sit on the sidelines and twiddle me thumbs. Because they can do it far more cheaply than I can.

The only place where work experience could work is in the casino. Work experience in the Melbourne casino seems to be paying off, especially for a lot of Asian high rollers. Once we can get work experience people running the TAB, people will be over the moon. I noticed a race run last week where the result was declared long before they stopped betting, and I think that with the work experience people there that would happen more often.

The real problem, of course, with unemployment, is that society is going through a phase at the moment where it believes that people who don't work aren't productive. I'd like to scotch that rumour entirely. People who don't work in a formal sense are often very productive. They contribute to things in the community. They contribute to things in a much wider net than corporate Australia.

Incidentally, I had hoped that the penalties for not showing up for the work-for-the-dole would include gaol, and I thought that would really help. Stick all the unemployed in gaol and the numbers will tumble down pretty quick. What I find amazing is still the persisting idea that there are a lot of jobs out there and people just don't know how to find them. I think that this is one of the great furphies of modern Australia.

Are you for the death penalty?

No, death's too good for dole bludgers: keep them alive, make them suffer. We have to realise that everybody has something to contribute. Some of us contribute in a work sense, and others in less formal ways.

I don't mind standing in a Medicare queue for twice as long as I normally would. I don't mind if the roads aren't done, I've got an old ute. But the difficulty is that people will eventually get a bit upset with this and think, surely there's got to be another way. The real problem at the moment is that unless you're a plumber pulling down $100,000 a year, with a mobile phone, you hardly rate at all.

But the big problem of unemployment is that the government is not being inclusive of unemployment. We're all in this mess together. It's not as though you can drop some people off and ignore them. And it seems to me that the government doesn't have all of us as a number one priority.

What are the rewards that you get from working, apart from money?

That's a very good question! I can't think of many.

A great stupidity of work is that we're going through a phase where the patterns of work are changing dramatically. When Roy and I started off we were able to do regular things, like Roy had a lot of success in sports so that opened doors. For me, I was able to call the dog meetings, this was a regular part of the week – every Thursday night I called the dogs, it went on for years and years and years. But now I'd be lucky to be able to call the dogs for five minutes before they either canned the dogs or found some other person who is more media friendly or whatever. No one can hang onto a job for more than about five weeks nowadays. Not because of their inability to do the work, but because the swirl of economic rationalism and new ideas just goes through at such a tremendous rate.

The Lithgow Bank is a case in point. The Lithgow Bank came up with a simple idea, a very Australian idea, combining three things – money, football and nudity. People said, it won't work. But when we opened up the first branch in Lithgow and had a lot of the lesser football names on a rotation basis as tellers behind the counter, well, we didn't know what to *do* with the money. We had to put up sheds, and we just shovelled it all in there with a padlock on it. When you see Ben Elias nude and Paul Sironen nude ... and people are queued out the front of the bank, round the corner, down the street, almost past the town hall there in Lithgow. We have created jobs that will last for life!

What role has education played in your life?

Education is largely the problem of one generation trying to teach to the next, things that the older generation thinks would be useful to have learnt when *it* was at school, to prepare them for their lives. So what you find is that education seems to lag about a generation behind where it should be. However, this is not a problem you can really do anything about.

But my feeling is that one thing that education *shouldn't* do is focus directly on a ridiculous set of standards. Education is now seen as producing products. This was brought home to me in a discussion about universities. One university was described as producing a certain sort of product as opposed to another university. Now, what the fuck are they talking about? Products? What they meant was graduates or students who had graduated. What a stupid way to see it. It's not as though they're making packets of Crunchy Nut Cornflakes. What education is meant to be doing is preparing people for life, and if they're seen as products, and if they're seen as measurable, that's got disaster built into it. Because as every teacher knows, one year is not the same as another year, they are all different and this difference should be celebrated.

Having said that, my own background at school was one of continual boredom, French lessons, Latin and maths that I couldn't understand. Physics lessons with a guy in a grey lab coat out the front while you did the experiment, particularly dull days spent dissecting frogs in biology. I wasn't able to be fitted into the scheme of things because I had no particular interests. A lot of it was spent with Sam Kokodas stabbing peanuts with a compass (which he got thrown out of class for), or walking around with a lot of coins sandwiched between two fingers until somebody went like *that* and punched them out on the floor ... 

School needs to be far more adventurous, and give people a sense of confidence. No matter what they bring to the HSC, their sense of wellbeing and the confidence to tackle anything in life should be developed. But if you push them into categories – well, you're below average to be in Grade 3 with your marks – I don't think we're going to get anywhere. Basically, education doesn't really begin until people leave school anyway. A lot of kids spend their time just waiting to become teenagers, then the trouble starts. Peace is disturbed.

Education is going through a dark age. I could not imagine spending enough money on it. Class sizes are increasing. Teachers expected to be drug counsellors, social services officers, legal representatives, and do a lot of parenting. At the same time, teachers' positions in the community have taken a terrible beating. In the end, if you can survive school, you've done pretty well.

What do you think about 'up-front' fees for universities and such issues?

Education should be a priority. I am, of course, delighted that the government hasn't touched the defence budget in recent times because I love anything that goes *bang!* But having said that, I don't think that you can spend enough on education.

The only up-front fees that I'd consider would be if people from other places want to come here and acquire skills and then go back to their countries. I think that it's a fair cop to ask them to pay for that sort of intellectual expertise. But the rest of it, I'd make it free to anybody who wanted to take advantage of it.

If your child had a drug habit would you want society to treat them as a criminal or as an ill person requiring treatment?

Obviously you have to treat people who are addicted to substances of any sort as ill. I'd strengthen the Customs services and try and employ some people who knew what they were doing – it appears that unless you are a Chinese swimmer you hardly have any attention paid to you. And I'd go after the Mr Bigs and Mrs Bigs. You've got to understand that none of the stuff gets in here without, I think the term is, 'juice upstairs'. So you have to question exactly how that operates.

Government needs to look primarily at the health implications. You could make comparison with problems of intravenous drug users and AIDS. Stressing the thing about not sharing needles and so on has been a successful campaign.

The government's got a terrible hump about media reaction in the drugs area. Why does the media react so stupidly to it? I could be persuaded the only reason is they like the current state of affairs. They can run all those bloody dreadful stories about people collapsing in car parks with toddlers alongside them. This is not something the community should encourage, exploiting people to sell papers or as a form of entertainment.

What do you think about looking 'outside the square' for new solutions – shooting galleries, drugs programs, whatever?

The difficulty is, until you get some sort of humanistic, sympathetic approach, these things are bandaid solutions. I'm not terribly keen on the idea of shooting galleries, only because government could stop at that and think they've covered the problem. We should see it as a medical problem. What you've got to accept is that society does a lot of risk taking, at all sorts of levels. And I think that we've got to minimise the risks, not pretend that no one's taking risks.

What do you think about tax reform?

Look, tax reform, I love it! You can't get enough talk about tax reform. People are so tax literate. They all know what's going on. That's the great legacy of the Hawke and Keating years, everybody knows some of the tax details. The GST, that's just a brilliant scheme. Let's face it, I'm a multimillionaire, I'd love it if my loaf of bread cost exactly the same as your loaf of bread, exactly the same as the unemployed person's loaf of bread. Yet when you've got millions, shelling out $1.95 for a loaf of bread is neither here nor there. When you're on the dole, shelling out a $1.95 for a loaf of bread with the GST slapped on it ... well, I mean, I'm laughing.

People don't propose these things from the point of view of not having a lot of money to start with. They propose them because they are on to an absolute rort. It's going to be tremendous. There's hardly going to be a product Roy and HG use that won't be GST exempt.

I've often said that *BRW* and the *Financial Review* should print lists every month of who paid the most tax. This is a tremendous idea. People would love to get on those lists and stay on them.

A lot of our problems would be solved if people paid their fair share. The whole thing's set up for financial wizards to find loopholes that allow their clients to pay no tax. They keep it simple for and stupid for people who can't afford to work their way around it, but if you're rich enough you won't be paying any tax. That's what I love about these tax proposals. You don't see people on the 380 bus discussing the merits of the GST. That just doesn't pop up as an issue, unfortunately. What happened in the cricket does, what happens in the rugby league, but I've never overheard conversations like, 'GST at 11 percent, that'll work an absolute treat, it'll iron out a lot of problems at the ATO'.

It's like the Asian meltdown. Roy and I made such a killing on the Asian meltdown. It was just like taking candy from a baby. Not small bits of candy, not a couple of candy sticks, but great logs and fat bloody pramfuls of it we were wheeling away.

Should Australia be a republic?

It's hardly an issue any more that Australia will become a republic. When you go to England you get an idea of how much of a republic Australia is. Peter Lalor obviously started the whole bloody republic thing off at the Eureka Stockade. But generally speaking the majority of people here have got over it as an issue. There are some who would rather be a constitutional monarchy. But 'a resident for president' is a very simple and noble ambition.

Could you imagine a situation where voluntary euthanasia might be desirable?

Voluntary euthanasia, with safeguards, is something that I totally support. I know I've been close to death many, many times. Once I screamed for the course doctor to put me out of my misery. Mercifully the course doctor had had a few sherbets and thought he was treating a horse and went to jab and missed and I'm still here talking to you today. Worst case scenario – how would you like to have the Ebola virus going through you? You wouldn't think that euthanasia was a good idea? You'd stagger out and sign on the dotted line at the referendum!

Look, the rich have always practised forms of euthanasia, the poor have just had to suffer with a drip of morphine in their arm. Modern medical practice will accept a slow death by massive doses of drugs, but they won't accept somebody being in charge of their life right up until the last minute and choosing their moment to die. The current state of play is just ridiculous. When a government won't allow euthanasia and has chopped palliative care, then I am very suspicious. In fact, there is a bill coming up in South Australia – I'm not sure when, it's an Upper House Private Member's Bill – which they think will be more foolproof than the Northern Territory one because it's a state not a territory and so the feds won't be able to overturn it.

The idea that the federal government might use a Ten Point Plan to circumvent the intentions of the High Court – is that desirable?

I love the High Court. You won't get me knocking it, seven blokes sitting down for a long day, having a bit of lunch, a bit of arvo tea, just thinking and talking about things legal. I don't care if they get $1000 an hour. Just to have them in charge of the nation's affairs gives me an enormous sense of comfort. They might look large, they wear funny gear, no one can understand what they say, but as long as they're thinking about it, I'm happy. It saves me having to worry about it myself.

The great thing about the High Court, of course, is the level of excitement. I don't know if you've ever been there or not? You know, they get a brief, you can see them go goosey all over when it's a real doozey, like a tax problem. They know there's no right and there's no wrong and they've got to sit there and make up their minds. All I can think of is the bagging that people like Bill O'Chee and Tim Fischer go on with is just pathetic. It's just jealousy. They'd *love* to have that amount of money. They'd love to have the time to consider whether sales tax on O-rings for a submarine is justified in the Defence Department and write about 600,000 words on it.

No, I just wish there were more High Courts. The latest appointment is Callinan, the playwright and restaurant guide author – and they're perfect credentials for somebody on the High Court. I don't care whether he's a black letter lawyer, I don't care whether he's even studied law. You can expect great things from Callinan and I just hope when Borbidge and Fischer start bagging him, as they will, that he will give as good in return.

Finally, H.G., what are your feelings on the native title issue?

Well, the difficulty here is, of course, is that the legal system before 1788 was one which obviously kept the place in fairly good nick. You didn't have any of the particular problems that we've got now. So in the last 200 years there has been a lot of wrestling with the problem of how recent immigrants are going to deal with the original inhabitants, for want of a better way of putting it. This is a complicated matter which is not served by trying to reduce it to idiotic points on a plan which largely seem to me to revolve around the issue of property, not the issue of principle. You have to go back to the principle and assert that principle pretty strongly. And this is what happened in the Mabo judgement. So you have to assert pretty correctly that the principle is that the original inhabitants have claim to the land if, as in the Mabo case, they can prove some sort of continuous claim on it. Obviously, there's got to be discussion points about what these claims involve. They should either have compensation or get it back to do with it what they want.

Now once you get into this area you've set a lot of cats running, because the legal system which has been overlaid here, and there's been several overlayings of it, doesn't allow for these things to be simply resolved. But when you look at Cape York, you see a group of people of Aboriginal descent and a group of people of more recent arrival, sitting down and talking about it. The difficulty is, when they arrive at an agreement, they have to enshrine it in some sort of conventional law. They've got a model which is very admirable and well worth considering in other parts of Australia. Another model was the case settled on the New South Wales north coast, where the claimants agreed on a certain amount of money that was put in a trust fund for the community.

What isn't going to work is if you get a discussion run by the National Party and certain farmers who won't talk to the community, who have made difficult arrangements with the banks, who have a lot of baggage to get through. But generally speaking, I think you've got to go to the principle, and then see where you can move on from the principle.

What's happening at the moment is they're trying to erect what you'd call parliamentary law, to get around the problems of not agreeing that this principle is a good idea.

Mercifully, I've been lucky enough to be rich enough to never have to worry about being a lawyer. That's pretty bloody rich. But one thing I will tell you for nothing is, people are going to make fortunes out of all this.

Thank you very much for your time.

Dr Pat O'Shane

Magistrate

'The pursuit of justice'

BRETT KELLY: *Is there an idea, person or event that had the single most profound effect on your life?*

PAT O'SHANE: Yes, there were a couple actually. The very first was when I was around 10, maybe a bit older, but I heard about the Rosenbergs in the United States – their conviction for passing atomic secrets to the Soviets and their subsequent execution. What I remember about it in particular is that at the time they had two young sons. I remember as a child reading the daily paper and seeing a photograph of these two young boys on the front page of the newspaper and being absolutely horrified because their parents had been executed. Because I was about the same age that had a profound effect on me. I thought about the Rosenbergs for many, many years and in fact subsequently as an adult read a great deal about the case.

So that incident I remember very clearly. I thought what a terrible injustice was done to those children and in fact, all these years afterwards, I know that there is still a great deal of controversy about whether or not the Rosenbergs were involved with atomic spying. I am not entirely convinced of that, myself, but that's probably not to the point.

The other issue that profoundly affected my life was always hearing from my mother about Paul Robeson – he was her hero quite obviously. He was the great American singer and civil rights activist and I think that he had visited the Soviet Union himself at some time and also sent his son to school over there, and he was condemned in the United States for his so-called Communist sympathies. As it happened, when I was about 19 years old he visited Australia and I went to one of his concerts and he held my hand and I was just like over the moon. He was my role model and I learnt that he was a law graduate, that he was a very fine actor, particularly Shakespearean actor, of course a very great singer and above all a very committed civil rights activist.

Is there a motto, quote or thought that summarises your approach to life?

Certainly, the pursuit of justice ... which sums up what I do in my life. I cannot view the world any other way than I do. Just this morning I was trying to think of how some people look at the world. I am horrified by instances that I see going on around me all day long – every day – that I think are so outrageously unjust, and yet many people seem to accept them. The greed, I suppose, is something that I cannot comprehend. It is beyond me to understand greed in a gut way. I mean, I understand it intellectually, but I can't understand it otherwise.

What is the most critical issue facing Australia in the next decade?

The greed and individualism that is promoted in our society. I think it is very destructive. I once thought I was living in an Australian society where people cared about each other, a society which was structured, in fact, to promote a sense of community amongst all of us. This has been, or is being, destroyed, torn apart.

What do you think are the best things about Australia today?
Well, there is still a sense that all Australians are entitled to a fair go. The fact that we don't *get* it is quite another issue, but there is still that sense there in the community.

In Australia we also have a very good record on human rights. That's not to say that we live in an ideal society – it would be foolish of us to think we did – and the fact that it doesn't exist does not mean that we should not continue to strive towards that ideal. So I think that is something we have got going for us in the future. I'd like to think we could retrieve the situation that we had, of good people dedicated to rebuilding a society built on principles of equity and justice.

What do you think are the things Australia could do better?
In rebuilding society I think we should consider revisiting social welfare, because in a society which is based on principles of equity and justice we would need to have a welfare system in place so that the stronger – in whatever terms we might define the stronger members of the community or stronger sectors of the community – support the weaker, and in particular look after those who are disadvantaged and dispossessed. In doing so we expand ourselves as individuals and as a community.

Is there a personal experience, either your own or that of a friend or family member or something seen in court, that really gave you an insight into the issue of unemployment?
Well, I grew up in poverty myself. My father was a seasonal worker, he worked on the wharves. Initially there was no guaranteed income for my parents. In those days, the workers literally had to scramble for tokens that were just thrown down on the floor. Anybody who managed to grab a token got a job for the day. But there were many, many weeks on end when my father did not have any work and therefore there wasn't any money coming into the house. So I grew up with that, the reality of unemployment.

I actually meet the problem every day of my working life. The overwhelming majority of people who come before the courts are people who are undereducated and certainly underemployed, although the majority of them would indeed be unemployed.

What are the rewards you have found in your work aside from the monetary compensation?
My whole job is rewarding, apart from the salary that goes with it. I have always said about this job that it gives me an opportunity to interface with members of the community at a very fundamental level. Hopefully I can do something to, in some way, make their lives a little bit better – although that may sound like a very strange thing for a judicial officer to be doing. But very often people are ground down by their circumstances and they are the majority, who ought not to be coming before the court – they really require intervention, welfare intervention, at some much earlier point in their lives.

I have always been of the view that the overwhelming majority of people now in jail should not be there. So many victims of poverty and dispossession, and it doesn't matter what colour or creed they are. They have been dispossessed of their self-esteem, their pride, their feeling of worth as human beings, by this society which places so much value on work and material fortune. These people have nothing.

So there are lots of rewards in being able to intervene in the lives of people, hopefully to make things slightly better, or at least not to worsen them.

Is there a level of unemployment that you think is acceptable in Australian society?
I think in any society there is inevitably *some* level of unemployment because without a doubt there are people who do not want to work. That is part of human nature. So I would expect that there will always be a very small percentage in any community that simply will not pull their weight, for whatever reason. The reasons could be psychological, physical or generally just their make-up, their personality or character, whatever.

I think that such people are much more likely to exist in a society like ours where people see that others amass huge fortunes in actual monetary or financial terms through straight-out corruption and other forms of deceit, and those people are lauded for their efforts. And I needn't name any names. I'm sure we can all immediately identify somebody that we could say he – usually it is a he – that he got there through deceitful means. And when others in the community see that, then they are likely to take the attitude, well, why should I work? I mean some of those very rich people are bludgers – there is no question about that – and yet society gives them all sorts of breaks. I have to say I don't agree with that point of view, but I must acknowledge that it is there within the community.

There are others who for whatever reason – make-up I suppose – will never ever work because they have not that kind of inclination. And that can happen in any kind of community whatsoever. I would think that those groups within the community constitute a very, very small minority. My reading of the situation would indicate that maybe, you know, every society needs to tolerate – or is going to *get* – around about 2.5 to 3 percent of people unemployed. And that is a tolerable level.

Is that less than what it is?
Much less than what it is at present. Yes, the unemployment levels that we suffer in our society today are due to the way in which the financial sector is deregulated, and to how people are running the stock exchanges, and the flow of money in the community is totally uncontrolled. In an era of economic and financial deregulation, people can do what they damned well like and others can go to hell. That basically is why people are unemployed. Again it is about greed.

Is there any merit in work-for-the-dole or national service schemes? Can you see that there might be some advantages in a scheme of that type?
No, I don't. It is really hard not to put it in any political context, because what you are talking about is a philosophical approach to life. Either people do it or people don't.

I mean, there are some political commentators who don't see that ideologies in politics run deep, they are not dead. I think that is the highly political deceit that goes on in our society, in particular in Western European society, where it is supposed that political ideologies are dead. I cannot see any truth in that whatsoever.

If people are going to be paid for the work that they do then they should have real jobs and be paid real wages for them, wages that are commensurate with the skills and effort that are required to do the job. And the job has to be socially worthwhile. The thought of people digging ditches and then filling them in again is just demeaning. It means nothing to our society and is utterly demeaning to the people who have to do that kind of work. Here I am just using a metaphorical situation, it is obviously not what is proposed. But how should I know if that will happen here? It has been done before.

In your experience is Australia a racist nation?
In my opinion, it certainly is a racist nation. I grew up with racism all around me.

Will Australia ever be a republic?
I think it is inevitable. It becomes quite a complex issue, however, when we start to talk about constitutions and how we design them to meet the various needs of our society and how we shape our governmental procedures.

Can you imagine a situation where having the option of voluntary euthanasia would be desirable?
I actually don't think it is desirable for people to kill themselves. We have a very high suicide rate, but here we are talking about people who are in extreme pain and usually at the end of their lives. People are entitled to not have to live the remainder of their lives in pain and discomfort such that there is absolutely no quality of life there.

People talk about the sanctity of life, and I think we get caught in a terrible bind because essentially we do not in fact subscribe to the concept of the sanctity of life. I mean we waste people's lives all the time, we couldn't care less about our children for instance, and in Australian society there seems to be a terrible hatred of children.  It seems to me, as a society, we do our level best to alienate our youth. We throw our old folks on the scrap heap of humankind. I mean, we have some real problems with those kinds of views and I think that you cannot talk about euthanasia without also thinking about these other issues.

An awful lot of emotion gets generated over the use of voluntary euthanasia. But in any event it seems to me it is a strange question, because I really don't see that there is anything which stops people from in fact ending their lives if they really want to do so.

Very often, of course, if they are very, very ill and have a great deal of disability, they don't have the resources immediately available to them and they don't have the physical ability to take the necessary steps to end their lives. Therefore that necessarily involves somebody else, and of course that is when all the problems arise. Should we allow somebody – should I allow you – to take my life for me, with my permission, at a point when I am no longer capable of living any sort of quality life?

At the federal level we have got a legislature and a judiciary, and my understanding was that for the successful operation of a constitutional monarchy those two entities should operate with some sort of separation. If the government proposed a plan to get around the intended application of the High Court's judgement, do you see that as a precedent? Basically, should the government be running the agenda or should they have respect for what the High Court decides?
Yes to both questions actually. I mean, the judiciary has one role and the government has a different role. The judiciary pronounces what is common law, or if some statutory law exists which they are interpreting then they define what it means. But in the case that you are talking about there was no statutory law and the judiciary simply enunciated what was the common law – what *is* the common law – that applies in this country.

Now if the government wants to circumscribe certain aspects of our lives within that common law then it has the duty to do so, it has the right to do so, because the electorate, the populace, has invested government with that authority. But I think that governments really have to keep faith with their constituents – they don't do it of course – none of them do it.

In the case that you are talking about, it seems to me that the government has attempted to denigrate the role and function of the judiciary within government, when the judiciary is part of government under the Westminster system that we have inherited.

I think those issues have become very much tangled and confused. It has been a deliberate political ploy and I think that the community needs to be very much aware that it is a political ploy. A lot of their democratic rights could well be in jeopardy if they allow governments simply to reject the rule of law.

I don't mean by that that governments are not entitled to reject decisions made by the High Court of Australia, but to bring the High Court of Australia into disrepute through political campaigns – I think that is a very dangerous thing for any government to do, or politicians to do, for that matter, in a community. Because somewhere along the line, at some time, the people will rely upon the High Court to pronounce upon their civil, political and economic rights, and that is something they ought to be very vigilant about. We need that recourse.

What is education, and what should it be for young people going forward?
Education overall is about giving people the skills to critically analyse the world, to be able to synthesise information and analyse it and come up with new ideas and new approaches, solutions to problems.

The narrow definition of education, and it seems to me it is becoming more and more narrow, is simply feeding people information and stuffing them with facts. In more recent times it has come to be applied to people who have technological skills. We are relying much more on computers to feed people information, or to be there as a data source so that people can retrieve the information from it, but I don't think that we are actually educating people in the way that I first defined.

In the world today, particularly in Australia, we are finding that the divide between the rich and the poor is being translated into our education systems. So those who can afford to send their children to private schools, who have the power to insist that governments allocate more and more of the education dollar to those private schools, also have access to those computers from which to access information.

Of course information is power or knowledge is power and knowledge these days is having information and having access to information and that has been denied to the overwhelming majority of people in the community.

What does that mean in terms of the community? I think we are translating into a situation where there are fewer and fewer people who have jobs and who are working longer and longer hours, and the majority of people who don't have jobs at all. And there has been no process, no plan, within our community to serve those people better in any way – by for instance giving them greater access to recreation facilities.

What role has formal classroom education played in your life?

Formal education has played a very great role in my life. It has certainly given me access to information and knowledge, but also it taught me how to be critically analytical. That is something I have learnt along the way, and I have used those skills to enhance my economic prospects through the sorts of jobs that I have been able to access. If I hadn't had a formal education, there is no doubt about it, I wouldn't be in the position I am in today.

Do you believe that educational opportunities are plentiful and well distributed in Australia?

No, they're not at all. In fact, in my job, I suppose the overwhelming majority of people we see are either uneducated or undereducated. A great number of them are semi-literate at best and probably innumerate as well. So the disparities in  the socio-economic conditions of our society – and education is a part of that, of course – are really seen in sharp focus in my job.

If a child of yours had a drug habit, would you want society to treat them as a criminal or as an ill person requiring treatment?

That's a really difficult question. I don't think that people with drug habits should be treated as criminals at all, but I do have serious difficulties in imposing a medical model instead, because in some respects I think that the medical model can be every bit as oppressive – or even more oppressive at times than the criminal model. At least with the criminal model there is a formal process through which people have to go before they are incarcerated, whereas with the medical model very often there are not checks and balances operating.

Something like the old psychiatric treatments ... ?

Yes, that's what the medical model does. I mean, if people are characterised as having a medical problem, then they have certain treatment regimes imposed upon them, and those treatment regimes can be extremely oppressive and dangerous. We don't have the sorts of checks and balances in the medical system that we have in the criminal justice system. And that is a difficulty.

Also I believe that when you impose a medical model you are generating an attitude of victimhood in a different, sometimes subtle, sometimes not so subtle way, that has greater long-term effects than victimising people in the criminal justice system. It can be a very insidious thing which takes hold of people's minds, individually as well as collectively, over many, many years.

It's about the impact of being told you are sick, as opposed to you are a criminal. Each, but most particularly the medical model, disempowers people in terms of exercising their own levels of responsibility. And it lets society off the hook as well. I think society never changes if it pathologises the victim – in this case, the user.

The reason people take drugs is a combination of individual pathology and the impact of socio-economic conditions on them. We see a very high correlation of youth who feel worthless in our society and high rates of drug abuse; also high rates of suicide.

I actually think drugs are not ultimately the problem, it is the socio-economic conditions of society that are ultimately the problem.

The way we have been fighting drugs for the last 20 years clearly hasn't worked. Is it time to look 'outside the square' and consider some other approaches?

It's long past time that we should be looking at alternatives for dealing with drug abuse in our community. We should have been looking at it a long, long time ago. We know that the reason why Australian governments do not implement alternative heroin treatment programs is because Australia is a signatory to some treaty where the United States in fact calls the shots and opposes the sorts of trials proposed in the ACT recently. It is a matter of politics, international politics – in fact, it's money. We know for instance, beyond a shadow of doubt, that the CIA has been very heavily involved in the drug trade and no doubt there are other government agencies around the world involved in the hugely profitable drug trade.

Is tax reform desirable, and should a consumption tax be part of a broader tax reform? What are your primary concerns?

I think tax reform is not just desirable but essential. We have very large corporations and exceedingly wealthy individuals in our community who simply do not pay their share of taxes. The majority of people do, because they are PAYE taxpayers.

We need massive reforms in the tax system, there is no question about that. What I find offensive is that people like Murdoch might pay all of 7 cents in the dollar tax, because of their ability to move money around the world via tax havens and to employ lawyers to simply evade tax.

The fact of the matter is they are the greatest tax bludgers in our community because they don't help to pay for any of the infrastructures this society needs, hospitals, schools, roads, fuel supplies and so on, and yet they take advantage of those infrastructures. They need them as much as you and I need them.

Should we have a consumption tax? Under no circumstances should we have a consumption tax. Consumption tax, again, reinforces the divide between the wealthy and the poor. In fact it makes that divide even greater, particularly for those who are less than wealthy but who are not poor – they are on the poor side of *this* divide, make no mistake about it.

Consumption tax means that the poor are paying more tax and the wealthy are paying less. If I'm on $10,000 a week and you are on $100, and we have both paid the same amount for our goods and services, quite clearly I am paying less, proportionately, than you are. So it is a very insidious tax and it would have very severe repercussions on the economic profile of our society. I am utterly opposed to it.

That is not the sort of tax reform that we need. There should be more equitable distribution of wealth in our society, but rather than the government working to ensure that, in fact they are simply working to ensure that the wealthy can become even more wealthy.

Our present federal government has more millionaires on the front bench than the previous government, and I dare say more than any other country except perhaps the United States. It's an outrageous situation. The present prime minister went on the hustings saying his government would govern for all, but they don't, they govern for the wealthy. And the proposal for a goods and services tax or a consumption tax is just one more aspect of that general bias.

Thank you very much for your time.

Siimon Reynolds

Principal & Co-creative Director, VCD Advertising

'Whatever the mind can perceive and believe it can achieve'

BRETT KELLY: *Is there an idea, person or event that has had a really profound influence on your life?*

SIIMON REYNOLDS: Well, a couple of events have had an impact on me. The first was that I was often told I was no good, and that was a huge motivator for me. I think a lot of people who become successful have been fear motivated, and I was certainly one of them. I had this fear that maybe these people were right, and so I did everything I could to try and prove them wrong. It was a great propeller. Then, you know, there's sporadic events I remember – getting a high mark one day when I did my three minute speech in school. That encouraged me to speak, which I have done some 50 times in the last year to audiences, almost all of which have paid. Then there's a thousand subconscious things that happen to you, that your brain says, yes, I get pleasure when this happens or when I do this, when I act like this, or when I say this, when I respond to people in this way; and I get pain when I do things a thousand other ways. So I believe that most of the things that have sculptured me are probably not conscious.

Is there a motto, quote or thought that really summarises your approach to life?
Well, I'm a big fan of Napoleon Hill who's quoted, 'whatever the mind can perceive and believe it can achieve'. What I'd add to that is perhaps not an elegant quote, yet I think it's very important: 'make sure you're rich in the physical, mental and spiritual parts of yourself' – rather than just one or two of these.

What are the most critical issues for Australia in the next decade?
I don't really follow what's happening in Australia at a micro level, I don't read the newspapers other than the business section, I don't join in social conversations about the nuisances or the ups and downs of society, so my comments are not about the next 10 years but about the next 1000 years. I would say that I believe that there is always only one critical issue, and that is the education of the individual. The reason we have all these problems is because of the often poor moral and mental education of individuals, and the degree to which a society's individuals grow is the degree to which we are able to overcome the ever-changing world problems. What are the problems of the future? I guess adapting to a changing society, handling ever-growing pressures, cultivating a self-image that can give you confidence to function effectively in the world. But that's not just the next decade, that's some of mankind's greater issues.

At a personal level, has there been an experience, or a friend or a relative who's battled with unemployment, that has given you an insight into the issue?
I did a speech recently for unemployed people, about 500 of them, and I was amazed at both their education level and their intelligence. What may be missing is confidence, self-image and tenacity – we need to address those three things, rather than try and make more jobs and work out schemes. Those are all well and good, and we've been doing it for the last 50 years, but one of the primary reasons

that a lot of people aren't employed is because they're missing in part those mental ingredients.

My other issue on unemployment is, people underestimate how good unemployment is as a symbol of a change in culture. For instance over 90 percent of America a century ago was involved in farming, now only 3 percent is involved in farming. You could imagine then that a lot of farmers became unemployed, but then if you actually followed the line of unemployment you could see that many people who are unemployed – like the American farmers – eventually got jobs in other industries. So now, a lot of the reason we have unemployment in Australia or any other country is because the structure of commerce is changing, people are moving or being pushed out of industries that are dying but will soon find their place again, broadly speaking, in industries that are growing. So I don't think unemployment from the macro level is that bad, it's just a sign of a changing world.

Have you found rewards in your work, apart from the dollars you get at the end of the week?

Absolutely. The great reward of working at VCD is the growth of the people. It sounds a bit wet but it's sharing their little moments of triumph and joy and helping them out with their little moments of grief. We're quite unlike a normal company, we place the personal happiness, personal growth, of the people we work with at our company as one of the main reasons that this company is even in business, and we gain just so much more satisfaction from our interaction with people than anything else. Do I want money? Yes. Do I want to have to worry about the cost of anything? No. It's a tool, it's a measure of success. Sophie Tucker once said, 'I've been rich and I've been poor, and believe me, honey, rich is best.' But at the end of the day, you know, money's not the driving force, achievement and contribution are the things.

Is there an acceptable level of unemployment?

Well, certainly, you'll always have some unemployment. But let us not forget, without being glib or callous about it, the significant growth that unemployment offers as a human experience. When people go through pain, they grow. That may seem a ludicrous thing to say, but there's a lot of people who now are in extremely important positions because of the profound lessons they learnt from being unemployed.

What is your view on some sort of national service, work-for-the-dole or training scheme for young people – where you get the dole working in the scheme, as opposed to getting it for nothing? Do you think there could be merit in a scheme like that?

Yeah, absolutely. Look, what people really get out of work is a sense of self-worth, in addition to the obvious material benefits, and that is where unemployed people are suffering the most, it's their own personal sense of worth. I believe that everything on earth, every living thing on earth, must create. You look at a plant and it's growing, you look at a flower and it's at least producing an aroma, you look at animals and they're working, you look at humans, they've got the choice. But I believe that we are made to work, we are made to create, we are made to contribute to society. If we can do anything to help people contribute, and working for the dole is certainly one way, it will make them a lot happier.

Do you think that over time the advantages could become obvious to people? At first they think it's not a good idea, but if they do it, it could be the best thing in the world for some people?

No, I think a lot of them will get advantages, and a lot of them will get a kick up the butt too ... if required.

Is Australia a racist nation?

I think every nation on earth is racist in parts. I've been to Japan and not been allowed into clubs because I was a Westerner. I've been to America and been looked at suspiciously by people who weren't white. You know, every country is like that. It's even very difficult to learn the secrets of Kung Fu if you're Australian, you know what I mean? So all around the world we have pockets of racism, and of course it will reduce as we become – as the media and transport advancement make us – a global village. But it will always be there, and possibly in more subtle ways in the future. But if we don't understand ... we are always scared of what we don't understand. We are always suspicious of what we don't know. It's inevitable and it's quite natural, although not beneficial.

Would you give me some indication of your educational background and what you see education as being?

Well, if I recall, and this was when I was 18 so we are talking 15 years ago, the Oxford dictionary defines education as 'to bring up mentally and morally'. I remember looking it up for a speech, and if you take that as the definition, then quite clearly the education you see is poor. What we have is the acquisition of facts, many of them useless for participating in a modern society. You know, while I can appreciate spending a small portion of my time understanding what so-and-so did in his life 500 years ago, the hours that I spent memorising I found virtually useless.

So from that point of view I believe that education needs to get a lot more practical, more realistic, more hard-nosed about the world. I think basic medicine should be taught, I think public speaking the ability to communicate, the ability to sell – should be a three unit subject. An understanding of all the major religions in the world is absolutely crucial – you know, we're all going to die, and something may happen on the other side of that, and we should at least be educated in what that may be. We need to understand many, many things that we are not taught.

By the same token I think a lot of students underestimate what they get out of school – I never really realised that mathematics was teaching you order, until about five years after school. I never realised the subtle benefits of understanding geography from the point of view of globalism, and all those kinds of things. But you know the greatest thing that school teaches you, in my opinion, is that if you do what you don't want to do, like schoolwork, then you'll be better off. And that is a great fundamental secret of life that people need to understand to make it – sacrifice.

What role has formal education, classroom education, played in your life?

I went to Sydney Grammar School and my headmaster's little line at the bottom of my last report card a few months before the HSC was 'if things don't improve then Siimon had better leave school'. So I bring a lot of baggage into this whole area.

But what were my experiences? I didn't want to go on to uni, so when selecting a career an important aspect was, do I have to go to university? And I ruled everything out that involved further study. I was basically down to the question, how do I make money without going to uni? The answer was advertising, real estate or stockbroking, and I chose advertising. But basically I hated going to school, I hated having to work at subjects I didn't want to work at, I hated having to conform, I hated having to toe the line, because many of the things that make you successful at school – not all of them, mind you, but many – are the opposite to what makes you successful in society. To step out and take new roads rarely was rewarded at school.

Was your school not keen on diversity of opinion?

Actually, the fact is I'd send my son to Sydney Grammar if I had one, and the reason is because, more so than most schools, it does allow diversity, certainly culturally – if you are a minority you're much better off at Grammar than most schools because there's a very great degree of acceptance. There is perhaps some intellectual racism going on there. If you are smart, even if you don't do well at school, if you're smart then everybody appreciates you regardless of your race.

Do you believe in fee-paying for university education?

Yeah, I believe you should pay for it. Look, if I give you a T-shirt, you might like it. If I make you pay $50 bucks for that T-shirt you'll appreciate it more. I know a lot of consultants who charge a lot of money, and one of the reasons is because they know if they charge a lot they will be appreciated a lot more. So I believe that when you pay to go to university there is a greater commitment. However there should  be systems in place so that those truly financially disadvantaged – who are far fewer than most people think – those people who are truly financially disadvantaged can still have the opportunity for education.

If your child had a drug habit, would you want society to view them as a criminal or as an ill person requiring treatment?

I absolutely see them as ill persons. But you know everybody's got drugs: some people's drug is fame, most people's drug is love, other people's drug is alcohol, money and so on. So we are all drug addicts, and these people have chosen one of a thousand avenues. This particular one happens to be illegal, so one needs to see it with compassion, with the compassion of someone who is in the same boat as you but has expressed it in a different way.

Is now a good time for us to look at a new approach to the drug issue, looking 'outside the box', looking for new solutions?
Yeah, absolutely, I'm a great believer that you model what works. For instance, we should immediately duplicate the British system whatever it is [in the context that they have a tenth of the deaths each year from heroin], in all its forms, then analyse a year or two years later what the effects of that were. You just continually look for the best people in the world in any area and then do what they do. Now that is a little clumsy, in that there are obvious differences between their society and ours, but I tell you what, it will lead to faster results than just making token changes to our own system.

Tax reform – would it make any difference to you if there was a consumption tax?
Ah no, I pay no attention to that kind of stuff. I mean the fact is it *would* make a difference. I'm sure technically it would. I might even notice it on occasion, looking at bank balances and overall financial performance. But I choose not to worry about things that I can never control. A person is only effective when they concentrate on what they can change. I have no interest in what the government does until I see something outrageous. I don't want to be disrespectful of them – I appreciate what they are doing, they're shepherding us, and I trust in their ability to do that.

Will Australia ever be a republic?
Yes, it's inevitable, it's absolutely inevitable. The reason is because the thought is implanted, thoughts implanted and nurtured tend to grow. And the other reason is, it's natural for a child to leave its mother.

What is the symbolic value of the flag? Is it really that important to the rest of the world, does it really send out that strong a message?
No, I don't think it's that important at all, but it is a critical part of the mental DNA. The mental DNA of humans is that they want freedom, any shackle that can be removed they will seek en masse to remove it and republicanism is just another version of that.

But do you think that moving to become a republic, changing the flag, is a symbolic gesture to the world that we are our own nation?
Oh yeah, it would be symbolic, and that's a critical word, symbolic. I don't think the world will give a stuff either way.

Could you imagine a situation where you'd like to have the option of voluntary euthanasia?
Yeah, if I reached the point where I was making no contribution to the world, if I was only a drain on the world and I wasn't growing, if I was a virtual vegetable or

in massive pain, then I would certainly consider that. It is an issue of such a critical nature, if you are in that position, that it deserves a hell of a lot more thought than I have yet given it.

Do you think the government should drive a Ten Point Plan that seeks to do something different to the umpire's decision, the umpire being the High Court, in relation to Aboriginal land rights?
No, we must trust in our judicial system. And who's the government? It's just another group of men and women having their opinion, and so why is it any better or worse than the High Court's opinion? There are some brilliant men and women on that bench and I certainly think they are as capable as the government of reaching the right conclusion.

If the government's got a Ten Point Plan to deal with Aboriginal land rights, should it have a mission statement or ten point plan to tell Australians where the country is going, how and why?
One of the great things that we are missing from politics is leadership. Leadership not at a tactical, political level, but at an emotional level. Why is it that when I read and hear on tape great speeches, they're so rarely Australian? The reason is because we're dealing with the details and we're not realising that it's not the politicians, no matter how hard they work, that will solve the country's problems, it's the people. And they will only solve them with inspired leadership.

Look at the world's greatest coaches. They wouldn't get a place in their own teams. But their ability is to coach, to manage and to bring the best out in people. Now at a government level you don't do that by fiddling around with tax and a thousand other little elements. You speak to the people and make them feel they are capable of more.

Those old fireside chats – who used to have them, Roosevelt, was it? – they really were the kind of things that move mountains, not the largely unbelieved promises 10 days before an election. That's about the only time we hear the greater vision, the so-called greater vision. People are deeply suspicious of that. In America there's a lot more respect for politicians in general, and part of it is because they don't stand there like children in Parliament bickering about trivia, they act as statesmen. And we could all learn from that.

Thank you very much for your time.

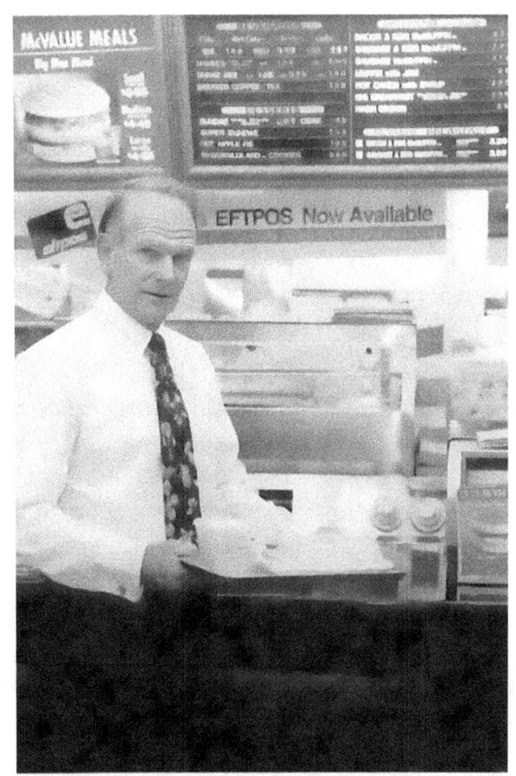

Peter Ritchie

Chairman, McDonald's Corporation

'Just do it. I can do all things'

BRETT KELLY: *Is there an idea, person or event that had the single most profound influence on your life to date?*

PETER RITCHIE: You mean in any stage of my life? No, I don't think so. Not one single event, no. My determination is probably my biggest strength and that comes from the hardships that my mum and dad faced – I think those things made me determined not to suffer in that way again, so I give my mum most of the credit for giving me that sort of strength. I'm not particularly gifted intellectually, just good enough to get through a university degree and that sort of thing, but determination is my biggest strength.

Is there a motto, quote or thought that really summarises your approach to life?
No, I think it can be almost misleading to try and put it into a sentence like that. Although I do like the Nike commercial theme – 'Just do it!' My mum, who was religious, gave me a religious quote that I did carry around for a long time, although I'm totally against religion now. But 'I can do all things through Christ which strengtheneth me' was what she gave me. I took the first part of it, 'I can do all things', and that does me now.

What are the most critical issues facing Australia in the next decade?
I think we have a crisis of leadership that's not being seen by too many people. That seems to me to be almost the most important thing, because unless we get better, stronger and more determined leaders, we're not going to get out of the shit we're in. There aren't many examples of what I'm talking about – the only politician that comes to mind is Jeff Kennett. For all his critics, I think he's exactly what Australia needs.

I see over here you've got 'do something, lead, follow, or get out of the way'.
That's another saying that I like. The emphasis is *do something*, lead, follow or get the hell out of the way!

What are the best things about Australia today, and are there things we could do better?
Look, we've got a wonderful natural resource here, wonderful, with so few people in it. We owe it to the country and to our young people to make a better fist of maintaining our standard of living, which I don't think we're doing. I think we're slipping backwards. What do we do well? We relax well, we're good at leisure and little else. And I'm proving in McDonald's that with the right environment and the right training young Australians are as good as, or better than, anyone else in the world, because McDonald's productivity in Australia is the best in the world. So we've got the ability there, but I don't think it's being tapped in hardly any areas.

So what are the things you think we should really try hard to be better at?
Bringing up our kids, to start with. I think fathers in particular are letting sons down by not providing the role model that they need, by not being there for them in their early years, and I would put part of the blame for our poor leadership right back to that. So we need to think more about the way we're bringing up our kids. Our education system is wonderful in technical things. We're great at teaching law and accounting and engineering, medicine, all those technical skills. We are terrible at the humanities, people skills, those things. They are more important, in fact, in making a successful life and country, in my opinion. When somebody like the [former] Federal Minister for Education, Amanda Vanstone, infers more than infers, she sort of said – 'the humanities are *not* important' she's got the bull by the horns, and we've got a real problem!

Is there a personal experience, either your own or that of a friend or relative or someone you might have employed, that has really given you an insight into unemployment?
Well, I see it all the time amongst young people. We have waiting lists in nearly every one of our stores in Australia, and over the years I've been involved in that area quite personally. Very often being criticised for exploiting young people. In fact I'm really proud of the job that I have done in training so many young people. That has now been recognised, thank God, because I went through a lot of years of just being beaten around the head over it. I see a lot of ability, a hell of a lot of ability, you know. I've got just the greatest young people working for me in McDonald's. But I also see an attitude problem there, and it gets back to education again, and right back to fathering. There aren't enough kids coming up with the attitude of, just do it, get on with it, it's there for you, it's available for you. I can understand why they don't have that attitude, with their upbringing and then with the education they get. It's a really long-term problem, and I'm a bit down about it at the moment, I must say.

Well, there's a question I think you've hinted at there, and there's been some press on it, but where's the dignity in making a hamburger? You know the argument: 'I have a university degree in whatever, why should I have to make hamburgers'?
What *do* you want to make with your degree? I know a lot of people think and I feel a bit this way myself – you're better off making *something* than sitting in a fucking merchant bank and playing with telephone numbers. Unfortunately that's where  so many of our graduates or high intellects end up. Manufacturing in general isn't seen to be that attractive, and hamburgers are at the worst end of that, of course. But you touched on something that may be at the heart of it all, and that is, first of all you've got to enjoy what you're doing, but then you've got to have pride in what you do, *whatever* you do.

So are there rewards in work, no matter what the job is, apart from the monetary reward?

Oh, hell yeah. If you saw the way the young people in McDonald's have developed, like Charlie Bell, now the managing director, 36 years old. Started work at 15 years of age. He hasn't got a university degree but he's got many millions of dollars and I'm extremely proud of him. His parents are too. His real skill isn't in making hamburgers, of course, it's in leading people. He's got a wonderful ability at that, largely from the training he's had at McDonald's. He's only one example, I've got many others. They can all go out and work effectively in any industry in Australia, I don't care what it is.

So you think there is something more to work than your pay cheque? If that's the case, should it necessarily matter what your first job is?

Absolutely not. If you're getting training of any sort and are able to develop personally, then it's valuable to you. That's a part of the attitude problem that I was referring to amongst young people. The social stigma perhaps attaching to something like fast food, you know, and that gets back again to the 'tall poppy' syndrome. I mean, we say that we're a very egalitarian society – there's a lot of bullshit in that, because you just referred to the social stigma attached to a particular industry, ours; there are others that are bad and some that are worse. But it shouldn't be that way.

Should we more broadly recognise people's contribution no matter what it is?

Yes, absolutely.

Is there an acceptable level of unemployment?

I'm not an expert on that – I don't know. I think there probably is a level where people are virtually in effect just changing jobs, you know. If you asked me to guess I'd say it's probably around 3 to 4 percent, about half of what we have now.

Peter, if there is some sort of value in work apart from the money you earn, do you think it would be worthwhile if there was a government scheme where young people could get the dole and still have the option of working somewhere for that money they get?

Oh yeah, no question about that. I'd go even further, at the risk of being seen to be extremely right-wing. I think that ... I didn't do national service myself, but I was in one of the final ballots and all of my peers that went through national service reckon it was so good for them personally, even just the separation from their family at that time of their lives. We in Australia don't do that well – in the USA they do that well, with the college system. Here in Australia we still mollycoddle our kids at 18, 19, 21 years of age – when in the bloody hell do they become adults? So I reckon a compulsory two-year national service for every person in Australia would be great! It would benefit practically everyone.

Would personal skills, attitude, be enhanced through national service?
Yes – and maturity, how to handle discipline.

Is Australia a racist nation?
I'm not really interested in talking about it even – I don't think we're different to anywhere else in the world.

What is education, does it have to be in a classroom, can it be on the job?
Yeah, you know, Charlie Bell has virtually been educated at McDonald's and I'd rank him amongst some of the best executives in Australia. I mean, he sits on the Business Council of Australia now and I'd rate him in the top 10 to 12 around that council table. So that almost says it all as far as I'm concerned. I think that academic qualifications – my time at the University of New South Wales was some of the best years of my life – but I say this publicly, I said it to graduating classes a couple of years ago, the biggest benefit I got from it was the network and the friends. The degree was just something to hang on your wall to prove that you have got some sort of preparedness to work, more than intellect.

Is tertiary education the answer to the 'success' question?
Well, it might sound contradictory, but I think that everybody should have some sort of tertiary education. But we set our tertiary standards too high, I believe. We should have those high standards still for those who are up to it, but we should let less capable people in at a tertiary level too. There are those lower calibre universities in the United States that still give a degree, so they make the individuals feel pretty good about themselves, and that's a positive thing. Yet everybody recognises the degrees for what they're worth, so it doesn't bother anybody. But we shy away from that system. I don't know why.

What do you think is the role of employers in education? Should Australian employers in general really pick up the ball and put their people through that sort of training?
No. Well, the fiasco over the training guarantee levy – that says it all about employers' attitude to training. The outcry over that, you know, they screamed like stuck pigs when they had to account for their training of people. I think that's deplorable. Australian employers are just not playing their part.

At a personal level, if your child had a drug habit, would you want society to view them as a criminal or an ill person requiring treatment?
Well, if it was *just* a drug habit, I'd want them very much treated as somebody with an illness.

Given that Australia appears to have lost the initiative on drugs, should we be sitting down and looking for potential solutions 'outside the box'? Is it now time to perhaps consider that?

Yes, it's a shame, that was just absolute closed-mindedness that they weren't prepared to have a go at that heroin trial in the ACT. I think we do have to try things, I don't know whether the answer is being found anywhere in the world, maybe we won't find it either. We should be having a shot at it, though.

In the broad area of tax reform, is it time we looked at our tax system?

Oh yeah, it's too involved. That's all I'd say about it, it does need reform – it's too involved. But I think most of the cry for deregulation has come from people who really want to pay less tax. It is not going to be the magical solution to Australia's problems either. I've heard too many business people speaking like the tax system is getting in the way. I don't think for a minute that it's really getting in the way. Except that it is, I suppose, costly to administer, but that's not that significant.

Do you think the current system really encourages young people to grow their wealth?

Well, as much as it ever has. I'd like us not to have a capital gains tax, but again I see that as part of the overall structure that should be looked at.

Australia as a republic? Do you think it will ever happen?

Absolutely. It should have happened before this.

Are there any benefits beyond the symbolic ones, that you can see?

I haven't even looked beyond the symbolic. Because it's all symbolic as far as I'm concerned. It's more of a statement of independence – that we haven't taken.

Is this like the kids still living at home with the parents?

Yeah, in part. You see, that Declaration of Independence that the Yanks did was more than symbolic, you know, it was something that all Americans could take to their hearts. When we finally get the strength to do it here in Australia we will have matured.

Could you imagine a situation where you'd like to have voluntary euthanasia as an option?

Yeah. I think that it ought to be allowed with the appropriate safeguards.

I'm talking about Aboriginal land rights, Wik and Mabo and all the rest of it. Howard's Ten Point Plan seeks to make the outcomes of the High Court decision different to what they would be otherwise. Do you think it is desirable for a government to circumvent that gap between judiciary and legislature?

I probably shouldn't comment at all. I know so little about the High Court decision and even less about Howard's Ten Point Plan. What I have picked up, the High Court is not infallible – it's only a bunch of people like ourselves – and I'd have to say the finding seems at the very least debatable. On the Aboriginal question in general, I think we've got a real national problem that may be insoluble. Largely because we've destroyed their culture. We can't put it back together, neither can they. So where do you go from there? Giving them the whole bloody country won't fix it. It's not going to be solved by giving them more and more and more.

Should the federal government have a clearly communicated ten point plan for the future of our nation?
That's the sort of leadership that I advocate. Most politicians steer away from it because it does set you up to be criticised, and there are some people who will always disagree. Politicians want to try and rope everybody in, and they think if you can be wishy-washy enough maybe you can do that.

Thank you very much for your time.

Imelda Roche

Chairman, Nutrimetics Cosmetics Group

*'If you are prepared to give more than
you expect to receive back you will
rarely, if ever, be disappointed'*

BRETT KELLY: *Mrs Roche, is there an idea, a person or an event which has had the single most profound impact on your life to date?*

IMELDA ROCHE: I cannot say categorically that there was a single event, but in terms of a person, my father's mother, my paternal grandmother, had the greatest influence. I spent a great number of my very early years with her. I won't expand on the reasons, they're not really important at this stage, but she probably inspired me with a feeling that you could achieve anything in life, that really nothing was beyond you, if you had the concept and you were prepared to commit the energy and dedication and maintain the focus that was necessary. They weren't her words of course in those days, but that's really what it amounts to.

Is there a motto, quote or thought that you feel really summarises your approach to life?

Yes, and it's one I use very often. 'If you are prepared to give more than you expect to receive back you will rarely if ever be disappointed.'

What are the most critical issues facing Australia in the next decade?

I think it comes down fundamentally to education, because that's where all understanding starts, and if the basis of comprehensive understanding is not available within the family unit – and very often it's not – the only other way it can come is through education. I do believe that education is a lifelong process, it's not something you do for a period of your life, it's a journey, and one of the things we need to achieve in education is well rounded people – citizens, however we may express that – but also people who understand that they need to be contributors before they can necessarily be beneficiaries.

Now what that translates to is that we need more 'doers' in this community, more people who are prepared to put in, and I think we're lacking that. One of my concerns is that with generations of the recent past, and I'm talking about perhaps since the end of the Second World War, I think we've created an expectation of entitlement that future generations will not be able to sustain, and I have really great fears for the kind of responsibilities we are putting on the shoulders of young people today, and which they in turn will bequeath to their children. So a couple of generations away, I think we've got real concerns in Australia, unless we change our attitude to one of believing that everybody who is sound of mind and limb – if I can put it that way – basically needs to look for ways in which they can be contributors.

What do you think are the best things about Australia today?

Despite the things I've just said, I believe that Australia is absolutely the best country in the world; it provides the greatest opportunity for people, even though we're a relatively small population. I also take the view that Australians generally do not really know what true hardship is. When we think about comparisons around the world; – and it is all about comparisons, because most Australians live well, comparatively – so when we talk about people on the poverty line in Australia, if we compare the standard of living of those people with people in other countries – let me start with the most obvious, China, India, Rwanda, North Africa – I mean, we don't know what hardship is all about, in this country.

One of our greatest challenges is really getting people's mind-set right, and that's not easy, but by the same token I still believe, despite all of those things, there's nowhere else in the world that offers a better standard of living and a better opportunity than Australia for those who recognise it and want to work for it. And you know, that's one of the most misunderstood four-letter words, *work*. It's very important. Whether it's physical, mental, emotional, basically we're all required to put something in.

What are the things we could do better? Is it attitude and mind-set?

Absolutely, attitude and mind-set. I think that as a nation we need to recognise that to compete effectively in the years ahead and in the next millennium, we need to be competitive, and that means we need to have a good work ethic. Now that's not to say it has to be back-breaking work, because that belonged to before the age of technology, but basically we have to have a good work ethic, to make sure that we're prepared to take on board the things that are necessary to truly make us a smart country. Because we no longer can consider ourselves the 'lucky country' – we are still lucky, but that's not going to carry us into the next centuries – we've got to become the 'smart country', and to achieve that we need a good work ethic, and we have to engender that in people, through education.

So is it a leadership issue?

Yes, it's about leadership and example.

In sport we're extremely competitive, unbelievably so. Can we not transfer that into all areas of endeavour?

We can if people believe that other aspects of life are as enjoyable as sport. You see it's all about the fact that we lionise our sporting heroes, we lionise our entertainment heroes, we don't lionise our business heroes. We don't even think about them – or we castigate them.

Have you found rewards in work apart from the money? What are they?

Well, the money to me is relatively unimportant ... when I say it's unimportant, it is one of the things I believe we have overly concentrated on in business.  Providing people an opportunity to be financially self-reliant, I believe *that* is very important. I believe being financially self-reliant actually gets right to the heart of self-respect and basically self-respect comes through it. I mean there's other ways of expressing it – as self-esteem, your self-esteem determines what you achieve in life, and if you're going to achieve your optimum potential you have to have high self-esteem.

So those of us who now have the better part of our working lives behind us need to recognise we still have a role to play. And that is in facilitating an environment for younger people to realise their potential, to provide them with recognition, encouragement, inspiration and support – and I don't mean financial support, because a lot of people aren't in a position to provide that, but emotional support. I think that is very, very important. People need to be encouraged to do well, and people need to feel that they want to strive towards recognition, not necessarily of themselves, but of the influence they can have on others around them.

Is there a personal experience of unemployment, or employing people, that has really given you some insight into that issue?
Well, I came from a family where dollars were very, very short, and I saw my mother, who was not really trained for any kind of work that was pleasurable or enjoyable, have to work in the most unattractive, menial kinds of jobs while she was mothering six children. And I suppose it really instilled in me a determination that, come what may, I was going to gain the knowledge, gain the skills at a fairly young age, that would put me on a path to having better control over my financial wellbeing. Watching the struggles of my mother, and also – I didn't marry until I was 28, I helped her – I had quite a substantial burden of assisting with my younger sisters and brother, *so* I suppose those things gave me a determination in life. There's another little cliche that's often used in selling circles: 'If it is to be, it's up to me'.

Is there an acceptable level of unemployment?
I wouldn't use the word acceptable, but I think there is an *inevitable* level of unemployment; there will continue to be some people who are unemployable for one reason or another. I believe communities have to be aware that there always is going to be a percentage of people in genuine need who must be cared for, and there are people who will not work for their own personal reasons. One of the dangers in education, even though I am a very strong supporter of the need for education, is that sometimes it propels people into unrealistic areas, where if they're trained to be an astronaut and they cannot find employment as an astronaut because there are very few, they won't do anything else. And that is a great danger. We're probably not training enough people to be *practical,* basically, and we're not training in some of the trades, while we're over-catering in other areas. So I think there needs to be a more meaningful balance.

A work-for-the dole scheme or national service, do you see that there could be an advantage at all in schemes of this nature?
Look, in principle I like it. I don't like the compulsion, unless you get to the view that there are people who are just bone lazy and want to live off the community, but I really am offended on behalf of people who are struggling to raise a family and have to pay taxes. I don't mind for people on higher incomes, but when the average family person pays a high percentage of tax to support somebody who is disinclined to help themselves, I find that difficult to accept. I don't believe in

compulsory participation, I would like it to be seen as an *opportunity*, but if you don't take that opportunity and you go too long without helping yourself in another direction, then you don't get society's assistance. So I think you give people an option for a period of time.

And you see such schemes as potentially offering a strong advantage?
I think there is no question that people who have nothing to do fill their time doing nothing. Once again it's the self-esteem issue. If you get people into a situation where they can be involved with people who are optimistic and energetic, where they know they're acquiring skills, that gives them the confidence to go on and it breaks the laziness barrier. It's very human to be lazy; that's a reality for most people. The less you have to do, the less you do. I mean all these old cliches are based on truisms.

What is education? Is it a matter of sitting in a classroom? Is it a matter of work experience or a traineeship or whatever? Is it basic skills? How do you balance that?
It's a well-rounded transfer and absorption of both knowledge and experience. Education is developing understanding, education is developing wisdom, education is developing skills and knowing how to implement those skills, education is developing a level of comfort in people, being comfortable with themselves and also, rather than just specialisations, developing basic life skills. Lots of people, in my observation, come out of the formal education system without basic life skills.

What role did formal classroom education play in your life?
Only up to the Intermediate Certificate. I attended school until I was 16, I went from the Intermediate Certificate into Fourth Form. In those days you did Fifth Year Leaving and did your matriculation in Fifth Year and went on to university. I actually left school to assist my father – he ran a small suburban newspaper and I left school at 16, when I had spent only a couple of months in Fourth Form – to assist him. So the only qualification I have is an Intermediate Certificate.

Was there something you learnt at the newspaper that enthused you, that you may not have found in the classroom?
I spent only a year doing that, and then I moved on to be employed in the Imperial Services. One of the things I learnt in junior high school was bookkeeping principles, so I went into clerical office management work there, and I moved on to the National Cash Register Company, training people to use bookkeeping machines and cash register machines. I worked in both of those divisions and I learnt a great deal in terms of skills and business methods and relating to people in that phase of my career, from about 20 to 23, and then I went on to become the first manager of Centacom Employment Agency. And that gave me great insights into people's needs and skills and interaction with business, and from there I went on to start my own business. 

I just want to add this, going back to what I was saying earlier. I believe learning is a lifelong experience and I am a prolific reader. I get involved in all sorts of things, a wide variety of things, which have all contributed to learning throughout life.

Are education opportunities plentiful and well distributed, socio economically, in Australia? And what will be the impact of increased 'up-front' fees in universities?
I think that they're reasonably well distributed. It could be better, and until you reach Utopia things could always be better. In terms of up-front fees, I believe some form of fee structure has to be considered because society cannot continue to support the level of education we may all desire. But by the same token I think there should be broad consideration for those who do have skills and are genuinely needy; maybe in some of those situations the entrance criteria could be reconsidered.

I must say it's a very complex and difficult question, because I really don't like the thought of excluding anybody with ability. But I do not think higher education facilities need to be a parking place for people who have no idea what they want to do and basically are using it as a temporary sort of – what should I say? pause in their lives. If we can devise ways to give access to those who genuinely want to use that training for very beneficial purposes and not those who want to be trained as teachers, knowing that we have an over-abundance of teachers and there is every likelihood they will never be employed as teachers and aren't prepared to do anything else. These are some of the dangers I think we have to consider very carefully.

Is Australia a racist nation?
Absolutely not, absolutely positively not. And some of the people who have been most prolific in their condemnation of Australia are the most racist nations you can think of. Without quoting specifically, I mean you would know exactly which I'm talking about. Many of our near neighbours are very discriminatory against their own populations – it's a joke for Australia to be called a racist nation. Every nation has its quota of extremists and we have a relatively small quota, but because we have freedom of expression and freedom of the press, those people have a high profile, one that is disproportionate to the influence they have. There's no question we've got our share of rednecks who have racist attitudes but they're a small percentage. Australians are very generous and very tolerant.

If your child had a drug habit, would you like her or him treated as a criminal or as an ill person requiring treatment?
Well obviously if it was one of my children I'd have to say as an ill person. Now I can say with some degree of satisfaction that I have four adult children who haven't had any such problem, despite the fact that I've been largely an absentee mother, because I've worked and travelled all of their lives. As a general statement of the community, I think it is an illness. Trafficking is a totally different thing and I would be very harsh in that regard, as I would with certain other categories of crime. For

those who become unsuspecting addicts I would be as supportive and as caring as I possibly could be, and I think that society should have that attitude.

The solutions we've adopted over the last 20 years don't appear to have worked. Do you think it's time we consider looking at ideas that are different, 'outside the box'?

Always. There's never a time when we shouldn't look 'outside the box' or outside the circle. Because what was available in terms of knowledge and understanding 20 years ago is very different from what there is today, and that will always be so. We should never have a closed mind to any new development. It's a question of looking at a scheme, seeing whether it has practical and rational application. If it does, let's try it, if it's affordable, and let's go for it.

Would a trial program, if it was controlled and the idea was to get people off drugs, be a problem?

Well, it would be a worthwhile objective, wouldn't it, to get people off drugs. I think one other way in which we can address it is to really make it not so attractive for those who are looking to make substantial amounts of money from it. So we have to look at ways in which we can diminish the attractiveness of it, and not have as many people looking at it as a good money-earning business.

Would you go as far as legalising it and giving it out to addicts, saying 'you can have it for nothing'?

Under strict controls, I basically would, although I wouldn't expect, if I were an addict, that you would give it to me for the next 50 years. And I would expect to be subject to some kind of disciplines, undertakings that may be required. Look, it must be a partnership. It can't be that one is taken on as a hopeless case.

So as long as the idea was to eventually get you off the drug?

Oh absolutely, yes.

Is tax reform desirable, that is, some sort of consumption tax? What do you see as the primary concerns that would need to go with that?

It's all a matter of what we call it. Whether we call it a consumption tax, or a GST, or VAT, or sales tax, we have a consumption tax right now. But it's absorbed below the line so people don't know the amount of consumption tax they're paying.  I think it's reasonable to put it above the line, so people know exactly what tax they are paying on goods and services. Right now, people don't think about the tax they pay on their motor cars, because they don't know. If you de-complicate the tax system for business, that has to be a forward step, because we have a very complicated tax system. The average person in business, unless they employ an expert, they can't keep up with the amendments to the Tax Act. Whatever we do, basically we should not increase tax *per se*, but reduce the compliance cost and really look to using taxes more effectively. Other than the cost of administration, a GST has to be a forward step.

Do you think our tax system serves us effectively?
No. I don't think it serves the government and I don't think it serves the people.

Should Australia be a republic, and if so, why would anyone care?
I think there are people who have strong emotional ties with our history and with what was. But their number is diminishing as each generation goes off to their 'just reward', whatever that may be, and a few years down the track you will not have too many people with those strong emotional ties. But to try and change something while a big proportion of people have those ties, that's what is causing anxieties. I don't think there is any question that in time we will be a republic. From my own point of view, I don't see it as imperative for Australia, I don't think it's a major contemporary issue. I really don't much mind if the majority votes we should have one, but I don't think the issue should be given the kind of profile and priority it currently has. There are far more important things to be addressed.

Can you see it happening before the year 2000?
It could. I think you would probably have about the same proportion very strongly for and very strongly against, and there will be a percentage in the middle. Whichever way it goes, we'll all adjust.

Can you imagine, or have you seen, a situation where voluntary euthanasia would be a good option to have?
That is a very difficult one. I would have to say that I'm right in the middle on that. I can see all the dangers in terms of how it could be abused. I'm also very sympathetic to the view that we cannot take life into our own hands and I have a Christian belief.

Thank you very much for your time.

Bruce Ruxton

Returned & Services League

'Honour the work'

BRETT KELLY: *I'm here this morning with Mr Bruce Ruxton, the State President of the RSL in Victoria, which has 60,000 members. What decade were you born in, Mr Ruxton?*

BRUCE RUXTON: What decade? ... the 1920s.

Would you briefly run through your educational background?
Yes, Melbourne High School through to Leaving Honours, then the army, then RMIT [Royal Melbourne Institute of Technology] after the war.

Would you briefly outline your career history?
I was in the army until the beginning of 1949 because I went to Japan for three years. I came home. I was in England for three years. Then I went into business with my father until about 1986. And then the RSL full time, unpaid.

Is there an idea, person or event that had the single most profound influence on your life to date?
You mean people who have influenced me?

Yes, was there somebody who particularly influenced you, or an idea?
My mother influenced me a lot; she was a strong influence on me. My first wife died eight years ago. I just can't think of anyone else who has been an influence on me. I've been sort of a lone ranger until my marriage last year.

What was the motivation to go into the army?
Well, the war was on and boys were leaving school and enlisting. Some would be dead by the end of the following year.

Is there a motto, quote or thought that really sums up your approach to life? The Melbourne High School motto was 'Honour the work'. I think I've done that, I've worked hard all my life.

What are the most critical issues for Australia in the next decade?
Well, there are two things. I think that employment is paramount, and immigration.

What are the best things about Australia as a nation today?
We've definitely got the best country on earth. I haven't been to another country – and I've been right round the world – better than this place. We're hell bent on wrecking it for some reason or another. We live in the best climate you could ever wish for, even Melbourne's climate. People don't own overcoats. We have everything running for us, only we're shooting ourselves in the foot all the time.

Are there a couple of things you see as the main things we're shooting ourselves in the foot over?
I think, looking back over the years, there is a hell bent rush to become a republic. Immigration. There would be no Pauline Hansons if governments had adhered to the wishes of the overwhelming majority of Australians over the past 25 years; she wouldn't be about. The other thing is employment. It's tragic that young people can't get a job in this country. And I believe that they're determined to have no tariffs, duties or subsidies by the year 2005, which will cause this country to have another million unemployed.

Have you any experience of being unemployed?
No.

You've never been unemployed? Have you ever done a job that you really didn't like, or done something to get by?
No, no, I used to work hard when I was young. Even going to school I used to work hard.

So what was your first job? Did you have a paper run or something like that?
Yes I did paper rounds, I've sold papers on street corners, I've mowed lawns in the streets, I've delivered bread on Saturday mornings, and I've caddied and I've duck dived for golf balls – which was quite an income in those days.

Have you found rewards in work that are beyond the money that you were paid for the work you did?
Well, as I told you, there's no money in being president of the RSL.

So what are the things that you get out of the job that make it worthwhile?
I help the veterans who go into hospitals and the like. I help them with their repatriation matters. There's a lot of things we get satisfaction out of in the RSL.

Do you believe that Australia is a racist country?
I think usually Australians treat people as they find them. I think that has always been on. There's always been a bit of a ridicule, you know, even between Australian and British soldiers. But on that point, I do believe that each country should be allowed to maintain their own race. We are Caucasian, I think we should leave it at that. We've never said 'no' or barred anyone coming in, but I think that the percentage coming in from Asia is far too high and I've been screeching it now, what, since the early 1980s.

Does your attitude to immigration make you a racist?
It certainly doesn't.

Do you have anything against those groups?

I've had a Malay boy live at my place for two years. I've had an Indian boy for nine months and at different times I've had indigenous people from New Guinea at my place.

What role has formal classroom education and training played in your life?

Education wasn't paramount when I was young. You could get a job, depending on what sort of job you wanted. The war certainly interrupted a lot of people's career education. A lot couldn't settle down afterwards, even though education was handed to us on a plate under rehabilitation. But as is quite obvious now, we live in a high tech world, we live in a computerised world, and if young people aren't up with it they are going to struggle.

Are these educational opportunities plentiful and well distributed?

I think the opportunities are tremendous today. Only a select few could go to the university when I was a boy. Very few. You know, you had to have parents with reasonable means. So the university was out for most.

If your child had a drug habit, would you want a society that viewed them as a criminal or as an ill person requiring treatment?

Certainly I'm totally opposed to the heroin trial. To me it's like giving a bottle of whisky to an alcoholic every day. Does that answer your question?

Yes and no. Further than the actual trial, should we be looking 'outside the box' for a new solution to the drug problem?

I suppose there's a case to treat the users carefully. This is sort of a subject I don't understand. But the drug pushers, as far as I'm concerned – hang them. Those two Australians in Malaysia couldn't have cared less for the lives they would wreck.

Is tax reform desirable?

Certainly. I'm all for the GST.

Do you think that it would be beneficial to your constituents?

If it is equitable, and provided there is a safety net for pensioners. I believe that it's got to happen. David Lange, the former prime minister of New Zealand, who is a friend of mine, said that Hewson was an idiot. He said, 'What we did in New Zealand was to bring the GST in after we were elected.' And that's exactly what he did. And it's worked satisfactorily in New Zealand, it's worked admirably.

In 1995 I led a large group of people through Borneo and all over South-East Asia, and one of them died on the way. It's a long story, but we had to bring his body over from Borneo to Singapore. The Singapore Casket Company handled the funeral. After fixing up all the details, I later got an urgent ring at the hotel – they'd forgotten to put the bloody VAT on the funeral account! I had to go back and pay another 60-odd Singapore dollars. So they don't miss much over there.

***What do you think the issues of the GST are for older Australians, retired people,
pensioners?***

What I'm saying is this. Provided that all the other taxes are eliminated, it may not
be all that much different from what we are purchasing now, particularly with food.
Now I don't know what they have in mind about food this time. Hewson let food off
the hook. Whether that's going to happen or not I don't know, but most other
places include food. But I do believe that Australians are going to be much better
off. Much better off.

Do you feel that Australia will ever be a republic?

Inevitability is not in my dictionary. If you're brainwashed long enough with the press
and so forth it seems that way, but if people take the whole issue of the constitutional
monarchy and the republic, if they take it and really read about it, I think they'll
change their minds.

All we hear now is that we have got to have an Australian head of state.
You hear it from Turnbull, Keneally, all the brains, and they don't say how they're
going to do it. Is the president going to be like the US president? Responsible
to the executive and not the legislature? Or like France where the president
shares it with the prime minister? Or like Ireland and Germany that only have a
ceremonial president? They haven't come out and told us what they want.

***Should the president be elected by elected Members of Parliament, rather than by
the Australian people?***

That's what they're proposing. The republican movement has been fighting among
themselves over it. But I think that's the consensus.

Is the Australian system of government superior to those other republics
you've mentioned – France, Ireland and America?

I don't see why we want to undo the system of government that has made
this country the most free country on earth. I believe we are freer than America.
Their Constitution was formed on mistrust and ours is on trust. And if you heard
Gore Vidal – he's a very famous US writer – on television when he was in Australia
recently, he reckons the US is the most corrupt place on earth. Who wants to
follow the American line? No one! I've debated with them all – please pick out
a republic which is the role model – and they can't do it. Sometimes they shift
on a view. I mean bloody Germany has been a democracy for 50 years, that's all.
Germany wouldn't know what democracy was until after World War Two. We're
one of the longest standing democracies on earth and I think we should leave
it that way. Safeguards, they're there for the individual.

Just take the flag. They are in trouble, the republican movement. Turnbull
made a statement that we've got to divorce the flag from the republic debate.
That is the greatest load of bullshit that I've ever heard in my life. It's the Union
Jack in the flag that's killing them. Killing them! If we were a republic today, I
would suggest that the flag would have gone last night. And I'll stick by it.

Should the republic and the flag be considered together?
They will be.

Could you imagine a situation where the option of voluntary euthanasia might be desirable?
Let's start at the beginning. The RSL nationally ruled against euthanasia, and supported the prime minister and the bill outlawing the practice in the Northern Territory that has now become law. Personally, I'm against euthanasia. Life's too precious as far as I'm concerned. That's paramount thinking with me. Not on religious grounds. Secondly, a lot of people trust doctors. I know doctors, I tend to think about some criminals out there that I trust more, you know. I think if we're going to follow the Dutch line it'll be disastrous. Palliative care is pretty good these days. I suppose it's a hard decision, but those people who are hell bent on wanting to die, why don't they commit suicide and leave it at that? If you give them a gun they won't pull the trigger. They want someone else to do it for them. No, I don't know. Someone's got to convince me yet about euthanasia. Of course there is a large religious argument, mainly from the Catholic Church, which I support, I suppose.

I think Christianity is based on life, anti-abortion and such. I'm antiabortion and I'm anti-euthanasia. See, before the war, if a bloke got a girl in trouble, he took her to one of these doctors that used to practise illegally. I could name a few. The bloke used to pay the doctor to fix the girl up, he paid the coppers, everyone was getting a share and everyone was happy. But I don't know about legalised abortion where you start to queue up and run clinics. This country, at present, its increase in population is only through immigration and that's wrong. Our natural birth rate is level and that's terrible, it really is.

The High Court ruled on Aboriginal land rights in its Wik and Mabo decisions. Now the government has turned around, Mr Howard has got a Ten Point Plan to deal with the outcomes of that. What do you see as the desirability, on the one hand of the actual rulings, and on the other hand of the government's plan?
Let's say if I was prime minister now, just been elected, I'd repeal the Native Title Act completely. I'd put a new one in place to look after those Aborigines still living in tribal conditions. I saw some on television last night, you know, just with a bit of a g-string and a spear, and one was putting a kangaroo over his shoulder. I think those people have got to be looked after in their native habitat, but as for all this absolute baloney that's going on about sacred sites and land rights and so on – no.

There are a lot of socialists-cum-do-gooders sitting on the High Court bench. The government has got every right to change a decision of the High Court. I wouldn't give them parking time, most of those judges. All except Sir Daryl Dawson. I wouldn't give any of them time, including the incumbent governor-general. As far as I'm concerned, if I was prime minister this afternoon, he'd be gone by next morning. OK.

Thank you very much for your time.

John Symond

CEO, Aussie Home Loans

'When God gives you a gift he wraps it in a problem, and providing you're strong enough to get rid of the wrapping, the rewards will be yours'

BRETT KELLY: *Is there an idea, person, or event that had the single most profound impact on your life and where you are now?*

JOHN SYMOND: It would be when everything in my life went bust, in the late '80s. That period of crisis in my personal life carried through I suppose for three or four years, and it started about 1989 – this was before a stroke, before Aussie Home Loans. Certainly the first couple of years of Aussie Home Loans were very traumatic, to keep the company going, to make sure it survived – which fortunately has happened – and now Aussie Home Loans is a very significant, vibrant and dynamic organisation doing good things for the community and it's great. But that was when everything went bust in business and broke the family, or the marriage I should say, and I lost everything financially, facing bankruptcy. I wasn't declared bankrupt but I still lost everything and so that was a very important event in my life, that really made me refocus on myself and the future. It changes the priorities in one's life.

Is there a motto, quote or thought that really summarises your approach to life?
Yes. There were plenty of times when I had to ask myself, am I trying to achieve something that's just out of reach? Am I being stupid? And certainly I learnt that you never ever give up, if you believe in something and you believe in yourself, you never give up. I look at my situation and you know from having lost personal wealth of $10-$15 million, and still owing $3 million after I sold off all my stuff, had I given up I wouldn't be in this position, I wouldn't have created Aussie Home Loans, I would probably still be in my former financial services business. I think we all go through periods of life when terrible events happen, but you don't give up, you never know what's around the corner. There's a favourite saying of mine, 'when God gives you a gift he wraps it in a problem, and providing you're strong enough to get rid of the wrapping, the rewards will be yours'.

What are the best things about Australia?
I think the best things in Australia are its freedom and the opportunity it offers those who really want to embrace that opportunity and take advantage of it.

Do you think there are things we can really be doing better?
Sure. I think the work ethic in this country isn't as good as many other countries, and I think the industrial relations laws inhibit us from improving that. I think average Australians are prepared to work hard providing they are amply rewarded and providing they know they can't rort the system, so I think ... you know, I go by the old saying, 'success is brought about by 90 percent perspiration and 10 percent inspiration'. And we really are not a high work ethic country. We are in a comfort zone; we take things for granted such as freedom and opportunity. To have unemployment where it is today is absolutely ridiculous, and it shouldn't be where it is, but it's because of attitude in the community – particularly a lot of the youth, their attitude is, I've got a degree in arts and I'm not going to get a job at

Hungry Jack's, as was on the '60 Minutes' program. Did you see that? I mean, that's just pathetic. You know, I went to eleven schools, two universities, and during high school I worked part-time jobs wherever, they were stepping stones. Some young people think they are going to get the pinnacle job of their lives as their first job, and I mean that's ridiculous; that attitude is very poor.

Is there an experience of unemployment, your own or that of a friend or family member, that has really given you an insight into the issue?

When I kicked off Aussie Home Loans I looked around and I could see that for young people and the other end of the spectrum – people in their 40s or late 30s – it was nearly impossible for them to get a job. And one of the satisfying things about Aussie Home Loans was trying to create employment for those who really felt it was nearly impossible to get a job. We are currently employing about 50 new full-time staff every month, and the last three years our staff has grown from about 80 people to 800. And having viewed unemployment as bad as it was, particularly when I was down on the mat myself, not completely out but looking that way, I really understood how important employment was for family lifestyles and keeping families together. That's why we have no hesitation in employing as aggressively and as rapidly as we do. I just think it gives young people, especially, a chance and those that have been retrenched, it gives them a hope that there's still a life when you are 40 and above.

Are there rewards in work apart from the monetary compensation?

What I try to give my people, other than financial rewards, is self-esteem, it's career, it's opportunity. Aussie Home Loans is starting to diversify in terms of giving you challenge, because you know if you leave your mind inactive it gets rusty, it just gets bogged down, you are in a rut. If you have stimulating employment with a challenge, particularly if you're with an organisation that's dynamic and it's achieving like we've achieved, not just a large team but impacting on a community in such a positive way, where the average household is saving hundreds of dollars every month because of us, it's absolutely fantastic – it's just not a job and a pay package.

Is there an acceptable level of unemployment in Australia?

There's always going to be unemployment in any country, because there's certain sectors of people who really don't want to be employed, but I would think around the 4 to 5 percent mark. We are currently at about 8.1 percent – and I am fearful this figure will get worse before it gets better.

What do you think of the idea of national service or some sort of work-for-the-dole scheme, could these schemes have benefits?

I really do think so, because not only does it raise people's self-esteem because they feel that they are actually contributing, it introduces a discipline that you don't just go on the dole and be encouraged not to work. I think it's critical to have work-for-the-dole, but I am not in favour of people being forced into these schemes – I'm not in favour of that, they should have the option. A lot of young people would benefit from training and discipline and opportunity. Some form of optional national service, alternatively work-for-the-dole, I think that would be excellent. Also I really believe that structural tax reform will help the whole country.

Is tax reform, including a GST, desirable?
No, a consumption-based tax is part of the solution, only part of the solution. It won't survive, it won't succeed, if it's just a consumption-based tax. It's really got to be a lower tax threshold plus a well-designed consumption-based tax. I mean, user pay, but having regard for the elderly and disadvantaged.

Do you think that our current tax system really encourages people to create wealth?
Definitely not. There is no incentive at all. In fact, we work long hours here, and we've got staff who work long hours, but they say really, financially, it's not worth them doing it. Because they might work an extra 25 percent and end up with a 5 percent increase in their pay packet – they'd be better to spend the time with their family and friends. It's definitely a disincentive at the moment.

What are your primary concerns with any tax reform agenda?
My main concern is, government needs to address tax reform as a matter of urgency. The current system is not working and is stifling productivity.

In your experience, is Australia a racist nation?
No, not at all. Every year we are growing to be a more multicultural country. A young country like Australia, it couldn't survive if we just relied on Anglo-Saxons to pick it up and get it moving. The country is too big, the opportunity is too great. The country can't achieve greatness going into the 21st century without a growing population, and really that can't occur without migration. But I don't believe Australia as a nation is racist in any way.

Is education necessarily classroom based, university and so on?
As I said before, I went to two universities and eleven schools. I believe I received my best education in life, growing up in a very close family environment of parents and seven kids. My parents were a very hard-working couple, the kids chipped in, helping in the back of the fruit shops, learning my parents' work ethic, seeing how they treated their customers, how they took pride in running small businesses, fruit shops. That seven-day-a-week work ethic, and understanding about customer care and customer needs at a very young age, from primary school, I think that was more powerful education than just going through high school and university.

My father, in fact, because of family circumstances, had hardly any education. He had to help his father who migrated from Lebanon and worked in country towns. So formal education is a help, but it is not the answer in isolation.

Do you think the increase in 'up-front' fees for courses is really going to help the best and brightest get into those universities?

The old system of the best and brightest, there is a strong argument for that. But if it's on an exception basis, where if a family is desperate to put someone through university, providing that person meets the minimum standard and doesn't crawl into the system, if they are prepared to spend a lot of money and if the facilities are there, and as long as they are not keeping someone else out, I think they should be allowed access.

In the sense that you have across the board 'up-front' fees, that everyone has to pay for access to a university course?

This comes down to what the country, the consumers, can afford – it comes back to a fair, sustainable tax system. If all the money goes out of your pay packet you can't pay up-front fees for education. If there were broad structural reform, with everything on a more fair basis, they wouldn't have to introduce fees up front. The only reason they're doing that is something is out of kilter, so they're putting their hand up for money again. And there's a lot of areas like that, where they are forced to get money because there isn't enough money to keep the system going. I think the system is wrong, fundamentally – the whole tax system and savings system in this country is wrong. When I spoke about tax reform earlier, that also encompasses savings reform as well. And I really think it comes back to that. User pays mostly works, except in education it really should not be a crippling fee. It must be an affordable up-front fee, and it can't be a disincentive. I mean, in an educated society we need kids to go through university. If we cripple them, we'll pay for it down the line.

If your child had a drug habit, would you want a society that viewed them as a criminal or as an ill person requiring treatment?

It depends on where the drug habit lies. Is it a drug pedlar or someone who is just weak, a drug user who got sucked into the scene? If they are drug users I think they all should be treated as ill persons requiring treatment, but if they extend beyond that to the point of being drug pedlars, I think they should be treated as criminals.

The drug problem has become immeasurably worse over the last 20 years. Is it time that we sat down and looked at other potential solutions?

I think we've got to look at _all_ solutions. With these new approaches, you run small trials, small tests. You've got to try everything, because this is just a monster problem. You can't say it's black or it's white, I think you've really got to look everywhere for  a solution.

Will Australia ever be a republic, and why would anyone care?

I don't feel strongly either way on this because I'm looking at what the effect or change will really be on the country. I guess probably all countries end up wanting their own image, and for that reason Australia will eventually become a republic. It's really a self-image issue. I don't think it's constraining our success, it's not stopping us from being a better country. It is purely about perception, and I guess I can see some merit there, but it's not any big deal. I can think of more pressing problems in society that need addressing more urgently than the republic issue.

Could you imagine a situation where the option of voluntary euthanasia might be compassionate or desirable?

There probably is a role. You just can't have it unilaterally, where you get some patients that handle illness better than others. But in a case where you have at least two independent doctors who say, look, there's nothing more that can be done, you're going to die and you are going to go through tremendous suffering ... I think there's an argument that it's fair to give people that choice.

On Aboriginal land rights, particularly the Wik and Mabo decisions, but at the level that the Howard Government has a Ten Point Plan to deal with the rulings of the High Court, do you think a government should be trying to circumvent a judgement of the High Court?

I think judges, like any other person, can make mistakes – or may not necessarily make mistakes but may not be accurate or correct. Whether Mabo is correct or incorrect, I'm no expert in that area, but I do believe any democratically elected government should have the right to address any issue in a manner in which they see fit. I don't think that the High Court should be running the country.

The government has a Ten Point Plan to deal with Aboriginal land rights, should they also have a ten point plan clearly communicating to people what their aims are for the future of the country?

Governments and politicians have a terrible reputation for broken promises and I don't believe the public would take any notice of a ten point national plan because it really would have no meaning. Politicians seem to be able to promise things they don't deliver and nothing happens – if my business did that we'd be in breach of the law and would suffer the consequences. I think there is unfortunately a cynical view of governments and politicians; they seem to forget what they've promised at election time and they deliver something different thereafter.

Thank you very much for your time.

Arthur Tunstall

Secretary Treasurer, Australian Commonwealth
Games Association

'Every day's a challenge'

BRETT KELLY: *Was there an idea, event or person that had the single most profound effect on the person you are or where you've ended up?*

ARTHUR TUNSTALL: Probably the gentleman hanging on the wall up there, who was the mayor of Woollahra when I was very young; my good friend Les Duff started me off in the sports world, and I think he was the gentleman who really gave me the idea of continuing and maybe achieving some outstanding position in sport.

Is there a motto, quote or thought that best summarises your approach to life?
'Every day's a challenge.'

What are the most critical issues that you see for Australia in the next decade?
The most critical thing is to get our unemployed people into a position where they'll feel more secure. The way the government is going, taking the tariffs off everything, we'll be unable to compete with the rest of the world eventually.

What do you see as the best things about Australia today?
The fact that we live in the greatest country in the world. When I'm asked overseas where I come from I always say, God's country. I do travel a lot, I've seen a lot of countries in my time, and I still believe that Australia is the best. We still have a certain amount of freedom of speech – certainly not as much as we did before. I think the political correctness idea has gone too far. People should be able to express their opinion without being attacked or victimised.

What are the things that we could do better?
The fact that you can't express your opinion without being attacked and being called a racist or some sort of other name.

What role do you think euthanasia might play in Australia in the 21st century?
I believe that if a person is suffering that badly there should be some bell that they can turn off themselves. I read a lot about it and I feel there could be cases where people might say, well, this is a good way to get rid of Mum or Dad and get their money. I think it should be left to the individual person. I saw my mother die with an incurable disease and I know what it's like to see people suffering. So it should be their choice and they should be able to do it without any fear at all.

Is employment necessarily something that has to do with hours or satisfaction or is there some other notion of employment that you think is most realistic?
I started when I was 14, working 40 hours a week in a factory. I don't think hard work does anybody any harm. There's plenty of jobs around this country if you want to take them, the real problem is that most young people want to start off as the manager of the company without working their way through that company.

So you were prepared to do the hard yards, so to speak?
I've done it in my time. Hard times, real hard times.

The current unemployment rate is 8.6 percent. Do you see that as being an acceptable level of unemployment in Australia?
Under the present conditions 8 percent might sound a lot but the fact is that it could be reduced, and I support the government in their idea of not paying the dole without doing some work for it. I've always believed that to get the dole you should go to your local council where you get your cheque and the council has the right to say, OK we are paying you union rates which in actual fact is twenty-five hours' work a week, therefore I want you six people to go down and clean the park, I want you six people to go somewhere else … I think the community should be getting something in return for the money that's being paid to those people from the taxes which are being imposed on the people who are working.

Are there any suggestions you could make, either for the government or for an unemployed person, that might help alleviate unemployment?
It comes back to your own initiative. I've just come back from Indonesia where there's no social security – if you're not doing something or selling something then you're going to starve. And that brings out initiative or enterprise in people which I think Australians do not use. We're a bit lazy. A lot of young people have knuckled down and made a success of their life, I don't see why everybody else can't do it.

What do you see as racism, and do you feel that Australia is a racist nation?
No, I don't think Australia is a racist nation. I explained to the minister, when he came to see me after the last Commonwealth Games, that he should realise and so should his colleagues that the laws they're passing are discriminatory against the white people in this country. And the more he gives to the Aboriginal people the more he divides this country. I mean, when I was young, Aboriginals were part of our way of life, but today it seems to me that a lot of people are saying 'the bastards are getting everything' and the more they ask for the more the government gives them. I think the government's a little bit gutless myself in not taking a stand.

So you think that there is potential for division?
The government has created division in the country by saying, we want you to do this and we want you to do that, and the Aboriginals call for the old thing, give me back my land. I think that both parties can work in harmony with each other. I've been taking Aboriginal boys away with me for the last 40 years and I've never ever had any trouble with them. A lot of them tell me, the older people tell me, that it's  the radicals that cause all the trouble. And that's a fact of life.

Do you think that the government's Ten Point Plan in relation to Aboriginal land rights, which effectively looks to overrule the High Court's decision, do you think that's really in the spirit of accepting the umpire's decision?

No. One of the problems is that the white population is being told that we did a terrible thing 200 years ago. I don't think this generation should be responsible for what happened 200 years ago. It's not the only country that was ever taken over, every country in the world's been taken over at some time or another – even England was taken over by the Romans. I think the fact is that Australians and Aboriginals can live together ... maybe I should say that everyone in Australia can live together. As I said, I don't have any trouble with the Aboriginal people I know. But as far as giving back the land is concerned, they had it for 40,000 years, they didn't do anything with it, and now that it's been built into cities they want to claim it back because it's worth a lot of money. Somebody had to discover Australia – we're all lucky it was England.

What do you see as being education and what role has formal classroom education and training played in your success?

I don't think schooling ever played any part in my life because I never liked it. It was the happiest day in my life when I left – I left school on the Friday, I was 14 on the Saturday and I started work on the Monday. I was even working when I was 12 years old because I didn't have any money and neither did my parents and the only way you're going to get it is either with your hands or with your brains. I didn't have too many brains at 12 and that's why I was working and that's why I started in the factory as a messenger boy.

And the same opportunity is there for anybody today, but as I said they feel that they are lowering their standards. I heard somebody say on television that they wouldn't take a job at McDonald's, they'd rather live off the government – that means that they'd rather live off the honest people who pay their taxes. There's jobs available if they want to work, and if they've got the initiative they can get on.

Do you think that educational opportunities are necessarily in a classroom or is life experience critical?

The school system is quite good if you've got the brains to sit down and decide what you want to be later on in life. But there's too many people that have been over-educated today. The only real education is out in the marketplace.

Are you against the idea of government-operated drug trials?

I've read a fair bit about it, and I was always of the belief that if you tell an Australian that beer's going to be short, he'll rush down and buy two cartons straight away. It's the same with pornographic literature – I can remember when that was banned but you could always buy it under the counter. The same thing applies here in this situation if you're going to give heroin to people to try and break their habits. I read about two people who were on methadone rehabilitation who said that, instead of knocking an old lady down to get money for a hit, now they can just go into the heroin centre and get it whenever they feel like it, so they're not going to break their habit at all. But again, if people can get it easily, maybe they won't take it.

It seems to me that you start off smoking marijuana, then try this and try that – I've never tried it, but they tell me that once you get into it, it becomes a part of your life. So I'm beginning to think now that this trial is totally wrong. The only thing is that by giving it away it might make things a little bit difficult for the people at the very top of the tree who never get caught – maybe they will suffer because they won't be making the big money. No doubt *they* never want to see it happen that they give free heroin away.

What are your feelings as to the desirability or otherwise of a GST?

If you're an employee your taxes are taken out every week so you have no chance of beating the system. The big man will always beat the system, that's been proved time and time again. Look at the taxes that are paid by quite a few rich people, because they are registered offshore. Whether it's a Labor or a Liberal government, they need the support of these people, so they're not too anxious to pass any laws that will rope them into the tax system. And until they do, you will never have an equitable tax system. It's the working man who suffers every time.

Do you feel that there could be cash businesses that don't pay their taxes?

Let's face it, there'll always be people who have cash and there'll always be people who are going to take it. If they can get away with it, that's their good luck. After all laws are made to be beaten, or so I'm told, that's why these people employ high profile QCs to get around the law, to beat the system. And there'll always be somebody that will beat the system no matter which way you go. I think a GST looks pretty good, but again the big man will always beat you in some way through his company overseas. So you'll never catch him.

Will Australia ever be a republic? And, if yes, when might that happen?

I think the reason why there's not too much concern about a republic at the present moment is because people like me from Anglo-Saxon backgrounds have been brought up to respect the flag and the Queen. When I went to school the class had to stand every morning and say, 'I honour my God, I serve my King, I salute my flag'. That's gone today – we've got a multicultural society who don't really care whether we're a republic or a monarchy. And when the time comes, if it looks as though the majority of people are going to say we need a republic, these people will automatically follow. There's no tradition for young people to be brought up today with respect for the flag and the monarchy. Now the monarchy will probably change further down the track, but I can't see it happening until after 2000. I think  the interest in it has died.

Thank you very much for your time.

Malcolm Turnbull

Chairman, Australian Republican Movement

'Never take a backward step'

BRETT KELLY: *Is there an idea, person or event that had the single most profound influence on your life?*

MALCOLM TURNBULL: The person that had the most profound impact on my life was my father, but I can't think of an individual idea or event that I could single out. I don't believe I have had any blinding moment of self-realisation.

Is there a motto, quote or thought that really summarises your approach to life?
I'm a very positive person. It's very important to be on the front foot, to be proactive rather than reactive. I guess if there was a motto it would be, 'Never take a backward step'.

What are the most critical issues for Australia in the next decade?
In a sense all the issues are tied together. The most important is coming to terms with our place in the global economy, which of course has very considerable implications for employment. National governments, even the largest national governments, realise they have very little control over their own economy. The global economy is increasingly integrated and that integration is proceeding at a very rapid pace. You know, it is very hard for a government in Australia to pull the economic levers, to make the same kind of impact that they would have been able to make 20-odd years ago. Globalisation is a major issue. Issues that arise are ones relating to competition. We have to be more competitive, a more efficient society, and in seeking that we see a lot of less skilled jobs vanishing. And to the extent that new jobs are being created, they are not being created for the people that have lost their jobs.

I think for Australians to develop a clearer understanding of their destiny and their national identity is important – the republican issue that I've been associated with for some time is a very important one. I think that's now drawing to a successful conclusion, at least I hope it is.

Obviously the issue of Aboriginal reconciliation is one that seems to me to be very close to being resolvable, in terms of people's attitudes. But that solution seems to be eluding governments at the moment.

What do you see as the best things about Australia, and what do you think we can do better?
The best thing about Australia is that it's a very tolerant and egalitarian society – obviously it's not as tolerant as it could be or as egalitarian as it could be – but I think compared to other comparable democracies, our democracy is the best, because of our more tolerant society. In terms of things we could do better, I think we need to be prouder of ourselves, more committed to our country and to our fellow Australians. We tend to knock our country and ourselves too much. Australians could take a leaf out of the Americans' book and be a little bit more patriotic and proud of their country – and that again is one of the reasons why I'm such a keen republican.

Is there a personal experience, that of a friend, family member, somebody you've employed, that has given you a good understanding of the situation of unemployed people? Is there an inevitable level of unemployment?

I don't have a personal experience with unemployment, I've always been employed – or at least whenever I've wanted to be employed. I do recall getting fired once when I was working as a labourer in the city market, for being impertinent enough to ask for a raise. I was pretty fed up, working on a truck loading and unloading bananas.

The fundamental problem that we've got is that society is changing so rapidly, and many people's expectations in terms of employment are just vanishing. Nobody, nowadays, can seriously look forward to lifetime employment. What we should be looking for is lifetime employability, so instead of people joining a bank or the public service or a big company and saying, well I'm going to work here for 30 or 40 years, we've really now got to say, I need to have the skills that enable me to be employable throughout my life. And that involves a much more proactive approach than people have traditionally been brought up to have.

In terms of what's an acceptable level of unemployment, well I guess you could say zero, but any economist will tell you that even in what they call full employment, people will be unemployed – it's what is known as frictional unemployment. It is occasioned by people moving from job to job, or being laid off for one reason or another, and the time it takes them to get another job. The level of unemployment that I think is most troubling is not the national level, but the level among young people – that very high figure amongst school leavers, people 18 to 24. That's the thing that we've got to address. And the puzzling thing is that those young people are the people who are best able to be trained and best able to fit into the new information technology-based industries where jobs are being created.

Do you see any merit in the idea of work-for-the-dole or national service type schemes?

All those things can be good in the sense that they get people into the habit of working. A big problem is where people basically lose the habit of working and – bluntly – become slugs, get used to not having to do any work. But the fundamental problem is that unless these schemes are training people, it's just a short-term fix. You take people and you say, all right, you're going to build roads or plant trees or whatever. Unless there is a job for them building roads or planting trees, or the skills they have learnt there are going to be useful elsewhere, what have they gained? The answer is, probably nothing. So I think the focus should be on training rather than just providing tasks.

In your experience, is Australia a racist nation?

Well, some Australians are racist, but I don't think we are a racist nation. This is a very tolerant nation, overall. You can get in any society a range of views. You take Pauline Hanson: that is a phenomenon that has now just about died and she never had a significant percentage of support on any poll. Australians by and large are tolerant

and we are a tolerant country. I certainly think we are a lot more tolerant than most countries in this part of the world – or indeed generally.

What is education in this changing, moving world? What role do you see for formal classroom education?
What is education? I know what that means, but what role has formal classroom education played in my life? Well, a large role, because I've spent a lot of time in classrooms. I've got three university degrees, so I've spent a lot of time in universities. I think, however, the most effective method of teaching is an interactive approach, teaching in small groups, tutorial groups and so forth, with one teacher and three or four students. Sitting in a lecture hall just having a lecture read to you is pretty pointless, and educators are well advised to concentrate on developing and using technology to enable greater interactive opportunities.

Are educational opportunities plentiful and well distributed in Australia? And if universities are useful, should we be having huge 'up-front' fees?
Well, not plentiful or well distributed *enough* is the first answer.

Up-front fees for universities? There is a real problem here, because I personally think that the universities need to continue the trend of becoming more competitive with each other, more independent, more privatised. I do not have a problem with university fees at all, as long as people are not penalised because they are poor. I like the idea of students, particularly university students, being treated like consumers, so that they have some money – whether it is theirs from middle-class families, or is given in the form of a subsidy from the government if they are not well off, or a loan. I think they should have that power to be able to say to a university, in effect, we think your courses suck, we're going to spend our money somewhere else.

This does not necessarily mean you prejudice the worst off, as long as the government makes good, gives the less well off the economic power that they otherwise would not have. As long as the issues of social equity were properly addressed I think it would definitely improve quality in the universities. You only have to look at Bond University, which as a private university has had the most horrific problems, financial problems, problems over tenure and so forth. Notwithstanding that, and not withstanding that it's charging very substantial fees, it has a terrific following and its students do very well subsequently. The law students have a greater take-up rate in that profession than graduates of any other university. One of the reasons it's been popular is because they have turned around and said, well, instead of doing a law degree in three years, you can do it in two years and have fewer holidays. And why should people not be able to do that? Now you're just starting to see the larger universities react to that.

If your child had a drug habit would you want society to view them as a criminal or as an ill person requiring treatment?
Well clearly, as an ill person requiring treatment.

Is it time to examine solutions to the problem outside the conventional tactics employed over the last 20 years? Drug programs and the like?

I'm not an expert in this field, but what I would like to see is a non-emotional discussion, a rational, objective discussion on the whole issue of decriminalising drugs. I'm not in favour of people taking drugs. But I'm very conscious of the fact that we spend billions of dollars a year on law enforcement. We lock a lot of young people up for using drugs that are – at least in some sections of the community – effectively socially acceptable.

And it isn't working, it doesn't appear to be reducing the incidence of drug use. Now you've got to ask yourself, if you took those dollars and spent them on education would you get a better result? I think everybody is agreed on the end state, which is that people should not abuse drugs, but the question is, how do we get there? You've heard all the arguments, but I think this is something that needs to be addressed. The problem is, it's like so many issues – anyone who suggests the current system is not working is accused of being soft on drugs. They are *not* being soft on drugs, they're simply saying, let's have a look at some alternatives. I think it's very important to have a look at alternatives.

Is tax reform desirable?

Yes, of course it is desirable. I might say there is another issue in fiscal reform, because the taxes are raised to pay for government services and many government services can be delivered more efficiently, and then there would be less need to raise so much tax. I think there is a great deal of merit in a goods and services tax. The idea of taxing consumption in that way has been the received economic wisdom for at least 25 years, so Australia is very much out of step in not having a goods and services tax. It is one way of catching an enormous amount of tax avoidance. There's a huge black economy out there which is very unfair to those people who are not part of it and who are paying tax.

What are your primary concerns in any tax reform agenda?

There are some anomalies in our tax system which need to be straightened out – for example we don't have proper roll-over relief, when people sell assets for shares. If I sell a business or a company to another company in return for shares, and make a capital gain on paper – say I make $10 million capital gain on paper – I would have to pay the tax on that in cash. Now I don't have the cash unless I sell the shares I received, and I may not be able to sell them. So what you should be able to have is roll-over relief, which will encourage people to take their companies public, encourage transactions, make it easier to raise capital, all of which is good for business. And then in the final event people will at some point of the day cash out, and at that point you tax them. This sort of relief is common in most other countries, the United States being a good example, and it is quite bizarre that we don't have it. The other big negative is that capital gains tax is far too high.

Should Australia be a republic? If so, why? And when will it happen?
Of course. People have heard all this from me before, but it's clear to me that all of Australia's symbols and institutions should be unequivocally Australian. We need to be a prouder and more committed country, and we cannot develop and enhance Australia's nationhood if we have the monarch of the United Kingdom as our head of state, that's perfectly obvious. I think Australia will be a republic by 1 January 2001.

Has there been or could you imagine a situation where the option of voluntary euthanasia would be desirable?
I'm not sure if you asked me whether I've considered suicide or not?

No, I'm just sort of saying, in general, does voluntary euthanasia offend you as an option?
I would say it's something that's easy to accept in a philosophical sense. I can recognise that there are a lot of difficulties in legislating for it and plenty of opportunities for it to be abused.

Is the idea of the federal government using legislation to effectively circumvent the intention of the High Court a desirable precedent? How do you feel about this in relation to the native title issue?
The High Court decision is subject to the law too, it is subject to the Constitution and the laws of the Federal Parliament, at least in so far as those laws are not contrary to the Constitution. So there is nothing wrong with the Parliament changing the law and thereby circumventing a decision or abolishing a decision of the High Court.

As far as the native title issue is concerned, again I am profoundly disappointed that a solution has not been found. And at the moment the government has failed on native title to cut a deal that will satisfy all parties. Or at least to cut a deal that all parties will accept – they obviously all won't be satisfied.

Thank you very much for your time.

Robert Turner

CEO, The Smith Family

'There, but for fortune, goes you or I'

BRETT KELLY: *Is there an idea, person or event that has had the single most profound influence on your life?*

ROBERT TURNER: Yes, I'd say it was when I migrated from England with my family in the late 1940s, moving from a working-class background in a depressed part of England and coming to Australia. I think my life probably took off from there.

Do you think that left you with some sort of rapport with those worse off?
Oh yes, it certainly gave me an insight. I remember being very embarrassed about our big cabin trunks as they were called in those days; ours was the only one with ACT on it. Everybody else had NSW and QLD and I didn't have any idea what those initials meant – I thought that ACT indicated that we were the only people on board who were assisted migrants and everybody else was paying their way. From there, and living in migrant accommodation, yes, it gave me a great insight into the situation of people without money, and the personal trauma they experience.

Is there a motto, quote or thought that summarises your approach to life?
I suppose one that recurs particularly in this job is, 'There, but for fortune, goes you or I', because it certainly is very true – a large number of people say, if I hadn't been so lucky in my life I could easily be poor and alone today.

What are the most critical issues facing Australia in the next decade?
The growing disparity between the very well to do and the not so well off. The increasing accumulation of wealth at the top end of the market and diminution in what poor people have. That's one critical issue, and the other one is that I think we are stuck with unemployment at a fairly high level. How we manage that problem, and what we do with those people who in the past worked and now don't, and how they're treated, is crucial.

What are the best things about Australia today?
Well, it's a paradox really, you know, the best and the worst are closely related. Freedom – the freedom which we have in Australia. As I travel around the world, something I've done in my job, I'm aware of the freedom and openness of society here and the great opportunities that exist – but freedom can also mean poverty and hardship.

Are there things which you think we could do better?
Well, the opportunities are not as open as they should be. There should be a greater opening of doors of opportunity to people from poor backgrounds. I consider that we really have a wonderful country and I see lack of equal opportunity as a main threat.

What's your experience and understanding of unemployment?
We're confronting it every day. In this organisation we really do get a good cross-section of the community because we run a business ourselves as well as offering assistance to the unemployed. We employ 500 people in the business part of our organisation, and sometimes it's hard to fill job vacancies. We advertise them and we don't get people applying. On the other hand each month we see something like 15,000 families that are in very difficult circumstances because of the inability of the breadwinner to get work. Unemployment of youth and the unemployment of middle-aged people without many skills is a huge problem for society.

Is there a personal experience, either your own or that of a friend or relative, that has really given you an insight into unemployment?
Yes. I've never been unemployed – I'm 60 now and I've had a job since I was 11 and I've never been without one all through my whole life. My son and daughter who are now in their 20s had great difficulty in finding jobs when they left school – and they had the benefits of tertiary education and all of the advantages that middle-class Australians have. If they had been less well qualified, and hadn't had much family support, and lived in an area a long way from employment, it would have been even harder for them.

Have you found, particularly in an organisation like The Smith Family, rewards in your work apart from the cheque at the end of the week?
Oh, absolutely. I mean, nobody in The Smith Family simply works for the money. It's not that sort of organisation. We don't pay the sort of salaries that would keep people who are just interested in financial rewards. In my job, if I'm successful in a fund-raising event or in a commercial activity earning good profits, I can see the results in immediate help for people and scholarships, putting needy kids through school, housing for the elderly, all of those things. I have the great luxury of being able to see the result of my efforts, I'm a link in the chain.

Is there an acceptable level of unemployment?
That question can be viewed from a lot of angles. Of course there's an acceptable level of unemployment, because you always have a small percentage of mobile people going from one job to another, but I guess I'd have to say that the present level is unacceptable. Again I think what you mean by employment – full time, 40 hours a week, employment in a career – is increasingly a thing of the past. People are more mobile and move from job to job. Part-time work is common. People like me are dinosaurs. I've been with The Smith Family 34 years – that length of service doesn't happen very much any more. I think there has to be, even in a well-balanced economy like Australia, an acceptable level of unemployment, but unemployment now has to be looked at much more on a global basis. We can't go on living the life of luxury in Australia while there are countries around us who are impoverished. 
There has to be more sharing.

Do you find the whole idea of national service or work-for-the-dole repugnant, or do you think there might be a scheme that could have some merit?
I'm right behind it. The training element is important. I think that being out of work and having time on your hands is debilitating. For people without training to simply have a job, get up each morning, meet other people in the same circumstances, is part of attitude training in itself. However we haven't been able to come up with an idea that's good enough to soak up that huge pool of unemployment amongst youth today and offer meaningful employment.

In your experience is Australia a racist nation?
Well, it's a label that Australians often wear – I think in a moral way every country in the world is a racist nation. People are more comfortable, feel more secure with people that they share a culture with, share a language with, and I don't think that's bad. I can remember when I worked in New Guinea for a while, you'd come back to Australia and you would want to mix with the people that you grew up with. So to that extent yes, I think we're a racist country.

I don't really think we're as bad as we're painted. I was watching SES programs recently, showing countries where there's real hatred and violence towards people. It affected me very badly, just watching it, and I don't really think we're as extreme as that. Some older people are very conservative and stuck in their ways, and find it hard to accept the cultural changes we are experiencing.

What is the role of education these days – formal classroom training, vocational training, a combination of these?
Well, it would be sad if education was simply looked at as vocational training. I think there does need to be training for a vocation, but a general education helps society to hang together. It builds people's understanding and acceptance of each other. I don't believe education can be reduced to training to go into say the stock market or banking. It's a good idea for education to be kept at a general level, particularly in primary and secondary school – a very broad type of education, leading into perhaps more of a vocational emphasis in later secondary and tertiary years.

Are educational opportunities plentiful and well distributed in Australia?
No. I think it's a great disappointment it hasn't gone that way. The fact is that at universities, where presumably our future high fliers and high income earners are being trained, attendance is very much weighted towards the sons and daughters of professional people. It's a myth that you'll make it regardless of where you come from in Australia. If you start life in a family that suffers poverty, there's a very big chance you're going to suffer it yourself in your education and consequently in your life. That's why in the last 10 years I've introduced into The Smith Family the idea of helping kids from poor families through school, through university, with scholarships, with money, with mentors so that they can be lifted up and break that cycle of poverty.

Do you think a university education is a handy thing to have and do you think higher 'up-front' fees are the best way to get the best people in there?
I don't agree with up-front fees. I think it's a barrier for the less well-off. I've got no objection to HECS, people paying for an education once they have the ability to do so in the longer term. I think that is reasonable, you can't expect the worker in the factory to be taxed to support high levels of education for well-to-do people. It's fair enough for students to make a contribution. An up-front fee does deter kids from poor backgrounds from doing courses through TAFE or university, and increasingly, a tertiary qualification is required by employers. It has replaced the HSC as the base requirement.

If your child had a drug habit, would you want society to regard him as a criminal or as an ill person requiring treatment?
I certainly wouldn't want society to treat them as criminals. I take the line that substance abusers need help and assistance, and I think that some aspects of the drug question are sensationalised. Young people think that there isn't much difference between having a joint and having a few vodkas.

If you accept that our approaches over the last 20 years haven't worked, is it time to look 'outside the box' for some other solution?
Yes, I think so. Personally I'm one of those who have great reservations about shooting galleries, and free heroin trials. I really can't see that working. Again it goes back to the impoverishment of people, both in financial and in relationship terms, and I think the answer lies in education, training. I agree that what we've done hasn't been good enough and we do need to take a new approach to it. I wouldn't vote against a limited trial of legalised use of softer drugs.

Is tax reform desirable, and if so is consumption tax the only option?
I'm not a tax expert but I have been listening to arguments. I attended a Tax Summit when the Hawke Government proposed a consumption tax. And I'm a supporter of a consumption tax, I think it is a way of getting all people to contribute. What has to be done though is to make sure that there's proper compensation to people at the lower end of the income table. Pensioners and beneficiaries on fixed incomes clearly need to be compensated for the tax they will then have to pay when they're purchasing their food and services. But if the presumption is that by having a consumption tax we drag a lot of people unwillingly into the tax net, there should be more money to spend on human services. So philosophically I agree with a consumption tax.

Will Australia ever be a republic? And if so, when could it happen?
I'm sure it will. I think that it's more likely to be triggered by some further catastrophe in the British royal family than anything else. I don't think it will make much difference to Australian citizens. There are not really any successful models as far as I'm concerned in the Commonwealth where becoming a republic has made a

huge positive difference. If there was something you could point to and say, well since Canada, say, became a republic the whole country's changed, they're more energetic, more enthusiastic – but I don't see that.

Can you see a situation where to have the option of voluntary euthanasia would be desirable?

Yes, I support it. I think the management of it, the way it is handled, needs to be done with great sensitivity and many, many safeguards. I have known people who committed suicide, took the euthanasia option, when they knew they had a disease that would mean that their lives would be a misery from then on, for them and for others. They took overdoses. I admire the strength of those people.

One of the arguments thrown up is that Western civilisation is based on the value of human life: you can't allow people to kill themselves when they feel like it. Are there real problems with that?

No, I guess I'm a pragmatist. I don't see very much value in life being advanced while the person is in constant agony, or in some cases not knowing who they are or where they are. Families, instead of remembering people for the great life they had, are left to remember the last few years or few months with horror. I think there's definitely a place for euthanasia.

Looking at the Howard Government's Ten Point Plan for land rights, which effectively seeks to change the impact of the High Court's decision. Do you think it's desirable in a constitutional monarchy, with a separation of judiciary and legislature, to have a government effectively changing the umpire's decision?

No, I don't. I think that the umpire's decision should prevail, but the umpire should be democratically elected. There is a broader issue, and I suppose another of my great frustrations in my job here is that I would have clearly loved this organisation to do something in a positive and constructive way for Aboriginal people in Australia. Despite all the work I've done and discussions I've had with people, I don't know what the real answer is. What do the Aboriginal people themselves really need? They speak a language that I don't understand, and I admit that I do not know what effect Mabo will have on Australia in the future.

Thank you very much for your time.

Anthony Warlow

Performing Artist

'Take time and smell the flowers'

BRETT KELLY: *Is there a particular idea, person or event that had the single most profound impact on your life?*

ANTHONY WARLOW: The most prominent event in my life was my cancer. It was a turnaround, but it actually was a turnaround for the better in this regard, because my whole philosophy of life and my career status was questioned at that time. Obviously when one's met with one's mortality one has to ask questions, and I did ask questions. I asked the question, *why?* And then I started to realise that I had ambition and I discussed this feeling with my physician. He said that was actually the beginning of my recovery, having ambition and wanting to excel at things. Even in that state it was a good sign, and so it kind of reinforced my philosophies – because I guess if anyone has gone through a situation like that, they could just throw the whole thing away and ... not be interested. I knew I was here for a reason!

So that did occur with my career. I thought, I need to sing, I want to sing, I want to be able to perform. Of course if it turned out that I couldn't, then my life was the most important thing. So it wasn't a dramatic thing like saying, if I can't sing I don't want to live. But it is easy to say that now. So that would be the most profound thing that has happened, and very few people can boast that kind of lightning bolt.

Was there anything in particular that you got out of that experience?
I learnt to slow down. I learnt to say no. In fact it is a strange thing, but in my career in particular, I have learnt to take risks, I have learnt to be dangerous. And being risky, within calculated reason, in my case I find has paid off and is paying off tenfold. By saying no, there is the possibility that the party who asks for your services will think, well, we won't ask again. But in my case they have said, we will just wait until you are ready – which is wonderful for me because it means I am able to do the best work that I can, when I am ready to, and it is not pressure time.

Previously, I found myself wanting, needing, *having* to work to a point where each show became pressure. The bane of my life is that I tend to be a perfectionist, I cannot stand doing anything that is not exactly right. But in this type of work you are climbing to a particular level and you need to maintain your status constantly. Some things have to be sacrificed. And you go through that period of thinking, OK, I will do this because I need to do it, it is a furthering experience, and so on. But by doing it, what am I sacrificing? So then when this happened to me, this whole illness, it reinforced this strength, this power to say no, I won't do it now, I don't care whether it is going to mean that I won't work again. So it was very powerful.

Is there a motto, quote or thought that summarises your approach to life?
Well, yes, 'Take time and smell the flowers'. It is a very, very old saying but I think if you have been through what I've been through – and I am not saying that that was particularly unique, many thousands of people have been touched by cancer – but it is only after something like this that you actually understand what it means to stop and smell the flowers. So, corny as it may seem, that really is the saying for me.

What are the most critical issues facing Australia in the next decade?
Well, the issues that I see are about whether we become a republic or remain in the hands of a monarch. And the frightening situation with the One Nation Party – and I do think that is frightening. I think we have to understand that we are a multicultural society and embrace that fact. Part of Australia's success, I believe, has been because of the influx of outside influences, Asians, Europeans, Americans, have all made huge contributions. I mean, where would Australia be today without immigrants? But we have given back too, and we have grown as a country. I tend, quite honestly, to pull my head in on these sorts of issues, but sometimes a country has to learn to be tolerant to a point.

Having a little child in my life, I have learnt about tolerance, acceptance. No one teaches a mother that – they teach them how to *have* a baby but they never teach them about what happens the minute the baby is in the world. And it is hard work! I look at my beautiful wife, she works so hard, and I look at my career, and the things that have got me to a point of excellence, sleep and exercise, all those things that as an artist, as an athlete, we accept as normality.

Then something comes into your life which totally disrupts that. It starts to rock the boat and so it unbalances you, and the *way* to balance is through tolerance. I think Australia needs to understand a little more about tolerance. It is hard, we are all selfish to a point, but if everyone just became a little more aware of the next person and not about what they want for themselves, it would help enormously.

So, a better understanding of one's rights and the responsibilities that must go with these rights?
Exactly right. The responsibility for other people.

What are the best things about Australia today?
The fact that we are a country that can debate, as we are doing at the moment. We have a wonderful democracy here and we are able to boast some amazing qualities. One only has to travel overseas and fly home again to understand what Australia is all about. It is a haven for me. It is a wonderful haven for everyone in the country, I believe.

I'm looking at unemployment. Most artists have some contact with this – your own, that of friends. Was there some experience that gave you a real insight into this?
I have to say that I have been one of the fortunate ones. I mean, in my chosen career, I've come to the conclusion that you need to have a philosophy about the work. Mine has three points: first, it takes *time,* and second, it takes *humility,* and also it takes *respect* for the people around you. Just respect for other people's place, time and property is a most important lesson. The fundamental values of 'treating thy neighbour as thyself'.

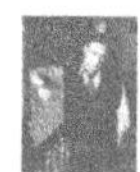

What are the non-monetary rewards you get from the work you do? People see successful people in terms of money, but I seem to be sensing that they also do something they like, and enjoy being good at it?

That is exactly it! I have been very blessed that I have been able to make a career and a living from what started as a hobby at the age of five or six – but I have taken this hobby as seriously as a scientist who wants to get to the moon. We all have to dream, without dreams there is no world. A sense of knowing where I want to go has been my fortune.

There is glamour which is attached to this business – people say, 'oh it must be great to get up and perform'. The research is something that I have actually discovered to be really rewarding. Sometimes when I'm offered a role I take maybe a month to decide I'll consider it. In that month, I go and find every book, every video, every CD concerning the character that I can put my hands on, immerse myself in all that, until some fibre of me says, yes, there is a connection – then I know I can do it. I find that thrilling.

The idea of national service or some sort of work-for-the-dole type scheme – do you think that could have merit at a philosophical level?

Personally, I have always been petrified of anything to do with war. When I was at school, it was the year before they abolished the cadet system and I was so grateful because, you know, being an 'artist', even then I didn't want to put on the greens and the boots. But I think there is merit in the philosophy behind work-for-the-dole, which is that you cannot expect to have everything for nothing. And I think some of the community nowadays, the young people, might be expecting more for less. It's wrong to say they don't want to work, I know the majority of them want to work and given the opportunity will work. But there is often one bad apple, and the publicity goes to that apple.

Is Australia a racist nation in your experience?

I think sadly it is. And when you remember that in years gone by, this country opened its arms to so many people – the Europeans who came in the '50s, and many others over the decades. Of course, at first they went into their own communities, which is natural. A friend of mine went to Germany to live for eight years and went first into a community of English-speaking friends. That's what happens. You cannot expect people to be instantly assimilated. It takes time and it takes effort.

It is very easy to forget the contribution of immigrants to our community. And the situation now with this so-called One Nation Party, you look at it and you think we have very quickly forgotten what made this country.

What is your idea of education?

Well, that's a hard one, because I think that the philosophy of education has changed. I can remember sitting in a class with 60 kids, where now you've got classes down to about 20. And you wonder how people could possibly have taught classes that size – it must have been frightening. I can only go on what I see on television at times, and my local community, but when you go into a shop and encounter a so-called educated person who says 'somethink' and cannot add up ... Look, I'm old-fashioned, but I think that sense of education has gone out the window.

I can remember some years ago, hearing that they have introduced Japanese into the school curriculum because Japan was such a powerful neighbour of Australia's, and that is terrific, but why wasn't it there all the time, instead of French, for instance? We don't have much to do with France as a neighbour. So maybe 20 years ago it should have been Japanese.

What do you think of significant 'up-front' fees for university courses? Do you think this is going to affect the quality and equity of educational opportunity?
Well, to be quite honest, I don't really know much about that. I mean, I have heard about it, but I didn't go to university and I haven't been touched by that situation to know whether the process is actually worth the pain of up-front fees.

If your child had a drug habit, would you want society to regard him as a criminal or as an ill person requiring treatment?
This is a very serious problem, and I think you have to look not just at the child, but at where the child has come from. You hear so many stories about parents who say, Jimmy was such a good kid, we gave him everything ... And that is probably the problem. The more you give, the more is expected. It's frightening that the youth of today expect so much.

If conventional tactics haven't worked over 20 years, should we look for new solutions to the drug problem? Do we need a shift in attitude?
I think we have to be open to new ideas to find a cure. It's a really hard issue. If you look at the Australian community, I didn't drink until I was 21. People nowadays are amazed that I didn't drink. The problem was that when I had my first glass of champagne at 21 it sent me reeling. So I thought well, I don't like this. And I really don't, I'm not a drinker. I will have a nice wine with a meal now and then, but I'm not a drinker.

Now it can happen that when you deprive people of something, as soon as they have the opportunity they go overboard for it. Take the Italian community, they often give their kids a little wine with their meals, and the children understand what it is, fermented grapes, it's part of their culture. By the time they're 18 they're not out there trying to find every pub and every glass of beer that they can, like many of their peers. It's a sad thing when kids become alcoholics.

Should Australia be a republic, and why would we care?
I don't necessarily think so. I come from an older, traditional family. Australia's done okay for so long, what really is going to change if we have a president?

I'm very proud to be an Australian, I've always said that. Twenty years ago people in the entertainment industry would leave this country to go overseas and become an American citizen or whatever, because they had found Broadway, or the

West End. I would always go as an ambassador at heart, because I learnt my craft in this country. I have had European influences to help me learn, but I've always had that philosophy of being an ambassador for this country, showing how great we can be. It's old-fashioned, I know, but it's the way I feel.

Voluntary euthanasia. Do you see a role for it, perhaps even legalisation, in the next decade?

I personally feel that it's the same as abortion. I think it's a frightening thing. They are my personal feelings. There comes a time when we have to accept that pain is part of living and you really don't understand life until you've gone through some pain. You can't feel good unless you've felt bad. I'm not trying to make light of the subject. I guess it comes back to my upbringing, a belief that no one shall take a life. There comes a time – and I've seen cancer patients who are very, very ill – but it happens that when morphine is given to them, eventually their bodies give up and the morphine actually puts them into a sleep. It's a very difficult issue. Personally, when it comes to euthanasia and abortion, I'm against both.

I'm looking at the native title issue on two levels. First, under our Constitution, we've got a judiciary and a legislature which are separated. If a government seeks to denigrate the role of the High Court, is that a good thing? And second, what are your general feelings towards the whole native title debate?

Once again, it comes back to respect. I'm sure there are rights on both sides. It's like the republic and the monarchy, we have gone for so long with a situation that has been perhaps tainted. I hope that in time it can be rectified and the communities satisfied.

This land was owned by the Aborigines. As far as we know, they were the first people here and they have the oldest culture in the world, people have been saying. So we have to respect that. But we, since 1788, have built this country and established this community.

That probably hasn't answered your question, but I'm as confused as the situation is.

So let's look at it two ways.

We all have to be able to live under the one roof somehow and it's not easy. We're all siblings and siblings fight. That's the fact!

Thank you very much for your time.